· THE ·
SANTA FE
TRAIL
REVISITED

Other books by the author

The Old Cathedral, 1965 (2nd edition, 1980)

The Story of Old Ste. Genevieve, 1967 (2nd edition, 1973; 3rd edition, 1976; 4th edition, 1987)

The Oregon Trail Revisited, 1972 (2nd edition, 1978; 3rd edition, 1983; 4th edition, 1988)

History of the Hazelwood School District, 1977

Legacy: The Sverdrup Story, 1978 (2nd printing, 1987)

Leif Sverdrup: Engineer Soldier at His Best, 1980 (2nd printing, 1986)

Maps of the Oregon Trail, 1982 (2nd edition, 1983)

Impressions of the Santa Fe Trail: A Contemporary Diary, 1988

Images of the Santa Fe Trail, 1988

Challenge: The Sverdrup Story Continues, 1988

Maps of the Santa Fe Trail, 1989

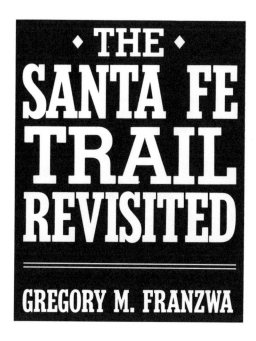

·THE·
SANTA FE
TRAIL
REVISITED

GREGORY M. FRANZWA

FOREWORD BY JAMES M. RIDENOUR
DIRECTOR, NATIONAL PARK SERVICE

THE PATRICE PRESS
ST. LOUIS, MISSOURI

Library of Congress Cataloging-in-Publication Data

Franzwa, Gregory M.
    The Santa Fe Trail revisited / Gregory M. Franzwa ; foreword by
James M. Ridenour.
        p.   cm.
    Includes bibliographical references.
    ISBN 0-935284-74-5
    1. Automobile travel—Santa Fe Trail—Guide-books.   2. Santa Fe
Trail—Guide-books.   I. Title.
    GV1024.F76   1989
917.8—dc20   89-39605
                                                        CIP

Published by
The Patrice Press
1701 South Eighth Street
St. Louis MO 63104
Printed in the United States of America

To Dr. Betty Burnett
editor, fellow traveler, constant friend

CONTENTS

James M. Ridenour

FOREWORD

In 1985 Gregory M. Franzwa came to Washington with a draft of a suggested piece of legislation which would have empowered the National Park Service to study the designation of the Santa Fe Trail as a National Historic Trail. Dale Crane, then as now the majority staff director of the House Subcommittee on National Parks and Public Lands, advised that the matter had been thoroughly studied by the National Park Service in 1963 and didn't need further study—the Santa Fe Trail clearly warranted National Historic Trail status.

So the St. Louis author, founder and at that time president of the Oregon-California Trails Association, went to work on the designation bill. It didn't pass the first year but it did the second, and on May 8, 1987, President Ronald Reagan signed it into law.

Franzwa was then retained as the cartographer for the three months of fieldwork led by the National Park Service Denver Service Center. During this arduous mile-by-mile examination he took careful field notes, knowing that one day he would write a driving guide from them. A year later, after his text was developed, he drove it all again, to make sure his odometer readings and directions were accurate.

Now, for the first time, Americans may drive the family car to the Santa Fe Trail, wherever it can be reached with safety and without trespassing. Sometimes they can get out and walk on the ruts. Sometimes they will be on highways and gravel roads which are directly on the route of the historic old wagon road. They can visit our wonderful National Park Service sites along the way—Fort Larned, Bent's Old Fort, and Fort Union—plus the army's celebrated old Fort Leavenworth.

They will feel the same mystique that our National Park Service team felt when they first explored the old ruts, the rubble from the forts and stage stations, the remains of one of the most glamorous eras of American history.

And they will come to appreciate, as indeed the National Park Service has, the wonderful work our Congress has done in establishing the program to recognize America's National Historic Trails, and in particular that marvelous old road to the Southwest, the Santa Fe Trail.

—James M. Ridenour
Director, National Park Service
August 1989

ACKNOWLEDGMENTS

To say that a work of this nature depends upon many helpers is trite. To deny it is dishonest. True, this book could have gone into print without help from anyone, a circumstance which would have been sheer delight to every snaggletoothed book reviewer. Well, SBRs, you have been foiled, and here are the people who did it, listed in geographical order:

Denny Davis received a draft of the first chapter, looked out the window of his Fayette (Missouri) *Advertiser* and saw rain clouds. He ran to his car to check the mileages posthaste. His corrections and suggestions were in the mail to me within hours.

Jean Tyree Hamilton of Marshall, Missouri, had a nasty foot problem, so she had a friend drive her the breadth of Saline County, from Arrow Rock to the Lafayette County line and beyond.

Roger Slusher of Lexington took over from there. He drove those complicated roads to Fort Osage, and added a few tidbits besides.

Much of the knowledge amassed by Polly Fowler of Independence was used in drafting the Jackson County text—the actual route was driven by Jeanne Miller, executive secretary of the Oregon-California Trails Association. Peggy Smith and Whitson Kirk helped too.

Bob Knecht of the Kansas State Historical Society in Topeka did his usual thorough job of providing documentation whenever we needed it. Of immense help in charting the military roads south of Fort Leavenworth was Bill Chalfant of Hutchinson.

Katharine B. Kelley, that marvelous birdwatcher from Baldwin City, persuaded one of her friends to drive her through Douglas County following the original text and found a few klinkers which she corrected with grace. Glen B. Norton of Overbrook, a total stranger, was contacted to see if he would help in Osage County, Kansas. He did help, providing valuable additions to the text.

Don Cress of Council Grove, who organized the Heart of the Flint

Hills Chapter of the Santa Fe Trail Association, leaned on chapter members to supply corrections to the text around that historic town. Fred and Virginia Shields of Lincolnville, who own the Lost Spring site, were helpful in clearing up some mysteries there. Bob Gray, that venerable trail enthusiast from McPherson, supplied historical materials to be included in the text, then critiqued the draft for me.

The Santa Fe Trail has no more devoted friend than Ralph Hathaway, a third-generation rancher from Chase, Kansas. He is the proprietor of the famous "Ralph's Ruts," swales through his land which are a magnet for people informed about the Santa Fe Trail. James W. Carmichael shared his information about the famous Battle of Cow Creek.

One of the most amazing of our Santa Fe Trail friends is Robert E. Button of Great Bend. This is one amateur archaeologist who is as talented as the pros. A prodigious collector, he also is an expert wood-carver. Bob patiently guided me through the maze of history surrounding the two Fort Zarahs.

George Elmore is a Larned native and full-time interpreter at the National Park Service's Fort Larned. George supplied all the geographical information needed for a good presentation of the Fort Larned story. And after I had screwed up the text, he unscrewed it cheerfully.

Our helpers in Dodge City included Noel Ary, Betty Braddock, and especially Jim Sherer, who used his car to tour the ruts west of Dodge and thus enabled me to write intelligently about that site.

Dale Eichenauer helped by confirming some text passages south of the Middle Cimarron Crossing. In Finney County I found David Brownlee to be very helpful in clarifying the route to the Aubry Cutoff. Jim and Hazel Tancayo, who own the site of Pawnee Fort, were extremely gracious and helpful. Jesse Scott, Jr., Garden City, provided cartographic information to locate the site of Pawnee Fort. Katherine Powell, the Finney County historian, came through with additional information on that site. Sister Aurelia Ottersbach, archivist of the Sisters of Loretto in Nerinx, Kentucky, provided documentation for the photos of the reenactment of the burial of Sister Mary Alfonsa Thompson.

Patricia Heath, who corrected the driving directions to the Indian Mound, also advised that historic Clear Lake is not only of the past, but of the present, too. Linda Peters was also a big help in the area around the Upper Crossing.

Ron French, Ulysses, who is an organizer of the Wagon Bed Spring Chapter of the SFTA, interrupted a busy Sunday to escort me to the old spring, to verify mileages on the new road leading to it. Ed White of Elkhart, who flew us over the trail in 1988, took time from his law practice to check out the text. Dick Bennin of the U.S. Forest Service came through with some maps which give a detailed picture of the Santa Fe Trail through the Cimarron National Grassland.

In Oklahoma our debt is deep to David Hutchison, Dan and Carol Sharp, and Joan Walton. Louise Dawson, a trail enthusiast from Kenton, gave some good advice on some of the delicate issues of site access in the Panhandle.

Susan Richardson, who runs the Meadowlark KOA in Clayton, New Mexico, paused during the busiest part of her year to explain the changes at McNees Crossing.

Help comes from strange places. Bill Goff of Kansas City, my special friend in the Oregon Trail studies, did a piece on the Taos Revolt in the March 1975 issue of the *Quarterly* of the Westport Historical Society, which somehow stuck in my files. Bill has been gone for a couple of years now, but he's still helping out.

Harry C. Myers, superintendent of Fort Union National Monument, went all out to help, even to the extent of rounding up a dossier of rare historical pictures. Furthermore, he carefully marked the trail on aerial photographic maps, pointing out visible rut swales.

Willie and Mary Gaskin, all gussied up and on their way to the races, stayed at their immaculate home in Raton for an extra hour on a Sunday morning, just to talk to me about the Willow Spring. They were using it to water their lawn at the time.

I have some special friends in the Trinidad-Branson area—Willard and Richard Louden. There are two adjectives which describe both those guys—brilliant and kind. Richard worked hard to try to solve the problems on the Military Road as it approaches Emery Gap. Both helped explore the Hole-in-the-Prairie area. All of us who love the Santa Fe Trail are indebted to the Louden brothers.

I blew one entire morning for Don Hill, superintendent at Bent's Old Fort, and his chief ranger, Bill Gwaltney. It was then that I realized how little I knew about the complicated dealings of Bent, St. Vrain & Company, and how much these kind men knew and were willing to share. They stuck to the job until I got it right. It wasn't easy for any of us.

Ava Betz of Lamar evidently doesn't mind late-night telephone calls, but when one is stuck with a problem in Bent County, Colorado, she is the one to call.

The work of some of the latter-day explorers was very helpful. The late Hobart Stocking's maps were of immense value. The late Kenyon Riddle contributed some interesting ideas and maps. Glenn R. Scott of the U.S. Geological Survey did a splendid job of charting the trail in the Raton and Springer quads.

But there are six special friends who really made this book. One is the irrepressible Paul Bentrup, official Ambassador of the Santa Fe Trail, annointed by the SFTA board of directors. He commandeered whole buildings and brought truckloads of papers to help me in the error of my ways. When something didn't sound right to him he would take off in his truck and start pounding on doors. He always came back with good information.

After one trip, to Hole-in-the-Rock, he relayed information on the missing stage station to me. I drafted it and sent copies to another special friend, Mark L. Gardner of Trinidad. Mark didn't like my new version so he took off in *his* truck and then phoned in a clarification, having walked over the site with landowner Butch Hall. Mark Gardner is a really great guy at three things: interpreting the Santa Fe Trail in the Trinidad-Raton area, performing period musical programs, and being a friend.

Then there is Dr. Jere Krakow of the National Park Service in Denver. Probably the most overburdened guy in the Denver Service Center, Jere nevertheless used some of his nights and weekends to critique the entire manuscript.

And Dr. Marc Simmons—without him I'm sure there would be no Santa Fe Trail. He has written so much on the subject, and so well, that I have a feeling he invented it. He also took time to critique the entire manuscript.

Finally, I am indebted to no one so much as to Dr. Leo and Bonita Oliva. Here they are, in the busiest time of the their 2,200-acre farm, with Leo getting out *Wagon Tracks* on his desktop outfit, trying to cut his wheat and put in his milo and beans, trying desperately to keep on schedule with his commission to write the definitive history of Fort Union. So I come trotting up with 300 pages of manuscript. Always the professor, he not only corrected the text, but wrote why he was making the changes. Never in my life have I come across such selfless people.

Finally, I want to thank the staff at The Patrice Press, who made the outfit run while I was in my cave drafting the manuscript. I am particularly indebted to Lisa Taylor, who designed the book and did the typography and pasteup.

My special friend, Dr. Betty Burnett, ran the office during this trying time, but also edited the manuscript, supplied much advice, and then made all the corrections as we verified the text with our several check rides.

I am not so naive as to think all those people did all those good things for good old me. They did them for the trail, for the sake of historical accuracy, and to make sure that those setting out on this adventure with this book in hand would not be disappointed. God bless them all.

—Gregory M. Franzwa
September 1989

ADVICE TO TRAVELERS

The time to start thinking about a trip down the Santa Fe Trail is winter, preferably early winter. The adventure will take between two and three weeks. A person should make the most of it by priming the thrill with some good reading.

The one book which gives the best overall view of the trail is William E. Brown's classic *The Santa Fe Trail.* Perhaps the most charming book ever written on the subject is Marion Sloan Russell's *Land of Enchantment.* Susan Magoffin's *Down the Santa Fe Trail and Into Mexico,* although now out of print, is must reading.

There are two books, in addition to this one, which certainly ought to be bought along on the trip. Dr. Marc Simmons's *Following the Santa Fe Trail* is a seasoned traveling companion. Our *Maps of the Santa Fe Trail* ought to be in the car, also.

Two good general histories are *Broadcloth and Britches* by Connor and Skaggs; and R.L. Duffus's *The Santa Fe Trail.* Both are long out of print but major libraries have them. My own *Images of the Santa Fe Trail* and *Impressions of the Santa Fe Trail* are fun reading and might enhance the enjoyment of the trail experience. *Matt Field on the Santa Fe Trail* and Josiah Gregg's *Commerce of the Prairies* are both out of print also, but are interesting accounts of the trail from the 1830s.

Dr. Leo E. Oliva's classic *Soldiers on the Santa Fe Trail,* also out of print, is the best view of the military experience along the wagon road. He and his wife, Bonita, collaborated on the delightful *Santa Fe Trail Trivia,* a fun book to read ahead of time and to have in the car. Lewis Garrard's *Wah-to-yah and the Taos Trail* has some thrilling passages describing his 1846-47 travels.

One of the best books written on one aspect of the Santa Fe Trail is David Lavender's classic, *Bent's Fort.*

Travelers interested in critters will want a good bird book in the glove compartment. The birds along the Santa Fe Trail range from eagles and hawks to pheasants, swallows, road runners, and dozens of varieties of small songbirds. The western meadowlark will follow you throughout Kansas. A wildflower book is handy to have also. The drive to Indian Mound during July is through an amazing field of wildflowers.

In southwestern Kansas small herds of antelope will be seen. Once in a while a jackrabbit will hop across the road. Mule deer and white-tailed deer abound along the way. The buffalo are fenced in these days. Prairie dog towns will be seen and heard.

For all those reasons, bring field glasses, the more powerful the better. Camera nuts will want long lenses and tripods.

People, beware of rattlesnakes! Rattlesnakes, beware of people! Each species seems to have adopted the idea of running like hell in the opposite direction. Not a bad idea. The snakes are usually more afraid of people and will head for the nearest hole unless their way is blocked. Rattlesnakes with no option but to attack usually give fair warning. When they can. Rancher David Brownlee advises that his snakes (around Fort Aubrey) have had their rattles sliced off when he runs his disc over the fields. It is a good idea not to try to kill them; maybe then they won't try to kill you.

When to Go

The one time when the Santa Fe Trail isn't much fun is winter. The best time to see ruts is early spring—from March to mid-May. The prairie grasses will not have overgrown the ruts by then. After the first killing frost of fall, perhaps mid-October, the grasses lie down, and again the ruts are striking. Both those seasons, however, have powerful winds. The temperature notwithstanding, the buffeting can be irritating. Summers, of course, are hot. But the lack of humidity makes the temperature bearable.

What to Wear

Be prepared for any kind of weather except tornadoes. Kansas has had a bad reputation for tornadoes ever since Dorothy left for Oz, but many natives have lived long lives in Kansas without seeing a single funnel cloud.

There can be extremes of hot and cold during any season. It rarely rains on the western two-thirds of the trail, but it can happen, and slickers and umbrellas should be in the car, regardless of the time of year.

Even in the middle of summer a windbreaker or light jacket should be packed. Spring and fall wardrobes must include gloves, overshoes, and heavy coats, preferably with hoods.

Outfitting the Vehicle

The routing in this book has been designed for the family car. No roads have been recommended which are passible only with four-wheel-drive vehicles. Some 50,000 miles of trail exploration for this book were undertaken with a 1987 Chrysler Fifth Avenue, a heavy, low-slung, rear-wheel-drive car.

That car has an odometer error of .3 mile per ten miles. For each ten miles driven, the odometer reads 9.7 miles. All distances in this book have been measured by the odometer of that car.

For proper extrapolation, the vehicle intended for this trip should be taken on a measured course of ten miles, preferably country roads, to determine the odometer error.

Make sure there is a good tool kit in the car, including a high quality steel lug wrench. Much of the driving will be on gravel and dirt roads, where nails abound. Changing tires with the Mickey Mouse lug wrenches supplied by the car's manufacturer can be a disaster. Get a good one, the kind mechanics use.

Carry an extra air filter. The dust on some of those roads is as bad as it was in trail days. The engine needs to breathe.

The vehicle should be checked over thoroughly before leaving. Put on a new fuel filter, change the oil and oil filter, and make sure the air conditioner is working properly. When driving on dusty roads, don't follow other vehicles closely. Keep the air conditioner on "vent," not "max." The ventilation mode admits clean rammed air from the front of the car and builds a slight pressure inside the cabin, which usually prevents dust entry from beneath the vehicle. When on maximum, the air inside the cabin is merely being recirculated and the dust comes in with a vengeance. When meeting other cars or passing feedlots, hit the "max" button, fast. Otherwise, leave it on "vent."

Equip the vehicle with a good automobile compass. There will be plenty of occasions when it will be needed. Disorientation comes easy on some of the roads.

Write to the departments of transportation of Missouri, Kansas, Oklahoma, New Mexico, and Colorado for copies of their official state road maps. Even though *Maps of the Santa Fe Trail* may be in the car, there are places where the highways are off the maps. Furthermore, the New Mexico Department of Transportation changed most of the state's highway numbers in 1988-89; the new numbers are shown on their 1989 road map.

Finding the Way

Generally, the book gives thorough directions for the traveler, but on occasion it is a good idea to follow your progress on a map. Getting unlost

The standard Boy Scout compass is ideal for taking bearings.

is not always easy.

Travel with a Boy Scout compass and learn how to use it. In several places the text asks the traveler to "take a bearing." That is a simple thing to do. Just spin the outer ring until it reads the indicated bearing, turn the compass until the red portion of the needle is over the red plastic, and sight along the arrow.

Some Cautions

Drive off the top half of the gas tank. Sometimes it can be as far as 150 miles between gas stations. It is infinitely more pleasant to stop frequently than to walk down a dusty road for twenty-five miles trying to find a station.

It also should be remembered that it is a long way between rest stops, and the inhibited are going to spend some very uncomfortable moments upon occasion. The uninhibited will do it the way the traders did it.

The big enemy of the traveler is going to be rain, particularly in Kansas. There is no problem on good gravel roads, of course, but sometimes the "gravel" roads turn out to be dirt, and after a sudden shower they can turn into mud. Driving on Kansas mud in a family car is exactly like driving on glare ice, with this exception: glare ice doesn't fly up and add a thousand pounds of weight to the underside of the car. There is no more fearful experience than to slide down a mud road sideways at thirty miles an hour, with the car completely out of control.

Some rather complicated driving directions are given at times. Frequently, after directions to a site are given, is the phrase, "Return to the highway.'' Unless other directions are given, this means return over the same roads taken to get there in the first place. Sometimes that can be complicated. If you get lost, turn to the automobile compass and the map book. Read ahead to find a fix and head for it to resume the adventure. On the way to a site, it is a good idea to note surroundings at turns, so they will be familiar upon returning. Landmarks such as road signs are rarely cited in this book, for they may not be there long.

The experience should be a team effort, and the navigator is fully as important as the driver. Don't try it alone.

Some Definitions

Some terms used in this book may not be familiar. In describing the trail, the term ''swale'' is used frequently. That is a smooth-sided, usually shallow, linear depression of the trail. The word ''rut'' is also used. Sometimes that can mean a swale, but usually it is an eroded swale. Wind and water have attacked the turf which had been broken down by wagon wheels and erosion has taken place. Usually this erosion is on the sides of the ruts.

The terms ''jog left'' or ''jog right'' are used often. That means turn left a short distance, then drive back to the right, or vice versa.

When referring to a river, the terms ''left bank'' or ''right bank'' may be used. These terms are constant and always refer to the bank when headed downstream.

One should be aware that while the name of the state is pronounced AR-kan-saw, the name of the river is pronounced Ar-KAN-sas. At least that's the way it is done by people who live near the river. Dr. Leo E. Oliva has given the matter much scholarly study, and has concluded that the river should be pronounced the same as the state. So far he has succeeded in convincing only Mrs. Oliva.

Organizations to Join

It is a good idea to join the American Automobile Association (AAA), not only for the maps and tour guides, but for help in the event a tow is necessary.

It is an even better idea to join the Santa Fe Trail Association. Those reading this book will notice the wonderful things the SFTA members have done to enhance the enjoyment of the trip. They will do it alone if they have to, but it would be much more pleasant if they knew all travelers were part of the fellowship. With membership comes four issues of *Wagon Tracks,* edited by Dr. Oliva; an invitation to attend the biennial symposium; and a membership directory. That directory could be very valuable; when traveling consult the local members for the latest trail news. Information on joining is in the back of this book.

Get Permission First

One theme recurs throughout this book—get permission first. Don't go on private land without it, for your own protection. The laws of trespass are tough and getting tougher. Because they are courteous people themselves, the leadership of SFTA has been encouraging courtesy among all who visit the historic sites of the Santa Fe Trail. Landowners have been urged to prosecute trepassers. Those ranchers have been very good to those of us who like to follow the trails, and deserve to be treated courteously. Some of them have been protecting their portions of the trail for generations and they are entitled to know who is on their land.

The names of most landowners have been deliberately omitted from the text. Take the time to check in the area (again, the SFTA roster will come in handy here) to find out whether the landowner should be approached. Almost all of them are wonderful people, and some may give you a lot more help than you really wanted. Others may say no, or perhaps not even answer the telephone. The SFTA leadership has worked hard to earn the respect of landowners. Please don't screw things up by going on their land unannounced.

Another factor should be considered. Cattle rustling today is probably more prevalent than it was in early settlement days. Rustlers now drive pickup campers with curtains on the windows. They herd a cow and calf in, slam the door, and the rancher is $1,000 poorer.

So don't take a chance by violating the laws of trespass. Every county seat has a jail. However, if you do decide to violate the law, be sure you have a Patrice Press order blank with you as you will want plenty of good reading while you rot away in the pokey.

Help Wanted

This book will be obsolete in places even before it goes to the printer. The built environment changes rapidly. Gravel roads become paved. Numbers on highways change. And even though the text has been checked by dozens of careful authorities, there are bound to be errors. Help your Santa Fe Trail friends by submitting corrections to the publisher to be included in subsequent editions.

—Gregory M. Franzwa
September 1989

Spelling and grammatical errors found in direct quotes have not been changed. Unless otherwise specified, all photographs are by author.

ACCOMMODATIONS

Because most of the Santa Fe Trail is away from interstate highways, and therefore from an abundance of accommodations, we thought we'd share some of our impressions of motels and restaurants along the way, based on nearly a dozen trips.

An advantage of leaving main traveled roads is that food and accommodations are very reasonable, sometimes even cheap. A disadvantage is that the selection is often limited and ''you get what you pay for.'' Most small-town cafes offer more fried food than a normal stomach can tolerate. Fortunately, many places today have a salad bar. Even though the lettuce may be wilted, at least it's green, and sometimes you can find a moderately ripe tomato. The salad bars at some of the ubiquitous steak houses in Kansas and Colorado are superb.

The gringo end of the Santa Fe Trail begins in Franklin, Missouri, and the Comfort Inn in nearby Boonville on I-70 is next to a small restaurant called, appropriately, the Santa Fe. This is a good place, symbolically speaking, to start your adventure, and the food is adequate. El Sambre Cantina in Boonville is better and will whet the appetite for the pounds of tacos, tostados, and enchiladas ahead. The pleasant Hispanic decor may help Anglos imagine the excitement of meeting a new culture circa 1840, when traveling for pleasure was almost unheard-of.

The Independence-Kansas City area has several historic sites relating to the Santa Fe Trail and many are concentrated in the Westport area. The Quarterage Hotel, located on the site of the old Yoacham's Tavern in the heart of Westport, is expensive, but a good place to splurge if your budget can stand it. Remember—you have lots of very small rooms and very old plumbing ahead of you, so you might as well revel in luxury when you can. Two nearby restaurants, the historic Sanford & Son, located in Jim Bridger's old store, and the Prospect of Westport, are especially good. And expensive. Kansas City is well known for its steaks and for its barbeque—Arthur Bryant's offers a good taste of the latter at an economical price.

If you want to keep to a reasonable budget, there are many fine rooms available at the motels found at the intersection of Noland Road and I-70 in Independence. Good restaurants are nearby, too. (A side trip we recommend while in Independence is a visit to both the Harry S. Truman Library and family home.)

Dozens of motels and restaurants can be found in the Kansas suburbs of Kansas City. Kansas has peculiar laws relating to alcohol consumption—some counties are wet, some are dry, and some are in between. Before you start visualizing a cold beer at the end of a long, hot day, you might check out the local regulations.

Our first Kansas stop on many of our SFT trips was frequently at the Best Western Hallmark in Ottawa. Its aroma of pine oil disinfectant was slightly less offensive than at the Best Western in Olathe. At McPherson we recommend the Red Coach Inn, a really fine, modestly priced motel with an indoor pool and hot tub. The restaurant adjacent is OK.

Council Grove is proud of its Cottage House, a restored old-fashioned hotel with a huge porch with gliders and swings. Dinner at the Hays House is a must—moderately expensive but delectable. Guests of the Cottage House may dine upstairs at the "club," where cocktails are available.

At Great Bend the Angus Inn offers some very spacious rooms opening onto the natatorium, if you get there in time. The Black Angus Restaurant next door has good food and good service—the Mexican food bar is highly recommended for those with a taste for the mild, Americanized kind. Those wanting more authentic, tears-in-your-eyes hot stuff better go to the Kiowa Kitchen.

Larned has a fine motel called the Townsman Best Western. Across the street is the DonDo Restaurant, where we enoyed many good meals cheerfully served. The Harvest Inn is awful.

We were not enthusiastic about any of the motels in Dodge City, although there are many. El Charro Restaurant is a good restaurant. At Garden City the Wheat Lands Best Western Motel was superb, as was the Grain Bin Restaurant next door. We were there on comedy night—pretty blue and geared toward the under-thirty crowd, but very funny.

At Syracuse the Ramble-N Motel is nice enough—a palace compared to the KenArk at Lakin. West of Garden City the restaurants, such as they are, slam the door at 8 P.M. If you miss that deadline, you'll be stuck with Dairy Queen. But that closes early, too (by urban standards), so don't let the time get away from you. Bed & breakfasts are available in the Syracuse-Ulysses area.

An oasis in western Kansas is the El Rancho Motel in Elkhart. Each modestly priced—and large—room appears to be different. We were given a suite on several occasions and one room had a sunken whirlpool bath. The restaurant next door used to be very good, but now the service is indifferent and the food only so-so. Try the Country Kettle in town.

The Oklahoma Panhandle, alas, is not a tourist spot and accommodations have not changed much since 1946. A number of motels line the highway, all old, small, and cheap. Both restaurants feature fried everything with gravy. There's also a Pizza Hut.

Once into New Mexico, things brighten a bit. At Clayton, La Paloma has a great buffet of Mexican food. You have to hang onto the sopapillas to keep them from floating away. The NuWay Cafe in the center of town is really good, with fast service (and fresh fruit!), and the restored Eklund Hotel dining room is marvelous. Unfortunately, its hotel rooms are not open for guests, and the motel selection in Clayton is limited, but adequate. Check the wind direction before you check in or you might feel you're sleeping in a feedlot. (Unfortunately, this is a problem in much of western Kansas, too.)

At Springer the only choice is the Dairy Delight—the cheeseburgers there will take you back to the 1950s when a cheeseburger was a meal in itself, instead of a piece of cardboard between two pieces of styrofoam. The ice cream treats are delicious too. There are a number of good motels and restaurants at Las Vegas. The food at Pino's Family Restaurant is abundant and good, but the service may have you wishing you'd gone somewhere else. The historic Plaza Hotel is not living up to its promise as "the" place to stay in Las Vegas. Our first visit there was perfect. Our subsequent three visits there were not, despite the fact that it's one of the most expensive stops on the trail. We found it difficult to sleep in a spartan room with an indoor temperature of 88 degrees when the outdoor temperature was 70 degrees. The dining room is a bit pretentious (after a week of down-home ambience, it seemed *very* pretentious) and you'll need to get out the iron.

Santa Fe is legendary for its accommodations and certainly has some of the best restaurants in the southwest. They range from the very expensive to the moderately so. We recommend the Old Mexico Grill, the Guadalupe Cafe, Maria's (this one will open your sinuses), and Rincon de Oso. There are *many* more; don't stop with these. We liked the superb High Mesa Inn for lodgings, and found the Residence Inn impressive, too.

A real treat on the trail is a stop at Casa del Gavilan,"the house of the hawk," which is an elegant bed and breakfast south of Cimarron. Built in 1908 by a Princetonian with taste and money, the place is loaded with history and beauty, both the natural and the hand-crafted kinds.

In the historic section of Cimarron is the restored St. James Hotel, great, but which is far too expensive for us, and the Kit Carson Motel, which is a bit seedy. The St. James restaurant is excellent.

At Mora we found an excellent small restaurant called Theresa Maria's, and at Pecos we were fortunate to come across a little roadside place called La Paz. At both places the food servers were exceptionally friendly, creating a very pleasant atmosphere.

Surprisingly, we never stayed in Raton, nor did we have a memorable meal there, so we can neither recommend nor disparage anything in that town. At Trinidad we prefer the Holiday Inn, although it is the most expensive lodging in town, because it's so comfortable and has a large indoor pool. The Mining Company Restaurant at the inn is good, but better are Chef Liu's, one of the best Chinese restaurants we've ever come across, and La Fiesta, if you haven't tired of enchiladas.

Lamar means only the Cow Palace. The rooms are fine and the restaurant, with an extensive salad bar, is one of the best on the route. The Lamar Truck Plaza is also very good—some creative soul there has turned a manure spreader into a super salad bar. LaJunta offers the modest Mid-Town Motel and a tiny restaurant in the center of town with very fine and low cost Mexican food, El Patio.

We hope travelers retracing the Santa Fe trail will share their recommendations with us, for the benefit of readers of future editions. *Buena Suerte!*

—Betty Burnett

INTRODUCTION
"THE SANTA FE TRAIL LIVES ON!"

It was bizarre, the way it happened. William Becknell, about thirty-four years old, had amassed a worrisome debt to many of his friends and associates in the vicinity of Franklin, the westernmost outpost of the new state of Missouri. He undertook one venture, a massive gamble, and won. He opened the Santa Fe Trail.

Becknell would have been aware of the dangers of trying to trade with the New Mexicans in Santa Fe. It was a practice strictly forbidden by Spain, and violation of that edict meant years in the Chihuahua dungeons.

But he also would have heard rumors that Mexico was about to overthrow its Spanish yoke and might have presumed then that the new regime would welcome the trade of Yankee goods for their surplus silver and furs. Certainly the people of Chihuahua and Santa Fe could obtain yard goods, hardware, cutlery, and other trade goods from Europe, via Vera Cruz. But it was only half as far from Santa Fe to Missouri. It made good sense to deal with the Yankees.

Becknell didn't know when the overthrow was going to happen, but he did know that the sheriff was only weeks away from his door. So he advertised in Franklin's weekly *Missouri Intelligencer* for fellow traders to join with him, and left Missouri on September 1, 1821. On September 21 Mexico became independent.

Becknell arrived in Santa Fe November 16, his gamble an unqualified success. The trade goods were sold at unbelievable profits and the following month he started for home with an even grander scheme.

His first journey was the beginning of the Santa Fe trade. His second, begun May 22, 1822, was made with covered wagons, and that was the start of the Santa Fe Trail.

His monopoly didn't last long. It took no time at all for other entrepreneurs to get the hint. Soon the Becknell path became a veritible highway, as each year more and more traders became involved.

Hauling tons of trade goods to Santa Fe behind slowly moving ox or mule teams was no picnic. There were streams to ford, and that usually meant spading ramps down and then back up on the other side. The weather could be awful—unseasonal blizzards could freeze animals by the hundreds, leaving men stranded with no way to move goods forward or back.

But the greatest enemy was Indians. This was recognized shortly after Becknell left on his second expedition, and Missouri's powerful U.S. Senator Thomas Hart Benton urged Congress to appropriate money for an expedition which would survey the new trail and enact treaties with the Indians along the way.

The Sibley party left from near Fort Osage in 1825, surveying and mapping the route as they went. The congressional order to mark the trail was unnecessary, they felt, for the traders themselves were already marking it with their wagon wheels. The trail was a broad, flat highway by the time the Sibley party went to work. Nevertheless, they erected dirt mounds along the trail, knowing full well that if the Indians didn't take them down the weather would.

They did enact two effective treaties—one with the Osage at Council Grove, and the other with the Kansa south of present-day McPherson. But those tribes weren't causing much trouble anyway. The ones who were didn't come to parley—hence, no other treaties were signed.

The map and field notes which surveyor Joseph C. Brown prepared so meticulously and so accurately lay unnoticed in the National Archives for a century until historians discovered them in the 1920s.

The first few years on the trail were relatively peaceful. Hispanic traders saw *Los Americanos* reaping big profits, loaded their own wagons in Santa Fe with silver and furs and took off for Missouri, to do exactly as the Missourians were doing, and soon there were as many New Mexicans on the trail as there were Yankees.

But in 1828, following an altercation on the Cimarron River east of McNees Crossing, all hell broke loose. Indians attacked whites and whites attacked Indians. At first there were merely shootings, and death came quickly. Later the Indians adopted savage tortures and kidnapped women and children, and destroyed trade goods, wagons, and livestock.

Relations with the Mexican government deteriorated, too. The United States cooked up one excuse after another until a state of war existed between the two nations. The Army of the West, under Stephen Watts Kearny, left Fort Leavenworth for Mexico, avoided the Indian-menaced Cimarron Cutoff and vaulted the Raton Mountains at Raton Pass. They were traveling over what came to be known as the Mountain Branch of the Santa Fe Trail. The American forces captured the old capital of Santa Fe without the loss of a single life. Tentacles of the U.S. Army went

Kansas State Historical Society

The Atchison, Topeka and Santa Fe arrived at Lamy in 1879, effectively putting an end to the Santa Fe Trail.

south to Mexico City and west to California—bitter fighting resulted in a resounding American victory, and New Mexico and California were ceded to the United States.

Then the trade grew exponentially. And with it, the Indian menace took on terrible new proportions. Now Indians were being required to move to reservations and take up agricultural pursuits in exchange for annuities.

This notion was resisted ferociously. Indians saw the white settlement coming, along with the extermination of the buffalo, the sustenance of Indian life for centuries. The battle now became one of desperation. If whites could not be stopped, the despised and degrading reservation life would be forced upon the Indians and the old ways would be gone forever.

In some years it was rare if a wagon train got through without being attacked at least once. Both Anglo and Hispanic traders called to their government for help and they got it. Forts were established at strategic points along the trail, from which escorts were dispatched to provide added firepower to the wagon trains. That in itself called for heavier use of the trail. Military freighting, to supply those outposts, quickly rivaled trade caravans in tonnage.

Another great battle was looming—the War Between the States. Fear of Confederate and Indian raiders shunted Santa Fe Trail traffic away from the Cimarron Cutoff and up on the Mountain Branch. But even the greatest war in American history didn't stop the Santa Fe trade.

What did stop it was the advent of the railroad. The Kansas Pacific went west first, and by 1867, only two years after the end of the Civil War, the Santa Fe Trail east of Fort Larned was history. Three years later the rails were at Kit Carson, Colorado, so that place became the eastern terminus of the Santa Fe Trail.

Then the Atchison, Topeka, and Santa Fe began warring with the Denver and Rio Grande for the right to penetrate New Mexico. The Santa Fe representatives got to Uncle Dick Wootton in the middle of the night and he granted them the right to surmount Raton Pass. The first train entered Santa Fe on February 9, 1880, and the odyssey was over.

Or was it? When Dr. Marc Simmons gaveled in the first symposium of the Santa Fe Trail Association on September 12, 1987, he said, "The Santa Fe Trail Lives On!" At that moment the Congress of the United States was contemplating legislation which would declare the old route a National Historic Trail. Simmons's rallying cry has become a slogan of sorts for the Santa Fe Trail Association.

Now, with the National Historic Trail status an accomplished fact, it is becoming evident that the trail really is living on, as thousands and thousands of travelers—Americans and people from foreign lands—take to the old trail once again.

Yes, indeed, Dr. Simmons—the Santa Fe Trail does live on.

FINDING THE TRAIL IN MISSOURI

COOPER AND HOWARD COUNTIES

There is no better place to begin a retracement of the Santa Fe Trail than the lovely old town of Boonville, Missouri. Here, on March 14, 1988, the National Park Service survey team began its Santa Fe Trail study.

Boonville is 104 miles east of Kansas City, between I-70 and the Missouri River to the north. Despite a few local claims to the contrary, it really isn't on the Santa Fe Trail. Certainly some traders had lived there and a few caravans may have started from there, but those were isolated instances and not very significant to the history of the trail.

Boonville still has many vestiges of its past. The old homes are warm and picturesque; the restorations are joyful to behold.

There are three I-70 interchanges at Boonville. Exit at the center one, Highway B. Proceed north 2.8 miles on Route B, which is also identified as Main Street. Turn right on Morgan, which is two blocks south of the Missouri River. Continue 1.5 blocks to the Old Jail, 614 East Morgan. This is the headquarters for the Friends of Historic Boonville and a good place to gain some knowledge of the history of the town.

Return to Main Street and turn right (toward the river) one block to High Street, then left. The street to the north of High is called Water Street, because it floods. High Street is atop the bluff, so it doesn't. A half-block to the west, at 409 West High Street, is the Ballentine House, or Commercial Hotel, now in an advanced state of disrepair. The center section is said to have been built in 1823, two years after William Becknell opened the Santa Fe Trail from Old Franklin. The main building was erected in the late 1830s.

The noted Missouri artist George Caleb Bingham reputedly was taught to paint in a building which stood next door to the Ballentine House, and according to town historians his first cash commission was a painting to hang in the tavern of the hotel.

Turn right at the next corner and proceed north on Fourth Street to the Missouri River. There is the turgid waterway which carried so many thousands of people on one-way trips to the jumping-off places to the American West.

Turn right on Water Street and proceed beneath the bridge which carries Missouri highways 5 and 87 over the Missouri River. The old highway bridge spanning the river was opened in 1924. The north abutments are on land that was once the north portion of the booming old town of Franklin, which flooded into memory in 1828. Halfway up the hill, in the soil beneath that bridge, are remains of the cobblestone levee of the 1800s. The steamboats docked for a block or two on either side of the present bridge.

Turn around (there won't be much traffic). Proceed west along Water Street for .7 mile, where the road turns to gravel. Continue through the entrance to Harley Park and turn right, following the direction sign to Lookout Point. Stop and park at the cul-de-sac.

East of the parking area is a high eminence, believed to have been an Indian temple mound. To the north is the Missouri River and the Santa Fe Trail.

The Santa Fe Trail, as defined by the National Park Service, left from a point 400 yards west of the north abutment of the Boonville highway bridge and proceeded northwest, just above the floodplain but still not on the high ground, paralleling the river for about eleven miles to the ferry to Arrow Rock. The trail is believed to be under the paved roadways which go in that direction. The view from Harley Park overlooks this route.

On the northwestern horizon is a tiny water tower. That is Arrow Rock, thirteen miles away.

Return to downtown Boonville. Since the bridge cannot be reached from Water Street, turn right for a block on 4th Street, then left a block to Main. Then turn north and cross the Missouri River to Howard County.

There are, or were, three towns named Franklin. The oldest was a booming city in the second decade of the nineteenth century. It was established in 1817 and by the end of the following year boasted 150 houses. The value of the lots had risen by more than 1,000 percent. An 1819 census enumerated thirteen stores, four taverns, two billiard rooms, a post office, a jail, and a newspaper, the weekly *Missouri Intelligencer.*

Prosperity indicated further precipitous growth during the 1820s, but a funny thing happened on the road to glory. The cantankerous Missouri River attacked it time and again, finally doing it in in 1828. It is referred to today as Old Franklin.

But Old Franklin didn't die immediately. This report is from the May

2, 1828, issue of the *Fayette Intelligencer:*

> The town of Franklin, as also our own village, presents to the eye of the beholder, a busy, bustling and commercial scene, in buying, selling and packing goods, practicing mules, etc., etc., all preparatory to the starting of the great spring caravan to Santa Fe. A great number of our fellow citizens are getting ready to start, and will be off in the course of a week on a trading expedition. We have not the means of knowing how many persons will start in the first company, but think it probable the number will exceed 150, principally from this and the adjoining counties. They generally purchase their outfits from the merchants here at from 20 to 30 per cent advance on the Philadelphia prices, and calculate to make from 40 to 100 per cent upon their purchases. They will generally return in the fall. We suppose the amount which will be taken from this part of the country this spring will not perhaps fall much short of $100,000 at the invoice prices.
>
> We wish them a safe and profitable trip, a speedy return to their families and homes in health, and they may long live to enjoy the profits of their long and fatiguing journey of nearly one thousand miles, through prairies inhabited only by savages and wild beasts.

Beginning in 1826 residents started moving a couple of miles to the northeast to the high ground, where they founded New Franklin. But they were too far from the river, that great highway to the West, and prosperity and growth eluded the relocated village.

So did peace and harmony. Some years after its founding a group of New Franklin residents, incensed over a taxation issue, pulled up stakes and established another Franklin a mile to the west. "Just Plain" Franklin has had an even more difficult time surviving, but it is still there, population 196.

But the place so important to this story was the original city of Franklin, once the booming hub of the frontier. Boone's Lick, a saline spring which is now a state historical park, served as a magnet to settlers from the east. Here, in 1806, came Nathan and Daniel Morgan Boone, the sons of the noted frontiersman Daniel Boone, to boil salt from those waters. Also involved were James and Jesse Morrison. Legend has it that the men followed the hunting trail blazed by old Daniel Boone about 1800, known today as the Boonslick Trail. Later, they helped establish the route of the Boonslick Road, the first formal highway west, leading to Franklin from St. Charles.

The men produced twenty-five to thirty bushels of salt per day using forty kettles and one furnace. They hired six to eight men at $15 per month to help and eventually expanded to the point where sixteen to twenty were employed at four furnaces, producing 100 bushels of salt per day. A bushel of salt weighed about fifty pounds and sold in the Missouri River settlements for $2 to $2.50.

The salt was produced by heating large iron vessels filled with brine over a stone furnace. Salt crystals remained after the water evaporated. Three hundred gallons of water produced sixty pounds of salt.

The salt lick was abandoned in 1833 but the Boone brothers sold out to the Morrisons long before, probably in 1811. Today there is only a trace of the old salinity evident in the water coming from the spring.

In 1804 a claim was staked out five miles west of the townsite of Old Franklin which later became Hardeman's Gardens, a formal botanical garden established in 1820 by John Hardeman. Serpentine walks paved with crushed shells laced through the garden. There was nothing like it in Missouri Territory, not even in St. Louis or Ste. Genevieve. Much of the garden was destroyed in a flood in 1826.

Today the University of Missouri operates a horticultural research station west of New Franklin where botanists are planning to replicate Hardeman's Gardens.

The Thomas Hickman House, built in 1819, stands on the property of the research station. The University of Missouri is now seeking funds to restore the house to its original appearance.

Just past the north abutment of the Boonville bridge is a road marked 463, leading to the right. Turn east on that road. Immediately on the left, on the northeast corner of that intersection, is a marker placed by the Daughters of the American Revolution (DAR).

During the early years of the twentieth century the DAR undertook a difficult and costly job—installing incised granite markers on the great highways to the West, including the Boonslick Road and the Santa Fe Trail. Members did their research carefully and well. This is one of scores of markers which still stand along the Santa Fe Trail.

Just .2 mile to the east, on Route 463, is Rivercene, a mansion erected in 1869 by Joseph B. Kinney, a Missouri River steamboat captain. Kinney owned twenty-one boats at one time. The house, now owned by Mike and Winifred Cenatiempo (she is a direct descendant) is shown by appointment only.

Return to Highway 5, at the north abutment of the bridge. Across the highway and to the right is the Kit Carson Motel, owned by direct descendants of the family of the famed westerner. Cross the highway, bearing left, and enter Highway 87 to the west. H. Denny Davis, publisher of the *Fayette Advertiser* and a noted historian of Howard County, feels that this portion of the highway is atop old Broadway, the important main street of the old town of Franklin.

About one-half mile west of the bridge is a large marker on the south

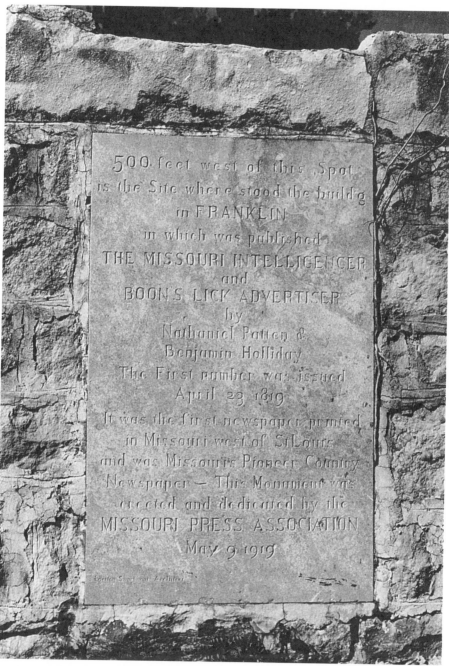

500 feet west of this Spot
is the Site where stood the build'g
in FRANKLIN
in which was published
THE MISSOURI INTELLIGENCER
and
BOON'S LICK ADVERTISER
by
Nathaniel Patten &
Benjamin Holliday
The First number was issued
April 23, 1819
It was the first newspaper printed
in Missouri west of St.Louis
and was Missouri's Pioneer Country
Newspaper — This Monument was
erected and dedicated by the
MISSOURI PRESS ASSOCIATION
May 9, 1919

William E. Brown

This marker commemorates Franklin's prospering newspaper, the Missouri Intelligencer. *It is on the site of Broadway, in the long-disappeared town of Franklin.*

side of the highway. The marker, erected by the Missouri Press Association, is on the approximate location of the *Missouri Intelligencer,* Old Franklin's daily newspaper. Copies of that paper are today a prime source of the history of the area.

Continue northwest. At 2.4 miles from the bridge, far back on the road on the right, is the William Jefferson Smith house, built in 1857. Smith was a prominent early farmer and one of the first to exploit the rich Missouri River bottomland on a large scale.

Just .3 mile farther west Highway 87 turns to the right; continue straight ahead on Route Z. Note that the road is just above the flood plain; this has to be the site of the Santa Fe Trail. About .8 mile from that corner, or 3.4 miles from the bridge, there is another DAR marker, on the right. It sits in the front yard of the Horace Kingsbury home. The single-story west wing of the house was erected in 1824 by Nicholas Amick, an early grower of hemp, which was once the leading crop of Howard County. The main section of the home was built by Kingsbury in 1856. Kingsbury Siding, one of the sites proposed for a Santa Fe National Historic Trail Interpretive Center, is named for him. The siding was built by the Missouri-Kansas-Texas Railroad in 1870 to accommodate Kingsbury's grain and cattle shipments.

At 5.7 miles from the bridge a gravel road marked 341 comes in from the left. Some two miles to the south is the original site of Hardeman Gardens. There is nothing to see there today.

Continue to the northwest for 3.8 more miles, to the settlement of Petersburg. There the blacktop turns right, but continue straight ahead onto a gravel road marked 330.

The Boonslick Historical Society is restoring the Cooper cemetery at Petersburg, including the original tombstone of Col. Benjamin Cooper, and those of his wife and sons. Famed as the first settler of the Boonslick country, in 1810, he built Cooper's Fort. Cooper County was named for him.

There is a marker at Petersburg denoting the site of Cooper's Chapel Methodist Church.

The farm where young Christopher ("Kit") Carson grew up is about seven miles due east of Petersburg. He was sixteen years old in 1826 when he bolted from his apprenticeship to a Franklin saddlemaker and joined Richard Gentry's caravan to Santa Fe.

Proceed due west for .8 mile. The water tower ahead and to the right is in Arrow Rock, across the Missouri River. A DAR marker is on the left. About twenty yards ahead and to the right is a marker commemorating Cooper's Fort.

Davis thinks that the site of the fort is out in the field to the north, but he also feels that no one knows exactly where it is. The fort was at-

Across the Missouri River bottom is a canebrake, the site of the landing for the ferry which crossed the river to Arrow Rock.

tacked and successfully defended during the War of 1812; in fact, those were the westernmost shots fired during that war.

Cooper paid close attention to Becknell's account of his first expedition to Santa Fe in the fall of 1821. Cooper was on his way with his own caravan to the Southwest even before Becknell could get his second trading venture mounted and rolling.

Proceed west another .7 mile, and cross the levee. There is a steel gate on the other side. Beyond that gate a dirt road continues northwest on private land. Go no farther. The road will peter out at a canebrake about a half-mile away. That marks the bank of the Missouri River and the site of the ferry used by early Santa Fe traders and operated by Henry Becknell, a brother of William Becknell. However, that is all private land, and there is nothing to see out there anyway. A better view of the site may be had from across the river at Arrow Rock. Return to Petersburg.

Route Z ends at Petersburg and Route J begins. Turn left on J. After about a block, turn left, or west, and follow the gravel road marked 328 for about one mile. Cross a concrete bridge and arrive at a T intersection. Bear to the right, still on the graveled 328. Cross a steel bridge .1 mile ahead. One mile farther there will be a sign on the right marking the beginning of state maintenance. Turn left (north) there and proceed .3 mile to the Boone's Lick State Historic Site.

Drive in to the parking lot and walk through the handsome exhibits

The Thomas Hickman House is near New Franklin, Missouri. It was built in 1819.

there. Follow the path down the gentle bluff to the historic spring itself.

The Boonslick gurgles, or more correctly oozes, from the base of a small hill. This unimpressive little spring was mighty important to the early history of central Missouri. Not only is this the location of Boone's Lick, but it also was the farm of William Becknell, the father of the Santa Fe Trail. And about eleven miles northwest of here is the farm which was home to young Josiah Gregg, who grew up to write perhaps the greatest contemporary account of the Santa Fe Trail.

Return to the park entrance and turn to the left. This is now a paved highway, Missouri 187. About two miles ahead is a stop sign and Highway 87. Turn right. This highway will lead (in 1.1 miles) through the little town of Boonesboro and eventually back to the bridge at Old Franklin. That combination of roads leading from Boone's Lick is the original Boonslick Trail.

At the intersection of 87 and Highway 5 turn left on Highway 5 and proceed two miles north to New Franklin, following Highway 5. Like its predecessor, New Franklin has named its principal street Broadway. Turn right. There, in the median, is the impressive monument commemorating New Franklin and the start of the Santa Fe Trail. Almost hidden behind that marker is a smaller stone, which marks the end of the Boonslick Road. (Technically, the Boonslick Road continued to Old Franklin, but departed from the earlier trail, to the east, to pass through Columbia.)

Head west from the marker in New Franklin and bear left .4 mile ahead. Just .4 mile farther and on the right is the entrance to the Horticultural Research Facility of the University of Missouri, in "Just Plain" Franklin. Proceed .7 mile ahead on the entrance road to the Hickman house, which is past the research buildings.

Return to New Franklin and turn south on Highway 5 at the stop sign. The highway turns to the right about a mile farther, where U.S. Highway 40 comes in from the left. At that point the Boonslick Road continued due south along the fencerow across the broad field. At the trees in the distance it fishhooked to the west, to align with Highway 87.

Return to Boonville via the Highway 5 bridge, proceed south on Route B to I-70, and turn west.

SALINE COUNTY

From Boonville proceed west on I-70 for 5.3 miles to the Highway 41 exit and follow the signs about fourteen miles to Arrow Rock. The first entrance to Arrow Rock State Historic Site leads to the camping area. Proceed another .4 mile north to the entrance to the town and turn right on Main Street. Continue east for six blocks. The Arrow Rock Information Center is on the left. Stop in to say hello to Kathy Borgman, executive director of Friends of Arrow Rock.

The Friends, in cooperation with the Division of Parks and Historic Preservation of the State of Missouri, lead walking tours of the historic old community daily during the tourist season. Membership is inexpensive; they need the support.

Six professional theatrical productions are held weekly in the Lyceum Theater, an 1872 church. Various plays are presented in repertory from June through August.

Cited by explorer William Clark in 1804 as "a handsome spot for a town," Arrow Rock had been an Indian rendezvous before it became an important stop on the Santa Fe Trail. The first permanent settlers arrived in 1815. The pioneer Becknell expedition stopped at the Santa Fe Spring in 1821, and most expeditions leaving Franklin in the 1820s would have taken the ferry and stopped at the spring also.

Across the street from the information center is the Huston Tavern, built by Joseph Huston in 1834 and recently restored by the state of Missouri. Not only is it outfitted as a museum, but it is also a fine restaurant.

Proceed on to the east to the stop sign at the last cross street and turn right. Two blocks to the south the road veers to the right. About a block ahead there is a Y in the road; bear right. Ahead is the famous Santa

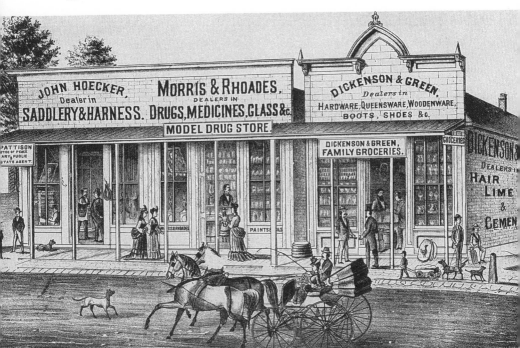

This sketch of Main Street, Arrow Rock, in 1876, was taken from the Illustrated Atlas of Saline County, Missouri.

The Santa Fe Spring was the magnet which drew the traders through Arrow Rock.

Fe Spring, still flowing. It issues, however, from a pipe in the concrete base of a small pavilion.

Make a U turn and return to the point where the road heads northwest. A post on the right bars the way to what was once the booming Arrow Rock Landing. Warehouses there in the mid-1800s were filled with goods shipped to the growing community. The river at that time swept up almost to the base of the hill—now it is far to the east across the bottom fields. There are still traces of those warehouse foundations at the base of the bluff, on land the state hopes to acquire for the expansion of the site.

Turn left at the first opportunity. Two blocks ahead and to the right is the 1839 courthouse, restored by the Friends of Arrow Rock and deeded to the state. Make a U turn, proceed back east and turn left at the corner. Continue north past Main. Proceed another block and stop just before reaching the intersection. On the right corner is the home of the noted Missouri artist George Caleb Bingham. The famous painter of frontier scenes lived here intermittently from 1837 through 1845.

This is a good time to discuss the famous stone gutters of Arrow Rock. Much has been written about William Becknell returning to Arrow Rock after his first trip to Santa Fe, taking a leather pouch from the back of a mule, holding it up, cutting it, and letting the silver coins roll into the stone gutters. The townspeople, it is said, were amazed.

Good trick, except there were no townspeople. There were no gutters. There was no Arrow Rock until 1829. If it happened at all, (which is unlikely, given Becknell's great financial stress) it happened in Old Franklin.

But those gutters certainly are in place now, a fact which will be painfully evident to any driver foolish enough to cross them carelessly. This text has been written to guide the traveler away from them. However, if they are crossed at an angle there should be no problem.

Turn left at the Bingham House onto High Street and continue west for nearly two blocks. The Matthew Hall House on the southeast corner of the intersection was built in 1846 by the pioneer doctor and has been restored by the Missouri Division of Parks and Historic Preservation.

Continue west until forced into a left turn. Proceed one block to Main Street and turn right. A block ahead is Highway 41—turn right. The way the traders left Arrow Rock is not known today; presumably they went west from the spring. The trail would have crossed 41 a couple of blocks south of Main Street, and the terrain indicates it would have looped due north to cross the highway about a block north of the west end of Main Street.

Jean Tyree Hamilton dug up this quote from an old history of Saline County:

The famous stone gutters of Arrow Rock flank Main Street. At right is the Huston Tavern, built in 1834.

The first business done and recorded was the appointment of Littleberry Estes, Daniel McDowell, and William White, Jr., as commissioners "to view and mark out the first road established in the County, petitioned by Lewis Rees and others, leading from the Arrow Rock [it was then not a town, only a rock] to the Grand Pass, by the place where Rees now lives, and from thence to the western boundary of the county, and make return to this court at the next term."

About one mile north of Main Street Highway 41 begins a gradual curve to the left. Just past the intersection of Route AC, on the right, is "Chestnut Hill." That is the home built in 1844 by the trader P. W. Thompson, on land he had purchased in 1826. It is one of many great homes still surviving which were built during the heyday of the Santa Fe Trail. Jean Hamilton and her late husband, Henry W. Hamilton, spent decades researching the trail in Saline County. The faint traces they found going up the rise to the west still can be seen from the back of the house.

On June 24, 1847, while in Santa Fe "traveling in foreign countries," Thompson was issued a certificate of membership in the Arrow Rock Masonic Lodge No. 56. A DAR marker denoting the route of the trail is in front of the house.

Proceed northwest on the highway for 2.5 miles. The settlement at the intersection with Route D is Hardeman, named after the family of John Hardeman. Just 1.5 miles to the west a gravel road enters the highway from the left. It is numbered 202. Take the gravel road west for .5 mile and stop at a cluster of farm buildings on the left. The stone building to the east is the smokehouse of the Neff Tavern, a trailside stopover popular with the traders.

Neff built his tavern in 1837 to capitalize on the Santa Fe Trail trade; the trail ran between the smokehouse and the barn. Continue a quarter-mile to the west. Bending down the grade to the northwest are three sets of parallel rut traces, now timbered gullies. It could be said that these are remains of the Santa Fe Trail, but Leo Oliva has pointed out that this was a more heavily traveled road terminating at Fort Osage, both before and after Becknell's journey. Certainly those wagons had a more telling impact on the land than the Santa Fe caravans which left from Franklin. A DAR marker is there also.

The Santa Fe Trail headed due north from there to cross Highway 41. Proceed west a half-mile to the gravel section line road and turn right (north) on Route 225 to intersect Highway 41 .3 mile away, and then turn left.

The highway crossed the trail a block to the east, then curved to parallel

Only the stone smokehouse, left, survives from the complex of buildings known to the traders as Neff Tavern.

41 about .3 mile to the north, for a distance of about 1.5 miles.

On the right a half-mile ahead is the Fahey farm. The house stands on a hill far from the highway. Faint traces of the trail are in the front yard.

The trail comes beneath Highway 41 1.7 miles west of the point where it was entered, at the intersection with Route E, coming in from the south. The trail stays with 41, sometimes a few feet on one side or the other, for another 1.5 miles. About 1.1 miles west of that intersection the Shiloh Cemetery is passed on the left, and then several extremely traces are seen extending up the grade to the west along the south side of the highway, terminating in the area of a small pond, which is 2.1 miles from the Fahey farm.

Another .4 mile and the trail is ahead on the right, at the Moore place. Faint traces are immediately in front of the house. It is there that the Santa Fe Trail leaves the highway to swing to the north to head several tributaries to Salt Fork Creek, thus averting difficult crossings. (That creek was bridged in the late 1840s, so the trail did not have to move so far north—it headed through the town of Marshall and Malta Bend instead. However, by that time most of the traffic was emanating from Independence and Westport, so those traces probably were never very deep, and certainly local traffic would have helped make them.)

Rock Creek was crossed more than two miles to the north. There are traces there, but no roads nearer than a half-mile away, and the land is all private. Proceed five miles ahead to Marshall.

Highways 41 and 240 separate on the northwest edge of Marshall. Stay on 41 to the north. Cross Salt Fork Creek. Four miles from the junction of 240 and 41 a gravel road crosses the highway. (The Santa Fe Trail crossed the highway a few yards south.) Turn left there. At the corner was the Maupin Tavern, a hostelry popular in the later days of the trail. It is gone now. There is nothing there but rolling terrain.

But at 1.1 miles ahead there is a set of rut swales which rival any seen in the West, the Harvey Springs-Weinrich traces. Five sets of deep-cut ruts go westward through timber down to the grade on the south side of the gravel road. Another trace is adjacent to the road.

There were two springs here, indicating that this would have been a choice camping spot for traders. The spring north of the road is called Indian Spring, because many Sac and Fox were seen in the area in 1846, when they wintered here on their way to their new reservation in Kansas. The Indians were under the protection of Maj. T. H. Harvey, Superintendent of Indian Affairs during the terms of presidents John Tyler and James K. Polk. Harvey owned more than 2,400 acres here. The spring on the south furnishes sufficient water for livestock and two residences of the current Harvey family.

Make a U turn and return to Marshall. Turn west on Business 65, join the main Highway 65, and continue west through the town of Malta Bend. Two miles west of there the highway curves to the south. Here the Santa Fe Trail parallels the highway, a few yards to the north.

Just 4.4 miles west of Malta Bend is the cemetery at the little town of Grand Pass. Here are broad, dramatic traces of the Santa Fe Trail running northwest down the gently sloping Missouri River bluff to Grand Pass Spring. Turn right on Route T into the town of Grand Pass and right again to the cemetery on the east edge of town. It will be on the right, on the south side of the road. A DAR marker on the northwest corner of U.S. 65 and Route T commemorates the Santa Fe Trail.

Jean Hamilton has written about the Grand Pass:

> There have long been references to the idea that the Osage and other Indians were able to wade across the Missouri River during times of low water, during the early historic period, near the present town of Grand Pass. The village of the Little Osages was about seven miles from here at that time. The stories were given credence during World War I when a Saline County man visited an Osage at Camp Funston. The Indian had never been to Missouri, yet knew much about his home environs. He explained that Grand Pass was near the great river crossing of his people and the details had been handed down by the elders of the tribe.

Return to Highway 65 and continue west. The trail is following the pavement closely, to one side or another for 2.1 miles to the Lafayette County line.

LAFAYETTE COUNTY

Although there was some local knowledge of the route of the Santa Fe Trail in Missouri prior to the National Park Service study, it was exceedingly well hidden. The efforts of H. Denny Davis in Howard County, Jean and Henry Hamilton in Saline County, and Roger Slusher in Lafayette County, have now produced cartographic data which locates the route of the trail.

Slusher first articulated the "facing houses" theory to the NPS team—when antebellum homes are found forming an east-west line, chances are their front doors faced the Santa Fe Trail, since it was the only major east-west highway which existed in western Missouri at the time those houses were built. Slusher found fifteen such houses from Dover to the eastern border of Jackson County. The Hamiltons found additional houses east of Dover and in Saline County. All define the route of the trail.

At the eastern county line the trail is on the same alignment as the highway and stays that way most of the way to Lexington. The first mention of a road in the annals of Lafayette County was found by Jean Hamilton, referring to a county court record dated April 24, 1821:

> Abner Graham was appointed overseer of the road leading from Fort Osage thru Sniabar township, from opposite James Connors to Fort Osage. He was required to keep the road in good repair, clean & smooth, twenty feet wide. At the same time James Young was appointed overseer of the road from Little Sniabar to James Connors. Wm. F. Simmons was appointed overseer of the road from Tabbo Creek crossing near Mount Vernon [south of the mouth of Tabo Creek] to the range line between ranges 26 and 27 . . . and from this point Thos. Fristoe was appointed overseer westward to Little Sniabar Creek. George Parkeson was appointed for the road from Tabo Creek eastward through Mount Vernon to the east end of Tabo township. [That would cover the entire distance from Fort Osage to Saline County.]

Continue on U.S. 65 to Waverly. U.S. highways 65 and 24 turn north in Waverly to cross the Missouri River; watch the signs closely to go west on Highway 24.

Motorists along this portion of the Santa Fe Trail will note a number of Lewis and Clark Trail signs on stretches of the highway close to the Missouri River. This isn't the Lewis and Clark Trail at all—the Missouri

River is. This is the highway retracement route.

A 1914 atlas of Lafayette County identifies as "Santa Fe Trail" a road that swings due south at the western limits of Waverly. That is believed to be an error, easily committed in that case, as the trail there had been in disuse as a covered wagon road for about seventy-five years before the map was drawn. From the standpoint of terrain, there is no reason why the traders would have followed such an out-of-the-way route. Route N is about seven miles ahead. Check the odometer there. Just 1.6 miles ahead is an antebellum house on the right, a considerable distance north of the highway. The town of Dover is about a mile west of there.

From now on there will be a number of pre-Civil-War houses along 24. They clearly define the route of the Santa Fe Trail as being the same as Highway 24.

About 2.5 miles west of Dover is the crossing of Tabo Creek. That miniscule watercourse was such a formidable obstacle to the pioneers that a ferry had to be established. That indicates that the stream (and its banks) were much less docile than they appear to be today. On April 24, 1821, more than four months prior to William Becknell's history-making expedition to Santa Fe, a license was issued to Adam Lightner to keep a ferry across Tabo, for which he paid two dollars. The ferrage rates fixed by the county court were three cents for one passenger and another three for a horse or cow; two cents per head of sheep or hogs; twenty-five cents for a carriage or cart; and thirty-seven and one-half cents for a wagon and team. (One of the ferrymen at Tabo Creek was Thomas Slusher, ancestor of Virginia Slusher Fisher, a member of the Santa Fe National Historic Trail Advisory Council; and Roger Slusher, of Lexington.)

About two miles east of the center of Lexington there is a new alignment to Highway 24, which veers to the southwest to bypass the town. Just before reaching that point there is a road leading north from Highway 24 to the tower of radio station KLEX. The Santa Fe Trail left the highway about a quarter-mile east of there and is directly beneath the tower, heading a little north of due west. Instead of following 24 as it veers to the left, continue straight ahead on Missouri Highway 224, toward the business district of Lexington. To the north, the Santa Fe Trail will cut sharply to the southwest and come back to join Highway 224 just after entering the city limits. To follow the trail back a half-mile or so, turn hard right on Martin Lane Road, just inside the city limits. It is also known as the Old Dover Road. Follow it to the northeast. At the point where the present road turns due north, the Santa Fe Trail turned to the southeast toward U.S. 24. Return to 224.

Highway 224 at that point is also known as the Old Dover Road. Proceed southwest to a street which slants away to the left and turn half-left there. That is also the Old Dover Road and the route of the trail. Continue southwest one block past Franklin Street, where the road turns half-right and becomes South Street. Proceed straight west to 23rd Street. There is a marker there denoting the site of the original courthouse and the center of the town the traders knew. Proceed on South to 20th Street and turn left, or south. The trail does that, too. A few blocks farther south, 20th veers to the right around a shopping center which is on the left. At the stop sign turn left onto Highway 13 and resume a southern course. Cross U.S. Highway 24 a little less than a mile ahead. Proceed .8 mile more to a point where 13 curves to the left. Continue due south on Route O for one mile, where the blacktop curves to the right around a striking Victorian mansion.

At a point where Route O begins to curve back to the southeast, a gravel road proceeds straight ahead. This is Route 82 and the Santa Fe Trail. Take it.

At the intersection of 80 and 82, .7 mile ahead, continue on 82. The intersection of 82 with 84 is exactly one mile ahead, and at that point the Santa Fe Trail bisects the intersecting roads and heads due west, through the fields. All traces are believed to be lost today. Return to Lexington.

An alternate Santa Fe Trail route heads up to the river in present downtown Lexington. Turn left on South Street from 20th for seven more blocks to 13th. Turn right, proceed north for two blocks, and then left on Main Street. Continue due west for 4.5 blocks and slant to the right on Broadway. A half-block ahead turn right onto Highland Avenue and stop. Here, on the corner of Highland and Broadway, is the location of the DAR *Madonna of the Trail* statue for Missouri. That's the good news. Here also is a red granite DAR marker. That is bad news, because it was moved here from Tabo Creek, and it should be moved back.

Throughout the length of the trail there will be instances of those markers being moved by well-intentioned but ill-advised people. All markers ought to be where the DAR put them in the first place. Those valiant women did their research well in the first decade of the twentieth century, when the markers were placed, and it ill behooves any individual or organization to tamper with their locations. Local and state chapters of the DAR ought to take the lead in a campaign to return the misplaced markers to their original sites.

This is known as the "river route" of the Santa Fe Trail and probably would have been used in dry weather, particularly if the traders had some business to do in Lexington (which predates the Santa Fe Trail).

Downtown Lexington has a fascinating heritage. The first home office of the famed freighting partnership of Russell, Majors, and Waddell stood on the northwest corner of the intersection of 10th and Main streets. The bank of the famous Aull brothers' mercantile empire was located where Pioneer House is now, at the point where 224 and 15 turn half-right, between Eighth and Ninth on Main. The Aull empire is closely identified with the Santa Fe Trail. Louis Atherton's *The Frontier Merchant in Mid-America* has a good summary of the mercantile and trading activity of the Aull brothers. Other structures are related to the Civil War Battle of Lexington.

The old trail followed approximately the route of Highway 224 to the southwest, paralleling the Missouri River. Follow the highway west for 2.3 miles to the Peckerwood Club, on the south side of the road. A marker next to the building denotes the site of "Simpson's Santa Fe Trail Spring." Whether it was named for Lt. James H. Simpson of the Corps of Topographical Engineers, or for Dr. Richard French Simpson, a military surgeon, has yet to be determined.

Continue west to the heart of Wellington, 6.7 miles southwest of Lexington, and turn south on Missouri Highway 131. Proceed .8 mile due south to Highway 24. Cross the highway. A few yards to the south is County Road 24, which roughly parallels the highway. Take it to the right. That is the main route of the Santa Fe Trail. It had crossed the formidable Sniabar Creek a half-mile northeast of there. That corner is about where the "wet" and "dry" routes of the Santa Fe Trail join.

Follow that gravel road west for six miles. The blacktop Route D will be at that checkpoint. Continue on the gravel to the west for about 1.5 miles, where the road turns to the right. A handsome DAR marker is in the front yard of a home to the north and on the right. Slant to the left around the old Anderson Cemetery and proceed another half-mile ahead to U.S. Highway 24. The trail has been beneath the road for all that distance. There are some large rocks on the gravel road; a safe speed would be thirty miles per hour. They come crashing up against the floorboards at an uncomfortable velocity at faster speeds.

Some say that the trail goes beneath the highway at that point. Some show it paralleling the highway a quarter-mile to the south for about two miles. From there to Fort Osage the location of the old trail remains a mystery. Turn left and proceed west into Jackson County.

JACKSON COUNTY

The trails in Jackson County are complex but they are not hard to find if the directions in this book are followed carefully. They will take the traveler to Fort Osage, to the Blue Mills, Independence, and Westport landings and along the roads from the landings to Independence and Westport. These directions will guide the visitor along the Santa Fe Trail southwest out of Independence to New Santa Fe, and south from Westport

Fort Osage, a federally owned fur-trading post, has been reconstructed by the Jackson County Parks and Recreation Department.

to the same town; and then southwest of Westport to Olathe.

Leave Highway 24 in the town of Buckner, which is about seven miles west of the Lafayette County line, by turning north on Route BB (Sibley Street). The Santa Fe Trail would have crossed BB about two miles north of Buckner; no one knows exactly where. Turn half-left (northwest) there. The Jackson County Parks and Recreation Department has done an excellent job of posting directional signs to Fort Osage; this is where they start. Follow those signs for about 1.5 miles to Fort Osage. Be prepared to spend a couple of hours there.

The site of Fort Osage was selected by William Clark of the epic Lewis and Clark expedition. The government ''factory'' was erected there in 1808. Situated on a bluff high above the Missouri River, it served as a federally owned fur trading post. A garrison of soldiers stationed there discouraged unwanted intrusions into the fur-rich frontier by British traders. The storerooms were adjacent to the fort buildings.

Fort Osage has been reconstructed virtually from bare earth. Sophisticated archaeological work was undertaken prior to reconstruction. There is plenty of evidence to prove that Fort Osage is today as it was in its heyday.

It is open from 9 to 5 daily from April 15 to November 15, and on weekends the rest of the year. There is a small admission charge.

Leave Fort Osage back to the south, to the stop sign two miles north of Buckner. Turn right there, at the Blue Mills Road, and head west. Just 2.7 miles ahead the road curves to the southwest. The Santa Fe Trail does so also, a half-mile to the north. Follow the winding road another 3.4 miles to the southwest to reach the dead-end Lentz Road. Turn right there and proceed north a half-mile (jogging to the right along the way) to the end of the road. An old, dilapidated two-car garage is on the right, built with rock taken from the foundation of the Blue Mills. Drive until the car is about even with the far end of the house on the right, and stop. Walk to the left, to the edge of the embankment leading down to the Blue River. A number of foundation stones are still there, near the top of the bank, and these are all that remain today of the Blue Mills.

The great three-story mill, built of walnut logs about 1832, was erected by James and Robert Aull. Aull is an enchanted name in the history of the Santa Fe Trail. John, James, and Robert Aull headed a prosperous mercantile firm in Lexington and expanded to stores in Richmond (nine miles northwest of Lexington) and Independence. They amassed much wealth outfitting the traders who were carrying goods to Santa Fe for sale. Their markups were as much as seventy-five percent more than eastern merchants were getting, but they were willing to give the goods on consignment and wait nearly a year for their money.

James Aull eventually decided to bypass the middlemen and go into the trade himself. He had the misfortune to be on a venture in 1846, when he was overtaken by the Army of the West and ordered to bring up the rear. By the time he arrived in Santa Fe business was terrible, so he decided to continue down the Chihuahua Trail. Along the way he was overtaken by Doniphan's legions and again ordered to bring up the rear.

Business was good in Chihuahua, however, until Doniphan decided to pull out his military detachment to fight elsewhere in the Mexican War, and left the Anglo traders unguarded. Aull decided to stand pat in Chihuahua. His judgment was good—sure enough, there was no Mexican insurrection to American rule. Instead he was murdered by four Mexican bandits as he was keeping his store.

The first of the Missouri River landings to serve Independence was the Blue Mills Landing, established in 1832. (Traders headed for Independence went overland prior to that time.) It is very difficult to reach today.

Return to Blue Mills Road and continue south and southwest for two miles to U.S. 24. Turn right. A block or two ahead the highway turns to the southwest. Just one mile from the point where 24 was reached, Kentucky Road slants off to the right, headed due west. Read the odometer at this point. Turn onto Kentucky Road and proceed west for .4 mile. Turn right around the Elm Grove School onto Whitney Road. Continue north nearly a mile, to 18th Street, where Whitney jogs to the left and then resumes a northerly course. Cross the Courtney-Union School Road at an angle and continue to the north, on what is now the Courtney-Atherton Road. Proceed generally north to a sharp right turn, at the locked gates to River Bluff Nature Reserve. Continue ahead on the Courtney-Atherton Road until reaching a point 3.1 miles from

Highway 24 and Kentucky Road. The Blue Mills Landing is about .7 mile due north and is not easily reached any way except by water. This is as close as anyone can get with an automobile today. But the road just traversed, according to Dean Earl Wood, is the road traders took (in reverse) to get from the landing to the old route of the Santa Fe Trail.

Return to Kentucky Road at the Elm Grove School and turn right. The Santa Fe Trail is roughly paralleling U.S. Highway 24, from .2 to 1.0 mile to the north. Exactly 3.2 miles to the west (or two blocks west of Pleasant Street) Kentucky Road starts to curve to the left. At that point make a very tight right turn to the northeast onto North River Boulevard. Proceed northeast for about a block to a Y in the road. Veer to the left, on the road which leads to the Missouri Portland Cement Co. Follow that road for about a block to an area paved with white rock on the left, at a sharp curve to the right. Park there and walk straight ahead to a marker on the embankment. Down below is the famous Independence Landing (also known as the Wayne City or Upper Landing.)

This overlook is one of the most impressive points on the trail, and Sugar Creek residents care enough about the view to keep the brush down. It is discouraging business. Now the steep riverbank is cluttered with trash from illegal dumpers. Good people like the DAR's Jane Mallinson do what they can to keep the place presentable; there just aren't enough Jane Mallinsons these days.

At one time blocks of buildings stood down below, where the cement plant is now. After the boats were unloaded the wagons headed to the northwest, gradually climbing the hill. When they were about half-way up they made a sharp switchback to the right and proceeded the rest of the way up to the top of the bluff. The road leading down to the cement plant (no admittance!) approximates the route of the caravans. The wagons would have gained the top of the bluff at this point, then headed south toward Independence Square.

Return to Kentucky via North River Road and head southwest, for a look at Independence Landing from water level. Follow Kentucky Road west for 1.1 miles. Turn right onto Vermont Avenue and pass through the Amoco refinery. Just before reaching the small Sugar Creek depot the road turns to the right and becomes the Cement City Road. This runs between the bluff and the Missouri River. Cross the railroad tracks and continue east. Check the odometer when abreast of the signal bridge, proceed 1.6 miles farther and stop at a graveled turnout. To the west on the bluff are the buildings of the cement company.

During the years of the Santa Fe trade the river swept in to about where the road is now, but now the water is a block or so to the north. The steamboats tied up here, as well as a block both upstream and down. On the bluff were many warehouses and other buildings for the now-defunct town of Wayne City. A ferry leading to the town of Liberty was about a block downstream. The levee was crossed not only by Santa Fe traders and their goods, but by tens of thousands of emigrants bound for Oregon and California.

Return to the refinery and head south to Kentucky Road. Turn left. A mile east, almost to the turnoff for the overlook, is North River Boulevard. Turn hard right and head south. In later years the trail did that too, but a more frequently used route arched to the east a couple of blocks. But that road was often a quagmire and, after the traders discovered the Westport Landing (also known as "Kanzas Landing"), some stopped using Independence Landing and started bypassing the town altogether.

The city leaders weren't about to tolerate that, so they macadamized what is now River Road, and eventually installed a railroad connecting the Wayne City landing with Independence Square. That didn't slow Westport's growth much, but it did keep Independence alive.

Cross U.S. Highway 24. Proceed two more blocks to College Avenue. The trail from the landing turned left (east) there. Turn east along with it and drive for six blocks to Bess Truman Parkway. Turn right, or south. Proceed several curving blocks to Spring and turn right. Continue south on Spring for three blocks and turn left onto Truman Road.

The trail went in many directions from the present traffic circle; the goal now is simply to get to the square. Proceed east for three blocks to Main Street. Turn right and park. Main is along the east side of the square, which is a block south of Truman Road. The visitor center of the City of Independence is on the corner of Main and Truman Road. Shuttle buses depart every few minutes for free tours of this historic city. (Some of the sites, however, charge modest admission fees.) The tour center is open from 8:30 to 5 daily. Many of the stops are Truman-related, including both the Truman Library and the Truman Home. Buses also stop at the Frontier Trails Center on the northeast corner of Spring and Pacific streets. This is the national headquarters of the Oregon-California Trails Association. Across the street, at 313 West Pacific, is a home occupied by George Caleb Bingham from 1864 to 1870, long after he had left Arrow Rock.

At 217 North Main, next door to the visitor center, is the 1859 Jackson County Jail and Marshal's Home, a restoration well worth a visit. There is a small admission charge.

But it is really Independence Square that exudes the mystique of the old trails to the American West and Southwest.

And speaking of mystique, this seems to be an appropriate time to introduce three of the four people whose auras accompany all travelers along the Santa Fe Trail.

The first is Josiah Gregg. The fifth of the eight children of Harmon and Susannah Gregg, Josiah was born July 19, 1806, in Overton County, Tennessee. Harmon's brother William moved to Howard County, Missouri, and shortly was joined by Harmon and his family. In December 1814 William was killed by Indians; Harmon Gregg's family holed up in Cooper's Fort to await the end of the War of 1812.

The Greggs remained in the Boonslick country until 1825, when they moved to a place five miles north of the great springs which two years later would become Independence, Missouri.

Josiah contracted a bad case of tuberculosis and became so puny he couldn't pursue the family occupation of farming. He left home for a medical education in Philadelphia, graduated, and returned to Jackson County to establish his practice.

By this time (no one knows the exact dates) Josiah would have been familiar with the romance of the Santa Fe Trail. His father had accompanied Becknell on his second expedition.

He, being a medical doctor, also would know of the effect of the dry air of the desert Southwest on the lungs of the consumptive. His editor, Milo Milton Quaife, said that he was so sickly that he couldn't mount his own horse, yet he opted to join a caravan bound for Santa Fe in the spring of 1831.

He pursued the career of a Santa Fe trader for the next nine years, and by 1840, at the age of thirty-four, he was a robust, healthy, and fairly wealthy man. He left the trade then, possibly to write his book, *The Commerce of the Prairies*, which appeared in two volumes in 1844. Said Quaife: "His style is simple, chaste, elegant, pleasing, and sometimes eloquent. His descriptions are complete and full, and never tedious. . . . Upon its publication the book was immediately recognized as a masterpiece, and that verdict will ever stand."

The life of a physician in the frontier town of Independence evidently lacked excitement, so when war was declared on Mexico in 1846, Gregg served as a war correspondent and accompanied the troops sent to Col. Alexander Doniphan in Chihuahua. He is believed to have returned to Missouri sometime in 1849; at any rate, he joined in the California gold rush.

He was at a mining camp in northern California in October 1849. Short of provisions, the miners decided to head west to the seacoast. Gregg led the seven-man exploratory contingent which reached the coast after a thirty-two-day drive. On December 29 they discovered Humboldt Bay (at present Eureka).

The group headed south, in the direction of San Francisco, turning inland toward the Sacramento Valley. Debilitated, this time by exposure, hardship, and starvation, rather than tuberculosis, Gregg lapsed into un-

Matthew Field

consciousness and fell from his horse. He died a few hours later and was buried somewhere in Lake County.

But he remains a vital component of the Santa Fe Trail adventure, for his book was the first, and indeed probably the finest, to be published on that great roadway.

Next onto the stage of the Santa Fe Trail walks Matthew C. Field. Like Gregg, he was a sickly youngster. At about age fifteen he was apprenticed to a New York jeweler. That was no fun, so he became an actor, and evidently a fairly good one. He was sponsored for four years on the Mobile-New Orleans-St. Louis circuit.

By the spring of 1839 he was in worse physical shape than ever before. If he didn't have TB he had the symptoms, plus a gastric ulcer. In 1839 Matt sold his watch and chain and headed for Independence aboard a Missouri River steamboat. He started down the trail early in August 1839, writing as he went. Unlike Gregg, he forsook the Cimarron Cutoff for the Mountain Branch, working his way through Big Timbers to the Bent brothers' palace on the Arkansas River. Then he possibly traversed the serpentine trail over Raton Pass, arriving in Taos first, then Santa Fe.

He hooked up with the noted trader, Dr. David Waldo, for the return over the Cimarron Cutoff. Back in the United States he went to work as an assistant editor for the New Orleans *Picayune,* where his accounts of his Santa Fe Trail adventures were published over a period of two years. His reputation as a writer solidly established, he became a partner in the new St. Louis *Weekly Reveille* in 1844.

Matt's health did not do well in Anglo civilization. He went East in the summer of 1844, sailing from Boston on a cruise calculated to bolster his physical condition. On November 15, 1844, two days at sea, Matt Field died. His shrouded body was committed to the deep immediately.

Susan Magoffin

Like Gregg, he continues to ride to Santa Fe often. His book, *Matt Field on the Santa Fe Trail,* lives on.

Susan Shelby Magoffin is a name that will evoke warmth in the knowledgeable Santa Fe Trail explorer. She had everything—blood that ran cobalt blue, youth, health, a wealthy husband. That she wasn't spoiled rotten is the wonder of the world, but she couldn't have been. Her daily diary, which appears in *Down the Santa Fe Trail and into Mexico,* reveals a warmth and compassion and love that had probably never before been seen on the trail, and certainly never recorded.

Susan was born July 30, 1827, on her father's estate near Danville, Kentucky. Several Shelbys had figured large in America's War of Independence, including Isaac Shelby, the first governor of Kentucky. Private tutors were retained to mold Susan's quick and retentive mind.

When she was eighteen she fell in love with Samuel Magoffin, a successful Santa Fe trader twenty-seven years older than she. They were married November 25, 1845. After a six-month honeymoon, Magoffin decided to go back to work. Their trip down the Santa Fe Trail together began early in June 1846.

Magoffin evidently regarded his bride as an object of prized porcelain. She had her own tent-house, a private carriage, books, toiletries, a maid, her own driver, and at least two servant boys. She may have had the feeling that she was writing American history, so well crafted is her diary. She was "sick"—pregnant, actually. Yet, she wrote almost every day. She thought she was the first Anglo woman to go down the Santa Fe Trail. So did everyone else, as a matter of fact, until the fall of 1987, when it was discovered that a Mary Donoho made the trip in 1833.

Susan's first pregnancy miscarried at Bent's Old Fort. She was at Matamoras, Mexico, in September 1847 when her second child died a few days after birth. She and Samuel were living at Barrett's Station, in west St. Louis County, by 1851, when her third child was born. Her health is said to have been damaged by the rigors of travel on the Santa Fe Trail, but she probably had internal problems unrelated to the experience. She bore her fourth child in 1855 and died shortly thereafter.

But her book lives on, as do those of Gregg and Field. Their comments will be included from time to time throughout this text.

The fourth traveler, Marion Sloan Russell, will be introduced at Fort Leavenworth.

Continue walking to the south along Main Street. The next street south, Maple, is the northern boundary of Independence Square. On the northwest corner of the intersection of Main and Maple is all that remains of the tavern and inn of Smallwood Noland. A small portion of the brickwork from the original structure can be seen in the northwest corner of the building, near the alley.

It is an important site, for here stayed Susan Shelby Magoffin:

> Tuesday evening [June 9, 1846] we went into Independence; there
> we stayed one night only at Mr. Noland's Hotel. On Wednesday
> morning I did considerable business; some shopping—little articles
> I had thought of only within a few days.

That hotel, which replaced one which burned a year earlier, was packed every night with 400 guests, two to a bed. It had a large porch facing Main Street; the inn's livery stable was on the west, facing the courthouse.

Matt Field left a detailed description of Independence in the spring of 1839:

> In the square you observe a number of enormous wagons into
> which men are packing bales and boxes. Presently the mules are
> driven in from pasture, and a busy time commences in the square,
> catching the fractious animals with halters and introducing them
> to harness for their long journey. Full half a day is thus employed
> before the expedition finally gets into motion and winds slowly out
> of town. This is an exciting moment. Every window sash is raised,
> and anxious faces appear watching with interest the departure. The
> drivers snap their long whips and swear at their unruly mules, bid-
> ding goodby in parentheses between the oaths, to old friends on each
> side of the street as they move along.

Gregg left Independence Square on May 15, 1831, a day he described as "one of the brightest and most lovely of all the days in the calendar":

This pastoral view of the Jackson County Courthouse in Independence was sketched about 1846. The view is believed to be toward the south.

At last . . . the miseries of preparation are over—the thousand anxieties occasioned by wearisome consultations and delays are felt no more. The charioteer as he smacks his whip feels a bounding elasticity of soul within him, which he finds it impossible to restrain; even the mules prick up their ears with a peculiarly conceited air, as if in anticipation of that change of scene which will presently follow. Harmony and good feeling prevail everywhere.

At that time another traveler described Independence as having "a courthouse built of brick, two or three merchant stores, and fifteen or twenty dwelling houses, built mostly of logs hewed on both sides."

It was the courthouse that caught the attention of the travelers. Sitting in the middle of the square, it is now more famed because it held the courtroom of the thirty-third president of the United States, Harry S. Truman. But of the courthouse of the emigrants—possibly the one Gregg saw and certainly the successor seen by most of the traders—fragments are still encased in that handsome brick structure across the street from Smallwood Noland's inn.

Continue walking south on Main Street past the courthouse. The street bordering the square on the south is Lexington. A block to the south is Kansas Avenue. On the southwest corner of that intersection is the town's old city hall. The little structure just to the west, at 107 Kansas, is the original 1827 log courthouse, which first stood at Lynn and Lexington, a couple of blocks to the northeast.

After the erection of the brick courthouse, the old city hall was used as a private residence. At one time it was owned by Samuel Owens, the ill-fated partner of the equally ill-fated James Aull. (Owens was killed at the Battle of Sacramento during the Mexican War, shortly before Aull's murder in Chihuahua.) The City of Independence, realizing the importance of the little structure, obtained and moved it in 1921. The stone fireplaces and veranda were not part of the original design. Judge Harry S. Truman held court in the building in 1932-33, while the main courthouse was being remodeled.

Proceed to Liberty Street, the west boundary of the square. Here the great caravans formed, heading south.

Complete the walk around the square and resume the automobile trip. Head south on Liberty Street from Truman Road. Before fences and private property lines regimented them to marked streets, the earliest caravans headed away from the square the best way they could. But shortly after Independence started its precipitous growth, the property lines dictated the route of the trail, so the caravans had the choice of turning west on Lexington for a couple of blocks to Spring Avenue, or continuing south two blocks past the square and turning west on Walnut. Either way, the goal was Spring. There they turned south. Just before reaching Pacific Avenue, today the location of the National Frontier Trails Center, they found a tremendous spring on the left. Across the intersection and to the south is a deep chasm, the route of the waters which once issued from that spring—the high banks give some measure of the volume of flow.

Continue south and turn right, or west, on Pacific Street. On the Southeast corner of that intersection, across the street from the Trails Center is the Bingham-Waggoner House, now open to the public.

Turn west onto Pacific for just a block, then go south again on Pleasant Street. The Santa Fe Trail is on a diagonal now, moving southwest through the Bingham-Waggoner estate to arrive at the intersection of Pleasant and South streets. Proceed south on Pleasant to its intersection with South, where it jogs to the right. Turn to the right but continue to the west, over the railroad tracks, for one more block to McCoy; then turn left. The trail is off to the right a few yards.

About a half-mile to the south, at a railroad crossing, McCoy becomes Santa Fe Road. At this point the street and the trail become one. Just past 31st Street is a wedge in the road—bear to the right for two more blocks to 33rd Street. Now the trail is a few yards to the left.

Bear right onto 33rd for two short blocks to Crysler Avenue and turn left, or south. The trail will intercept at 35th Street. Soon it will turn to head due south, a few yards west of Crysler.

Proceed south to 39th Street and turn right. Drive four blocks west to Blue Ridge Boulevard and turn left. The Santa Fe Trail intercept is a couple of blocks south, at 40th Terrace.

Blue Ridge Boulevard was built atop the Blue Ridge. The traders preferred the ridges to the valleys, so historian Dean Earl Wood's findings match the terrain—the Santa Fe Trail and Blue Ridge Boulevard are identical all the way into the heart of Raytown. There the trail turns west—so should the traveler today, onto 63rd Street Trafficway. The trail would have turned gradually in its earliest days, but Raytown was settled and fenced off early, so the bulk of the Santa Fe Trail traffic would have had to jog quite frequently in this part of Jackson County, as indeed the motorist must today.

A half-mile west of Blue Ridge Boulevard, just past the Regency East Apartments, is a Y in the road with a ''No Left Turn'' sign. The foolhardy may try to brave Raytown's finest, but the wisest will continue ahead one block to Elm, turn left for a short block, then right again. The traveler will be on Blue Ridge Boulevard and the Santa Fe Trail once more.

Within the next half-mile the road will gradually curve to the south. Just before the end of that curve there is a traffic island. Bear to the right past this triangular island and then turn south, or left, onto Blue Ridge Cutoff.

Shortly after the turn a granite DAR marker will come into view. A log cabin is on the left, a short distance to the south. It is designated ''Aunt Sophie's Cabin.'' Aunt Sophie was a slave of the Archibald Rice family. She lived in one of a number of cabins ringing the property and died in 1896 at the age of seventy-seven. This is said to be her cabin. A new roof was added in 1987 and several of the logs were replaced. Some of the bark is still on the newest logs.

To the east of the cabin is the Rice-Tremonti House, lived in continuously from about 1837 until 1989. It was purchased by the Friends of Rice-Tremonti Home Association, Inc., in the latter year and is now being restored one room at a time, as donated funds become available. Whitson J. Kirk, Jr., is leading the effort.

Matt Field remembered the place:

> About half a day's travel brings the Santa Fe bound traders past the flourishing plantation of Farmer Rice, where leisure travellers often linger to enjoy his sweet bacon, fresh eggs, new milk, and the other nutritious and unsophisticated luxuries that always appease appetite without encumbering digestion.

Rice acquired the land in 1836 and built a log house and three slave cabins (possibly Aunt Sophie's) in 1837. Matt Field came in 1839, of course, and five years later a prospering "Farmer Rice" made major improvements, bringing the property to the appearance it has today.

Continue south for about five more blocks to Gregory Boulevard and turn right. Proceed west for a half-block to the entrance to William M. Klein Park and turn left. At the end of the drive is the Cave Spring Interpretive Center. Visit the exhibits in the handsome building, then stroll down the shaded paths to the Cave Spring.

For a long time Cave Spring enthusiasts have tried to find primary documentation that this was used as a campground by either Santa Fe Trail traders or Oregon-California emigrants. So far none has surfaced. Yet, it stretches the imagination to suppose that it wasn't. The spring is powerful and would have been surrounded by good wood and grass in trail days. It is about ten trail miles from Independence Square. Travelers leaving at dawn could have arrived in early afternoon. But most didn't leave at dawn and many couldn't get away before noon. It would have been an inviting target for the first night's camp.

Return to the Blue Ridge Cutoff and continue south to East 87th Street, which is the north boundary of a shopping center. Turn right there, past a traffic island in 87th which is only a few yards long. Immediately after reaching the end of that island turn left, or south, onto an alley-like road which appears to be an access road to the back side of the shopping center. Actually, it is the Santa Fe Trail. Take an odometer reading upon leaving 87th, and exactly .3 mile to the south the trail turns to the right. Turn with it. It makes a left soon. The trail continued to the southwest there, but there is no way to follow it exactly. Continue due south for a block or two. Just past the Palestine Cemetery turn right onto 93rd Street.

Proceed over a railroad overpass. The Santa Fe Trail knifed in at about 200 yards ahead, headed to the southwest. Continue to the next intersection, which is Hillcrest, and turn left.

The Santa Fe Trail crossed at the high point of Hillcrest, just north of Bannister Road. Continue south to 103rd Street. Do not consult a map here; people who do so tend to want to give up and go home.

Just .4 mile west turn tightly to the left onto Hickman Mills Road— just before reaching U.S. 71 and I-435. Proceed beneath the I-435/I-470/U.S. 71 interchange. Continue south to about the 11000 block, which is Red Bridge Road. Turn hard right onto Red Bridge and pass beneath U.S. 71. Cross the railroad tracks on Red Bridge and turn to the left at the next traffic signal, which is Grandview Road. Drive just one block. Then turn right—on Red Bridge Road again.

Meanwhile, the Santa Fe Trail passed beneath the interchange of U.S. 71 and I-435, headed southwest.

Tens of thousands of covered wagons made this deep depression in present Minor Park, Kansas City.

Follow Red Bridge Road for 1.4 miles from Grandview, or about a block east of where Wabash Avenue comes in from the north. That is where the Santa Fe Trail neared Red Bridge Road, turning west to parallel it about fifty yards north. At the bridge over the Big Blue the trail is some 300 yards to the north. That, then, would be the site of the famous Red Bridge, built in 1859, during the later days of the trail. It was a wood structure, covered with a shed and standing on three stone piers.

Red Bridge Road passes over a railroad track at the same point the trail crosses. It was headed diagonally through William E. Minor Park, on the left. Slow down at this point and observe the northeast corner of the park. Soon there will come into view one of the most dramatic swales of the Santa Fe Trail—a deeply-worn groove extending for nearly a block, impressed by tens of thousands of wagons bound for Santa Fe, Oregon, and California. A DAR marker is in the bottom of the swale. Proceed west to the park entrance, turn in to the left and park. Walk east about a block from the parking lot to the swale and just stand in it silently, preferably alone. A little get-acquainted session with Susan, Matt, and Josiah Gregg.

Return to Red Bridge Road and continue west to the next traffic signal, which is Holmes Road. Turn left and head south along the western boundary of Minor Park. The trail is closing in from the left. Holmes will make a short jog to the left and the trail will make its intercept a couple of blocks past 117th Street. That will be Santa Fe Road. Turn right and head southwest. No question about it, this is the Santa Fe Trail; exactly the route of the old trace.

Pass the intersection with Wornall Road about a half-mile to the west. Another .6 mile and the trail bisects the site of New Santa Fe, the last bit of civilization in "the States," and the last chance to get a swig of legal booze. Nothing remains there today but a horsey subdivision and a cemetery which is old, but which postdates the trail days. In the parking area on the right are some interesting trail-related informational signs. The original land patents for New Santa Fe were dated in December 1844.

A few yards to the west is State Line Road and Kansas, and one phony French chateau after another—unless the traveler is in a proper frame of mind. In that case there will be no houses, no swimming pools, no barbecue patios. There will not be a tree or habitation in sight, only the boundless prairies ablaze with emerald grasses and wildflowers, one undulating hill after another. And a broad brown earthen highway, some say a city block wide, cutting through the land, completely defoliated, sometimes pocked with slashes of muddy water, sometimes smooth as a billiard table. No buffalo yet, no Indians either. Perhaps a gentle May breeze sends waves across the oceans of grass, only a hint of the exasperating Kansas winds to be encountered to the west.

This route is believed to be the path of the first caravans on the Santa Fe Trail. By the mid-1830s many were heading southwest out of Westport, in addition to Independence.

Westport came into use by traders who pushed straight west from Independence; later they found a fine landing on the Missouri River where downtown Kansas City is today, and Independence was bypassed altogether.

Pauline Fowler of Independence, leading student of the trails in Jackson County, doubts that there was much use of the Independence-Westport Road by traders or anyone else, but certainly it had some use. Francis Parkman wrote of seeing emigrants coming to Westport that way. A description of that road is found in *The Oregon Trail Revisited* (1972, Patrice Press).

The Westport Landing should be visited and the trail followed from there to the old town, and then to the southwest.

It is difficult to get to downtown Kansas City from the site of New Santa Fe, but it must be done. Trying it without a map or during the rush hour could be suicidal. The Automobile Club of Missouri has a fine new map of the Kansas City area, but it is the size of a bedsheet.

There are three places of great interest to see before going downtown: Fitzhugh's Mill, the Alexander Majors House, and the Shawnee Mission.

Turn right on State Line Road and head north from New Santa Fe. Pass beneath I-435 and turn right a few blocks ahead, onto 103rd Street. Drive east for a long block and turn right into the easternmost entrance to the parking lot for a shopping center, just west of the bridge over Indian Creek. Pull to the east curb and park.

Just to the east of the shopping center are the foundations to Fitzhugh's Mill (also known as Watts Mill). A historical display there contains one of the millstones. Efforts are now underway to rebuild the mill, which was erected in 1832. It was sold to Anthony Watts in 1850 and operated by his family for the rest of the life of the mill, well into the twentieth century. Edgar Watts donated all the ironwork to the national scrap drive during World War II. The mill was torn down in 1949.

The Magoffin entourage camped here in 1846, on their last night in the United States. Nobody knows exactly where the Magoffin train left the States, but they certainly spent an evening here. Susan wrote a description of the Magoffin entourage while encamped here:

> We now numbered, of ourselves only, quite a force. Fourteen big waggons with six yoke each, one baggage waggon with two yoke, one dearborn with two mules, (this concern carries my maid) our own carriage with two more mules and two men on mules driving the loose stock, consisting of nine and a half yoke of oxen, our riding horses two, and three mules, with Mr. Hall the superintendent of the waggons, together with his mule, we number twenty men, three are our tent servants (Mexicans). Jane, my attendant, two horses, nine mules, some two hundred oxen, and last though not least our dog Ring. A gray hound he is of noble descent; he is white with light brown spots, a nice watch for our tent door.

Return to State Line Road and resume a northward course. Twenty-one blocks ahead, at 8201 State Line Road, is the home of Alexander Majors, the leading commercial freighter of the Santa Fe Trail and a partner in the Pony Express venture. Continue to the north property line, just before reaching the sleek new Sprint headquarters building, and turn right into the Majors House parking lot.

From this building, built in 1856, freight baron Majors ruled a freighting empire that stretched across the American West. With his partners, William Waddell and William H. Russell, he competed for and won the freighting contract to deliver military supplies to the Southwest. Soon thereafter he transferred his thousands of head of oxen and wagons to Fort Leavenworth.

The house was occupied continuously by Majors's descendants until the late 1970s. At that time it became the property of the Alexander Majors Foundation. Meticulously restored under the direction of architect

Majors House Foundation

Alexander Majors

Majors could see thousands of his oxen and hundreds of his covered wagons from the windows on the west side of his house.

Terry Chapman in the 1980s, the house is open to the public from 1 to 4 P.M. Thursday through Sunday. There is a small admission charge.

The trail from old Westport to the southwest, through present Shawnee Mission, Overland Park, Lenexa, and Olathe, is extremely difficult to follow. Much of this land was developed since World War II, the the streets do not follow the familiar grid pattern of older city plans.

However, there is one section of the Santa Fe Trail, appropriately bearing that name, in Overland Park. It isn't very long, but it is long enough to get the feel for the old trail. From the Alexander Majors driveway turn left (there is bad visibility here) onto State Line Road. Proceed south only to the first corner, which is 83rd Street, and turn right. Lamar Avenue is 2.6 miles to the west. At that point the Santa Fe Trail comes beneath 83rd Street. Continue west for a half-mile and cross Metcalf. The trail is still beneath 83rd. Continue on 83rd for five irregular blocks, pass Valley View Drive, and the street will curve to the northwest. At that point the trail curves to the southwest. Stay on 83rd for two more short blocks and it will end in a T at Santa Fe Trail Drive. Turn left for two blocks. The trail is again beneath the road, headed southwest.

Proceed to the southwest for about .8 mile, at which time the road angles slightly to the right to head due west. The Santa Fe Trail itself continues to the southwest, through a maddening array of curving residential streets, country clubs, and shopping centers. Drive to the west on 87th for a block or two to Grant Avenue and turn right. Take Grant north to 79th Street and turn right for about a mile to Metcalf. Turn left on Metcalf and proceed north to the 6300 block, which is U.S. Highway 56. (The Highway 56 signs are prominent and give plenty of warning.) That is also Shawnee Mission Parkway.

Turn east on Shawnee Mission Parkway and follow the signs to Shawnee Mission State Historic Site, about 2.5 miles to the northeast. Turn left on Mission road and proceed one block north, turn right, park, and visit the mission.

The mission was established here in 1838. The federal government joined the Methodist Church in establishing a manual labor school here for Indian children. Building began in 1839, and over the next twenty years children from many tribes came to learn English, manual arts, and agriculture. There were sixteen buildings in the complex at one time; now there are three. The original tract was 2,000 acres; now it is twelve. Nearly 200 Indian children were enrolled at the height of its activity. The school closed in 1862.

The surviving buildings were extensively rehabilitated by the Kansas State Historical Society in 1985. Site interpretation is well done by the staff; a visit is very rewarding.

Return to Missouri via Shawnee Mission Parkway. The name of the street will change to Ward Parkway just across State Line Road. Continue east on Ward Parkway past famed Country Club Plaza, the nation's first shopping center. Stay in the right lanes and pass Roanoke Parkway.

Turn left on J. C. Nichols Parkway, on the east edge of Country Club Plaza. That is a tough street to find; those looking at the right-side street signs will pass by Baltimore, but they shouldn't, as J. C. Nichols Parkway is on the left there. Follow that street north and it will become Broadway, and then arrive at Westport Road. Turn right, proceed for a few blocks to Main Street, then half-left and follow Main north nearly three miles to Truman Road, which is the 1500 block. Proceed east one block to Walnut, then turn left and go south to Eighth Street in downtown Kansas City. Turn right; drive one block east to Grand Avenue and then left. Proceed north for eight blocks to the Grand viaduct, which veers to the left over the railroad tracks. There, under the ancient Heart of America Bridge, is the Westport Landing. This is the birthplace of Kansas City.

The landing was several blocks long—a high-and-dry stone ledge five or six feet above normal water level that had an air of permanence about it. When John Calvin McCoy opened his new store in the town of Westport (three and one-half miles south) in 1834, his first consignment of goods was deposited on this rock ledge by the steamer *John Hancock*.

A ferry was operating here in the 1830s, and in 1839 McCoy bought a license to operate a ferry at the foot of Broadway, about six blocks upstream. William Chick built his log house at Walnut and Second streets, a block upstream. Francis Parkman visited there during his famous trip in 1846.

That was the year of the Mexican War, and the landing boomed from a population of 300 to more than 700 in December. Its name was changed in that year to Town of Kanzas. By 1850 the boom was on in earnest, and if the old town of Westport wasn't worried, it should have been. In less than thirty years it would be gobbled up by Kansas City.

The road from Westport Landing to the town of Westport is obscure, but the topography indicates that it probably went south on Grand, then angled to the southwest toward Sixth and Delaware. Return over the viaduct; the original road probably is directly beneath it.

Third Street is the first stop sign; veer to the left there to remain on Grand. Continue south to Fifth Street and turn right. Three blocks to the west turn left on Delaware. Pass over another viaduct. Main Street is on the south side of the viaduct; continue to the south through Penn Valley Park to Linwood, which is 3200 south. The Santa Fe Trail, according to Dean Earl Wood, is beneath Main Street, more or less, all the way.

Turn right on Linwood for four blocks and then turn south again on Broadway. At 34th Street, turn right and head west for two blocks to Pennsylvania. That is what the trail did. Turn left on Pennsylvania and proceed to Westport Road and the heart of old Westport.

It is a good idea to park anywhere in the vicinity, and it is a better idea to do so in the daytime, as it is a very popular night spot for Kansas Citians. If fact, the last car that found a parking place in Westport in the evening was declared a National Historic Car, bronzed and placed in the Kansas City Museum.

There is now a vacant lot on the north corner of the intersection of Pennsylvania and Westport Road. At one time that tract held the best hotel in town, Harris House, bought by Jack Harris in 1846. The name was perhaps a little pretentious, in light of the fact that it was made of logs. It burned and was replaced in 1852 with a fine red brick three-story building, which Harris ran until 1864, when the Civil War put an end to Westport's trail traffic. Border troubles shunted it to the north, particularly to Fort Leavenworth.

A half-block north on Pennsylvania is a new shopping mall, Manor Square, but in 1846 it was the site of a log building known as Vogel's dram shop. Here Francis Parkman learned that his grand tour of the West was not to begin in Westport at all, but in Fort Leavenworth.

Across Pennsylvania to the southwest is Kelly's Saloon, on St. Patrick's Day the most riotous tavern in Jackson County. Of greater importance, the building was erected in 1851 to serve the Indian trade in Westport. Three years later it was bought by Albert Gallatin Boone, a grandson of Daniel Boone, who had been in Westport for seventeen years. The building was modernized about 1892.

Next door to the west is Stanford and Son restaurant, built in 1850 by Cyprian Chouteau. Jim Bridger, the celebrated mountain man and scout, bought it in 1866 after he had returned from the mountains. His son-in-law operated a grocery store in the structure for several years.

To the southwest down Westport Road, at 560, is the elegant new Quarterage Hotel. Somewhere below the rear of that building is the ground on which stood Daniel Yoacham's tavern, built in 1833 as a one-story log building. Yoacham evidently found no shortage of customers; he made it two stories in 1840.

This is what Parkman wrote in the fall of 1846, when he came tooling in from Bent's Old Fort on the Arkansas:

> At length, for the first time during about half a year, we saw the roof of a white man's dwelling between the opening trees. A few moments after, we were riding over the miserable log bridge that leads into the center of Westport [over Mill Creek, which flows

Westport's pride—this bronze statue in Pioneer Park—commemorates John Calvin McCoy, seated; Alexander Majors; and Jim Bridger, right.

beneath Westport Road at the low point, about a block southwest of the Quarterage]. Westport had beheld strange scenes, but a rougher looking troop than ours, with our work equipments and broken-down horses, was never seen there. We passed the well-remembered tavern [Yoacham's], Boone's grocery and old Vogel's dram shop, and encamped on a meadow beyond. Here we were soon visited by a number of people who came to purchase our horses and equipage.

Heading back to the northeast, note the triangular Pioneer Park on the left side of Westport Road at Broadway. There is a map of the western trails in terrazzo at the point of the triangle, and in the wide part is as handsome a piece of statuary as can be found on the Santa Fe Trail.

Three men are depicted there in heroic scale: John Calvin McCoy, the man who platted Westport (he is shown with a bronze copy of the plat in his lap) and early Westport's leading trader; Jim Bridger; and Alexander Majors. The park is the result of a determined campaign staged by the Westport Historical Society and the Native Sons of Kansas City.

Just .2 mile northeast of Pioneer Park is the corner of Main and Westport Road, where today stands a large drugstore. At one time the home of Jack Harris stood here, but the land became so valuable that it became impractical as a homesite. Instead of tearing it down, which would have been the logical thing to do in the late 1920s, it was moved.

It is now a block west, at 4000 Baltimore. So just before reaching the corner of Westport and Main, turn hard right onto Baltimore and proceed a short block to the Harris House.

The Westport Historical Society, an organization that doesn't seem to be able to lose for winning, acquired the structure and has succeeded in completing an authentic restoration of the building. It is open to the public most of the time. There is a small admission charge.

Young Lewis Garrard remembered the Westport of 1846:

> Every morning we rode to Westport and saw the different Indians, in fanciful dresses, riding in to trade and look around (on their handsome ponies). Some of the squaws were possessed of good features, though gross forms; and both men and women were debased by liquor. The laws are not stringent enough on this point. The unsophisticated Indian, too much exposed to the seductive language of the unprincipled trader in liquor, soon barters away all his valuables and annuity money.

It can be presumed that after 1846 both Santa Fe traders and Oregon Trail emigrants headed south from Westport over Wornall Road. During the years when Polly Fowler was archivist for the Jackson County Historical Society she discovered a court document ordering Wornall widened to thirty-three feet in that year.

Return to the intersection of Westport Road and Pennsylvania and turn south for two blocks. Jog to the west, or right, for a few yards on 42nd Street; then angle to the south again on Wornall Road.

This old ox road originally ran south out of Westport with no jogs at all. It was in regular use by 1834, if not by emigrants, certainly by the farmers who lived along the way.

Wornall slants off to the right in the 4600 block at 47th. This is the heart of Country Club Plaza. Proceed several blocks west from there to Pennsylvania, then turn left for one block to Nichols, then one block east to Broadway and turn right. Proceed south on Broadway and cross Ward Parkway. At that point the name of the street changes from Broadway to Wornall Road.

Continue south on Wornall past Loose Park on the right, and turn west (right) along the south boundary of the park at 55th Street. About a half-mile west of Wornall, or a short distance east of Sunset Boulevard, is the house numbered 1032 West 55th Street.

This is the former home of Seth Ward, a man who became wealthy operating the sutler's store at Fort Laramie on the Oregon Trail. A sign in front of the house indicates that the small building in the rear was built and owned by William Bent.

David Lavender's masterfully written *Bent's Fort* gives little indication

The home of William Bent, 1032 West 55th Street, Kansas City, stands behind a house built by Seth Ward.

that William Bent ever lived here, so The Patrice Press asked veteran Jackson County researcher Pauline Fowler to investigate.

> With the information I have at this time [July 31, 1989], it is my opinion that the small house on the north of the big house was first built and occupied by some member of the Matney family. They owned the land for eighteen years.
>
> William Matney, Jr., sold the land to William Bent by warranty deed on 6 April 1858. It seems probable that Bent bought the land as a base for his visits to friends in Westport, a home for his daughters in school, his farm overseer, or, as a stopover accommodation en route to St. Louis and eastward on buying trips to and from his Purgatory ranch.
>
> Accepting this possibility, it seems reasonable to assume that the north house was already there for his occupancy and that it had been built and occupied by the Matney family. His will shows that he owned 652.6 acres of land, more than a section, including two lots in Westport. He obviously was a man of considerable means.
>
> Mary Ward, Seth's wife, became the owner of record in 1870, when she bought the property from Bent's widow.

Return to Country Club Plaza on Wornall Road, continue through the Plaza again to Broadway, and proceed north on Broadway to 43rd Street. Turn left and drive west several blocks to Southwest Trafficway. Turn right on Southwest Trafficway and follow the signs to I-35, which is joined at about the 2800 block, near the north side of Penn Valley Park. Continue north on I-35 to I-70 and take the option to the west. Take an odometer reading at the Kansas state line. Nearly twelve miles ahead pass the I-435 interchange, and continue four more miles to the start of the Kansas Turnpike. Turn north on leaving the toll plaza onto Kansas Highway 7. Stay on Highway 7 for sixteen miles, to the main gate at Fort Leavenworth.

FINDING THE TRAIL IN EASTERN KANSAS

FORT LEAVENWORTH

The U.S. Army has demonstrated a remarkable enthusiasm for sharing the history of Fort Leavenworth with the American people. At the entrance to the fort is an information booth. A box holds free full-color maps of the post which were prepared by the army.

The Fort Leavenworth Historical Society has available a fifteen-stop self-guided tour booklet, including a map, with photographs and well-written descriptive legends. It can be purchased at the post museum. The tour is 2.5 miles long and takes thirty-five minutes by car (with stops at each point) or two hours afoot. The hike is more rewarding.

Fort Leavenworth was founded May 8, 1827, by Col. Henry Leavenworth and 188 personnel of the Third Infantry Regiment. Leavenworth's orders were to establish a cantonment to protect Santa Fe Trail wagon trains from Indian depredations, among other things. Thus was founded the first military fort west of the Missouri River. Leavenworth was ordered to establish the fort on the east bank of the river. There was no suitable site there so he violated his orders and built it here—at what Oliva considers an ideal location for a river post.

Maj. Bennet Riley tried to use infantry to escort a wagon train in 1829, and it became obvious to the army that its foot soldiers were no match for the Plains Indians, who were superb riders. Therefore, the First Dragoon Regiment was founded here. It later became the U.S. Cavalry.

From here large ox trains started moving over the Santa Fe Trail, clearly establishing that this mode of freighting was superior to either mule- or horse-drawn wagons. Oxen were cheaper, they survived better on the prairie grasses, and the Indians didn't covet them as they did horses and mules. For these reasons and the fact that they were so powerful, they set the pattern for motive power for the settlement of the American West.

The famous entourage of which Francis Parkman was a part departed from here. Through Fort Leavenworth passed tens of thousands of

Marion and Richard Russell

emigrants headed for Oregon or California. The heaviest use of the Santa
Fe Trail, however, was military freighting

Perhaps the best-known role of Fort Leavenworth was its participation in the Mexican War. Several regiments were raised here under the
command of Stephen Watts Kearny, and dubbed the Army of the West.
Here began the bloodless occupation of New Mexico; here began the
bloody conquest of Alta, California.

And yet, not once have the French cannons barked in anger; not once
has this historic place been attacked, by anyone.

Here we meet the fourth person who will accompany us to Santa Fe—
perhaps the most delightful of Fort Leavenworth's visitors, Marion
Russell. This little girl, age six or seven, arrived with her mother and
brother, Will, in the spring of 1852. Eighty years later she remembered
it well:

> During our enforced wait at Fort Leavenworth, Will and I had
> became acquainted with Captain [Francis X.] Aubry. He was our

The ironwork in this wagon, now in the Fort Leavenworth museum, was unearthed at nearby Trail Creek. That was the staging ground for the Russell, Majors, and Waddell wagon trains which supplied military installations along the Santa Fe Trail.

very good friend. We took our childish woes to him for solace, visiting him in his great covered wagon.

The avenue leading into the fort has been named for Gen. Ulysses S. Grant. Continue north on Grant for 1.3 miles to Reynolds Avenue and turn right. One block to the east, just past Gibbon Avenue, is the Frontier Army Museum, on the left.

Many vehicles are on exhibit there, but the principal one is a huge covered wagon of undetermined manufacture, typical of those engaged in military contract freighting on the Santa Fe Trail. The metal was unearthed from the land around Corral Creek, the staging ground for Russell, Majors, and Waddell. The wood parts and canvas are new.

After touring the museum, proceed east on Reynolds for the balance of the block and turn left on Sherman. A few yards ahead and on the right are two of the four French cannons at the post, one of the fort's great mysteries. They were cast in 1774 in Paris, but no one knows today how they came to be at Fort Leavenworth, or even when they arrived.

Proceed north on Sherman, bear to the left, and then to the right onto Scott Avenue, following the Missouri River bluff. Turn right at the first opportunity, which is Riverside Drive. Proceed to the bottom of the hill, where the road turns to the north again, and stop.

Fort Leavenworth historians have done a wonderful job of interpreting the history of this old post. These markers call attention to the deep swale leading from the landing to the high ground on which the base was built.

There on the left is a deep swale of the Santa Fe-Oregon Trail, mounting the bluff from the landing. It is believed to have been graded from time to time in covered wagon days, to make it easier for the teamsters. To the right are the remains of warehouse foundations. Through the buildings which once stood here flowed thousands of tons of materiel to be transported to the military out on the plains.

At one time the waters of the Missouri River were within a few yards of the foundations; now they are far to the east, with an extended mud flat intervening.

Follow Riverside to the north. It will curve to the west to return to the top of the bluff. Turn right on McPherson Avenue and continue due west to McClellan Avenue. Turn left. A short block ahead is Sumner Place, the north boundary of the Main Parade Ground.

Continue ahead to the next street, Kearney (they misspell the street at Fort Leavenworth, as they misspell the city in Nebraska), and turn left, around the south side of the parade ground, for one block. There is a triangular area at the intersection, on which stands a heroic statue of Gen. Ulysses S. Grant. More than 10,000 people witnessed the unveiling of the statue in 1889.

Here is the intersection of two major trails. An earlier Santa Fe Trail proceeded due south from here to Fort Scott in the southern part of present Kansas. It is believed that caravans bound for the Southwest took this road as far as New Santa Fe, then proceeded west over the main trail.

A later road went due west from here to Fort Riley, west of Manhattan. The Santa Fe caravans left that road near Topeka, then continued south to intercept the main trail west of present Burlingame.

That is the route taken in 1852 by Marion Russell and her family:

> The dread cholera was raging in Fort Leavenworth the day our white-hooded wagons set sail on the western prairies. Our little city of tents dissolved like snow in a summer sun. Captain Aubry broke camp first; his great wagon swayed out onto the trail. We heard his powerful voice calling orders to follow. Wagon after wagon rolled onward and it was not until the last of Captain Aubry's wagons was well on the trail that the first of the government wagons followed. Our leader drove four mouse-colored mules which scampered like frisky dogs and tried to run away.

Turn hard left onto Sumner Place just before reaching the statue and proceed north, along the east side of the parade. The two frame houses on the right, known as the Syracuse Houses, were built in 1855. Lt. Col. George A. Custer and his wife lived in one of them briefly in 1868. Ahead on the right, at the corner, is the Rookery, built in 1832. It is believed to be the oldest occupied structure in the state of Kansas. Young Lt. Douglas MacArthur lived here briefly, but he did not attend the U.S. Army Command and General Staff College. In fact, he is one of the few twentieth-century generals who did not attend the school.

Return to McClellan Avenue via Sumner Place, which borders the parade ground on both the east and the north, and turn left. Several blocks to the south turn left, onto Pope Avenue. Proceed one block to Grant Avenue and turn right.

Drive south for .9 mile to Pershing Park, proceed on Dickman only a few feet, then right on Warehouse Avenue. Continue south for about a block, to the point where Warehouse curves to the left, and stop on the bluff above Corral Creek.

Here, in the great dish to the south, is the staging area for the giant freighting operation of Russell, Majors, and Waddell. Thousands of cattle and hundreds of large freight wagons could be found here during the 1850s. The animals were yoked up, hitched to the wagons, and herded up the bluff, where the wagons were loaded and dispatched in caravans for the Southwest.

Make a U turn, return to Grant, and proceed south to leave Fort Leavenworth. It is now time to visit the Leavenworth County Museum, in the city of Leavenworth. Grant will become 7th Street. Just before reaching Spruce Street, or Route 92, 7th Street will veer to the southwest, cross 92 (Spruce), and the southbound street will become Fifth Avenue. The Leavenworth Museum is at 334 Fifth Avenue, a few blocks ahead and on the right. The museum is an ornate sixteen-room mansion built in 1867. It is open from 1 to 4:30 daily, except Mondays, and closed entirely from Christmas until late February.

Return to Spruce Street, turn right, and continue east for four blocks to Fourth Street, which is also Route 7 and U.S. Highway 73. Turn right and proceed south for about fifteen miles and cross over the Kansas Turnpike. Continue on Route 7 for another 2.5 miles to Kansas Highway 32 and turn left. Proceed east for 6.6 miles, along the north bank of the Kansas River.

In the meantime, the Fort Scott Road started heading to the southeast just after leaving the Leavenworth city limits. Now Highway 32 has closed the triangle, and the trail heads for the river along the east side of the Grinter House, which sits high atop a hill to the left.

Moses Grinter came here in December 1830 from Kentucky and the following month was operating the first ferry across the Kansas River. He ran the business from 1830 to 1870, extracting 50 cents per person and $2 per wagon for the crossing. Emigrants to Oregon and California used the ferry in the 1850s and 1860s.

Grinter built his great brick house in 1857 and operated his ferry until the 1870s. He died in 1878; his widow, Anna, continued to live in the house until her death in 1905. The house came under the administration of the Kansas State Historical Society in 1971.

The National Park Service survey team found only one trace of the trail leading to the Grinter House. There is a road on the east side of the house. Take it north for a half-mile to the next corner, Swartz Road. Turn left and proceed a little over .1 mile west. The ruts may be seen on the right, angling through a vacant lot and heading directly for the Grinter Ferry.

Attorney William Y. Chalfant of Hutchinson, Kansas, is perhaps the most knowledgeable authority on the road from Fort Leavenworth to the Santa Fe Trail via the Fort Riley Road. His description is as follows:

> The later road from Fort Leavenworth to Santa Fe followed the Fort Leavenworth-Fort Riley Military Road to a point opposite modern-day Topeka before dropping south, and was that followed by the Cheyenne Expedition of 1857. The departure point from Fort Leavenworth appears to have been at the southwest corner of the post. Robert M. Peck, a private with the First Cavalry at that time, stated in a series of newspaper articles which he wrote in 1901 that

his column of four companies, under command of Major John Sedgwick, crossed the old drill field at the southwest corner of the post.

From that point they continued westerly on the established trail to Fort Riley. They crossed Salt Creek about three miles from the post, then continued on until reaching Stranger Creek some twelve miles farther. The trail crossed the creek next to the tiny town of Eastin (later renamed Easton), and from there moved generally southwest through the present town of Winchester, then to Hickory Point, and then to Ozawkie. There they crossed Grasshopper Creek, later redesignated Delaware River.

From Ozawkie the road continued generally southwest until it reached Indianola. Indianola was on the north side of the Kansas River, about where the Goodyear Rubber Plant presently is located, and was just north of one of the principal points at which the Oregon Trail crossed that river.

For those going to Santa Fe, there were two points of departure from the Fort Riley Military Road. One drops nearly due south from Indianola and joins the Oregon-California Trail, crossing the Kansas River via Papan's Ferry (now believed to be just downstream from the Topeka Avenue bridge).

The second crossing point was Smith's Ferry (and later one or two others) located to the west of present Topeka. Smith's Ferry was in fact about six miles west of Papan's Ferry.

At a point approximately opposite Smith's Ferry, the second split occurs, where the trail left the Fort Leavenworth-Fort Riley Military Road and moved south to the ferry. Once on the south side of the river, the road moved first southwesterly, then southeasterly, passing the Potawatomie Baptist Manual Labor Training School, which was located about a mile to the south and east of the crossing. This it did in order to strike the road running southwesterly from Papan's Ferry at a convenient point.

From the junction the road followed a generally southerly direction through the small town of Brownsville (the present Auburn), and thereafter continued south-southwest until striking the Santa Fe Trail itself approximately six miles west of Burlingame, at about the point where the town of Wilmington later grew up.

Wilmington did not exist when Major Sedgwick's column followed the trail on its outbound journey in May 1857, but had been founded and the buildings constructed by the time Col. E.V. Sumner led two companies of the Cheyenne Expedition back to Fort Leavenworth following the termination of operations in September 1857. The intersection of the road from Fort Leaven-

worth and the main branch of the Santa Fe Trail was less than a
mile from the crossing of Soldier Creek by the Leavenworth Road.

Return to the west on Highway 32, but only as far as I-435, about
two miles away. Turn to the north for about three more miles to I-70
and turn west again. These directions are leading to one of the most
beautiful history museums in the world.

Follow I-70, which becomes the Kansas Turnpike, to the South Topeka
exit and take I-470 to the northwest from there. At Wanamaker Boulevard,
about six miles away, exit to the north. Proceed a few blocks north to
Sixth Street and turn to the left. The Kansas Museum of History (KMH)
is a few blocks to the west.

Few states have a more dramatic story to tell than the state of Kansas.
And few state historical museums tell their stories better than this one.
The KMH seems to do everything well, but it excels in its educational
programs. Children feel at home here, where history is portrayed as a
grand adventure. Furthermore, this museum has a strong twentieth
century collection, a facet lacking in many other states. It is open from
9 to 4:30 weekdays, 12:30 to 4:30 on Sundays, and closed on major
holidays. Admission is free.

(Those who are traveling on the main trail could drive to the Kansas
Museum of History via U.S. Highway 75, about ten miles east of
Burlingame.)

JOHNSON COUNTY

Return east to the Bonner Springs exit of the Kansas Turnpike and
turn south onto Route 7.

Just 13.5 miles south of the turnpike turn to the east onto Kansas Route
150 to Olathe. (That is a cloverleaf, so the exit is made to the right.)
At that point 150 is known as Santa Fe Street, and it is indeed the Santa
Fe Trail. Proceed 1.2 miles from Route 7 to a diagonal street called Kan-
sas City Road. Turn left there. This is still the route of the Santa Fe
Trail through Olathe. Proceed about .8 mile northeast.

Those following the AAA map will note that the Mahaffie Farmstead
and Stagecoach Stop has been marked as being on the wrong side of
the street. It stands far back along the north (left) side of the road, not
the south.

J. B. Mahaffie came to Olathe from Kansas City in 1857. He built
this fine stone house eight years later, the centerpiece of his 570-acre
farm. It served not only as his home, but as a stagecoach stop from 1865
until 1869. Three main lines stopped here. One ran from Westport to
Lawrence; another from Westport to Fort Scott; and the third from

The Mahaffie House, Olathe, was considered one of the best of the stage stops on the Santa Fe Trail.

Westport to Santa Fe. The basement was used as a dining room and kitchen for the stage passengers.

The house is owned and is being restored by the city of Olathe. It is open most afternoons from 1 to 5 P.M. There is a small admission charge.

Return to Santa Fe Avenue by turning left on Buchanan at Olathe East High School. Turn back to the east and proceed over I-35, staying on Route 150 for 6.7 miles to U.S. Highway 69. Turn right, or south. This is the Santa Fe Trail out of New Santa Fe.

The exit ramp for Stanley Road is 1.8 miles south of Route 150. That is a trail intercept. Take that ramp down to Stanley Road, also known as 151st Street, and proceed to the west for .8 mile. There is a historical marker there pointing out an intercept of the Santa Fe Trail. Continue another 1.8 miles to Quivira Road and turn south a half-mile to Morse. A dozen years ago this was a dying town of a half-dozen buildings. Now it is a thriving residential area.

The trail cut through the center of Morse, angling a little north of west. Return to Stanley Road and turn back west, or left. Proceed one mile and pass the Johnson County Airport. The old trail cut through

the airport heading northwest, and crossed Stanley Road just past the
west boundary of the field. It proceeded some fifty yards north of Stanley
Road and turned west to parallel it. Then it turned back southwest to
cross Stanley once again at the intersection of Black Bob Road. (Lackman
Road is on the left.)

Continue one more mile on Stanley (still 151st Street) to MurLen Road
and turn south, or left. (The surface changes from blacktop to gravel
in a half-mile) The trail makes an intercept .7 mile from that corner.
Continue to the next corner, which is 159th Street, and turn west, or
right, for another mile. The trail parallels the road here, about 100 yards
to the north, but about .1 mile before the corner of Ridgeview Road
it bends to the south and crosses 159th. Turn south on Ridgeview, and
the trail will cross the road another .1 mile down the road. Continue
to the next corner, 167th Street, and turn back west, or right. One mile
west of the corner is a railroad track. Cross U.S. 169, also known as Craig
Road. Proceed .1 mile past that highway and the trail crosses 167th Street.
The next corner is Lone Elm; turn south there. There is a marker on
the southeast corner of that intersection.

On that corner, behind the marker, is the famous Lone Elm Campground, generally reached by traders their first night out from Westport.
The campground was a large one—it extended back along 167th for
perhaps a quarter of a mile, and down Lone Elm for another quarter
of a mile.

For many years the campground was called Elm Grove, or Round
Grove. But by 1843 only one small tree was still standing here.

It was still there in 1846, according to Susan Magoffin:

> This is the first camping place from Fitzu's, which is at the border
> of Mo. and the place at which our wagons stayed the night before.
>
> There is no other tree or bush or shrub save one Elm tree, which
> stands on a small elevation near the little creek or branch. The
> travellers allways stop where there is water sufficient for all their
> animals. The grass is fine every place, it is so tall in some places
> as to conceal a man's waist.

The spring which made the campground so attractive to nineteenth
century travelers now is in a concrete cistern in the approximate center
of the section of land. The creek, fed by the spring, leaves the section
just south of the marker. This is private land, but an inquiry at the farmhouse might yield permission to visit the cistern. It is a nasty hike, fraught
with brambles, and is hardly worth the time.

Lewis Garrard found a little more water at Elm Grove than he had
bargained for:

This was a most desirable spot for camping, as wood, grass, and a running, limpid stream were close at hand. . . . we encamped at the "Lone Elm," in the midst of a hard rain which poured on us the entire day; and, the wagons being full of goods and we without tents, a cheerless, chilling, soaking, wet night was the consequence. As the water penetrated, successively, my blankets, coat, and shirt, and made its way down my back, a cold shudder came over me; in the gray, foggy morning a more pitiable set of hungry, shaking wretches were never seen. Oh! but it was hard on the poor greenhorns!

Proceed .4 mile south on Lone Elm Road to an intercept with the trail, which is bearing about 240 degrees at that point. Continue south to the next corner, which is 175th Street, and turn right. Go west one mile to the next intersection; the trail crossed about twenty-five yards east of the corner. Continue west another mile to Clare Road; the trail now is near the grove of trees about a quarter-mile south of 175th.

Continuing on 175th Street, cross over I-35 in the next mile. The Santa Fe Trail is about a half-mile south but changing course to the northwest, to cross 175th just .7 mile ahead. At the next section line the road is about fifty yards north, bending back to the soutwest. It crosses 175th again .3 mile further west.

By this time 175th is bearing the designation Main Street (of Gardner) but, of greater significance, also U.S. Highway 56. The trail is going to stay near that highway for most of the way to New Mexico. After it crosses 56 it crosses the railroad tracks, heading to the point where the Oregon Trail split away from the older Santa Fe Trail.

Continue the balance of that mile on Main Street past the heart of Gardner to Center Street. Turn left on the viaduct which vaults the railroad tracks. This is an intercept of the Santa Fe Trail. It is heading due west at this point.

Turn right onto Cherokee (183rd Street), which is .7 mile south of Main Street, and proceed 1.1 miles, to cross over the Santa Fe Railroad. The trail is off to the right, or north, about fifty yards, and paralleling Cherokee.

A half-mile farther cross another railroad and then immediately cross U.S. 56. Stop in the small triangular roadside park on the other side of the highway and read the state informational sign, relating to the split in the trails.

Resume the westerly direction, but only for .2 mile. There is a house on the right, then a fence on the half-section line. There is a winding dirt road just west of that fence which leads into the field. Just .2 miles ahead is the famous junction. Not a single piece of evidence indicates it, however. Those who make the effort to reach the site are urged to seek permission of the landowner first.

Les Vilda, the delightful Ambassador of the Santa Fe Trail Association, talked to the farmer shortly after the small dam out in the field was installed. Vilda was told that the site yielded a great quantity of rusted wagon parts and other artifacts.

At this point the road to Oregon heads due west; the Santa Fe Trail moves to a bearing of 240 degrees, or southwest.

The site of the junction moved eastward over the years. In its earliest days it was probably still farther west. Irene D. Paden, in *Wake of the Prairie Schooner,* reports that she talked to an old-timer during the 1930s who told her he remembered the junction being in the school yard in Gardner. It kept moving to the east as the trails aged.

Conversely, the road from Westport through Olathe is believed to have joined the Santa Fe Trail a mile or more to the east in the earliest days. However, by the time of the 1856 General Land Office survey, it is shown merging at this point, in what amounted to a six-way intersection. In 1843 the so-called Great Migration stayed with the Santa Fe Trail until crossing Bull Creek, to the southwest a little over a mile.

Return to the gravel east-west road and continue west to the next intersection. That is where the Santa Fe Trail crossed, heading southwest. Then continue west another .4 mile to a little bridge over Bull Creek. The trail crossing, according to the 1856 GLO survey, is about .3 mile due south.

Proceed west .5 mile to the section line road (Dillie Road) and turn left. One variant of the trail, which left the road to Oregon a half-mile past the main junction, cuts across this intersection to tie up with the main trail nearly a mile to the southwest. Proceed a half-mile south on Dillie Road. On the left is the Lanesfield School. Built in 1869, the school is the only structure left of the town of Lanesfield on the Santa Fe Trail. It was extensively restored in 1989 by the Johnson County Museum System. The press release issued on the opening of the restored building carried a quote from a former student: ''The Santa Fe Trail ran about 100 yards from the schoolhouse and it was interesting to see the wagon trains pass when we could get outside to enjoy the sight.'' The museum is open weekends and admission is free.

The GLO survey shows the trail passing about where the DAR marker is, at the south edge of the school property. The 1988 National Park Service survey team found a gentle swale going through the school yard just south of a large evergreen tree, which is a few yards north of the marker. It aligns well with the route taken by the trail from Bull Creek. A walk back through the field northeast of the school property reveals several indentations which could have been swales of the Santa Fe Trail.

There are very few places on the thousand-mile trail where all the threads come together. South of the Arkansas River (and often in other places, too) the caravans moved four abreast for defense against Indian attack. In prairie country, whenever the road became too rutted or dusty, they would move to one side or the other of the trail for smoother going. Chances are the DAR marker is on a trace which has disappeared, one of at least two that lead southwest from Bull Creek.

Continue south to the T in the road and turn west again on 191st Street. At 1.5 miles the Santa Fe Trail is off to the right about .2 mile. Two miles farther is another intersection. The trail crosses just before reaching it. That intersection marks the Douglas County line. Turn south for one mile to U.S. 56 and then right.

DOUGLAS COUNTY

The Santa Fe Trail in Douglas County, Kansas, has been researched over many decades by Katharine B. Kelley and the late Amelia J. Betts of Baldwin City. These two remarkable women traversed the trail in their county, painstakingly replacing the white paint which was originally in the lettering incised in the granite DAR markers to make them more legible. There were seven sites which had not been adequately marked. They spent their own money on handsome, durable markers which are now at those sites—a sum taken from their teacher retirement pay, their business enterprises, and memorials from friends. Few have made such sacrifices for the preservation of the American heritage.

Proceed west on U.S. 56 three miles from the Johnson County line. The Santa Fe Trail crossed the highway just west of the intersection with a section line road. Nearly a mile ahead on the left is a turnout into Black Jack Park. A DAR marker is there, backed by a Betts-Kelley metal sign citing the significance of the site. Proceed west to the next corner and turn left.

Park alongside the road a few yards south of the grove of trees, opposite a sign on the east side of the road. The sign is in one of the four deep swales of the Santa Fe Trail which course through the pasture. The field, owned by Douglas County, is burned off almost every spring; the ruts are very dramatic in March and April, and can be seen even when the grass reaches three feet high in mid-summer.

Proceed about .2 mile further south and turn into the native prairie on a dirt road. There is a sandstone marker out in the prairie a few dozen yards. The inscription indicates it was placed by George Sibley when he was leading the federal survey of 1825. Actually, it is one of two rocks hauled to the tract after World War II by the man who donated the prairie

*Infrared film was used to make this dramatic shot of the ruts in Black Jack Park,
east of Baldwin City, Kansas. North is at the top of the picture.*

to the state. He attempted to commemorate the Sibley effort, but in the process some people have been misled. Sibley marked the trail only with earthen mounds to satisfy the requirement of the legislation authorizing the survey. He knew that the mounds would soon disappear and that the trail hardly needed a marker anyway, as it was in heavy use by 1825.

Retracing the swales back to the road, it will be noticed that one veers off to the right, to enter the grove of trees where the markers are, and exits at the intersection. All four traces disappear outside the park.

Black Jack Park marks the start of a section of the trail known as "The Narrows." To the north flows the Wakarusa River, the first major water crossing of the Oregon-bound pioneers. To the south is the Marais des Cygnes, another substantial watercourse. Tributaries of those streams flow north and south, respectively, like tentacles. The high land in between is known as the Narrows, which extends for nearly a dozen miles through Douglas County. That dictated the course of the trail through the area. There were few tributary ditches to ramp and cross, but there was a lot of mud after rain. In trail days the top of the ridge was flat and the drainage poor. "The soil held water like a rubber blanket," reported one traveler, "and in wet weather the trail along the ridge was almost impassable."

Return to Highway 56 and resume a western course. A little more than a mile ahead the highway veers to the right and so does the trail, about .2 mile out in the fields to the northeast. It is staying atop the ridge. The trail nearly touches the highway as it turns back to the west, on the outskirts of Baldwin City.

Turn north just past the city limits sign onto County Road 1750E (Eisenhower Drive). A block ahead is the heart of Palmyra, a long-vanished Santa Fe Trail town. Here is the second of the seven Douglas County DAR markers. Proceed past the high school to the next corner and turn right on a dirt lane leading to a farmyard. Just before reaching a fence turn to the right onto no road at all, and proceed south along the fencerow to a picturesque well on the left. This well was dug by Palmyra settlers to encourage those on the Santa Fe Trail to stop in the town. The well is old; the structure around it is new.

Continue to the next cross street and turn right on Quayle Street. Cross Eisenhower and proceed west a block to the T at County Road 1055. Turn right and proceed north for .4 mile to the point where the diagonal County Road 358N slants away to the northwest. Take it for a few yards, pull in to the right and stop at Trail Park, the triangular area to the north.

This place was named in 1907 when the land was donated to Baker University in Baldwin, which agreed to maintain it. Both Kelley and Betts are Baker alumni, and here is another of their signs. The diagonal road is over the original route of the Santa Fe Trail.

The late Amelia Betts devoted many hours to replacing the white paint in the legends incised in the DAR markers in Douglas County, Kansas. She and her friend, Katharine B. Kelley, used their personal funds to erect many permanent markers at selected points in the county.

Proceed northwest for .6 mile, where the road curves to head due west. The trail continues on the diagonal. Proceed to the next fencerow and park. (This is private land; permission should be gained before hiking on it.) Walk due north to the crest of the hill, where the alignment is an extension of the diagonal gravel road. In the foreground are the ruts of the Santa Fe Trail, lining up perfectly with the diagonal road to the southeast.

Continue west to the next intersection and turn right onto 1600E for .3 mile. Then angle back to the northwest on another gravel road (450N). This road is atop the original Santa Fe Trail. Continue northwest for .4 mile, then due west .2 mile. The trail has been beneath the road for more than a half-mile. Turn right on 1550E at that point, as the trail cuts diagonally across the section. A half-mile to the north turn left again on 500N, jog to the right .4 mile ahead for just a few yards, and then proceed due west for another mile. The trail generally follows the high land on the north side of the road.

On the west side of that section turn right onto 1400E and drive north for a half-mile to the intersection with 550N. On the right is a sign identifying the site of Brooklyn, which is out to the southeast less than a

This gravel road follows a diagonal course north of Baldwin City. It is over the route of the Santa Fe Trail.

quarter of a mile. On August 21, 1863, Quantrill's men passed through here. They had some matches left after they had torched Lawrence, so they burned Brooklyn, too. Legend has it that only one building was spared, the combination store-saloon.

Turn west at that corner onto 550N. The trail cuts through the intersection heading northwest, still following the ridge, and immediately turns west to follow the road just to the north.

On the right, just after turning west, is a spring, believed to be the muddy area mentioned by Gregg:

> . . . we encountered a region of very troublesome quagmires. On such occasions it is quite common for a wagon to sink to the hubs in mud while the surface of the soil all around would appear perfectly dry and smooth. To extricate each other's wagons we had frequently to employ double and triple teams, with all hands to the wheels in addition . . .

Cross the blacktopped Highway 59 1.5 miles to the west. About .6 mile ahead the trail is on the right. A tall gray fertilizer tank and two grain silos are atop a hill, and a gully angles to the northwest. Between the road and the gully are ruts running from the northeast to the southwest.

Continue west to a T in the road. A DAR marker was once in the middle of the road at that corner. It has been moved to the other side of the ditch to the west. It marks the site of Willow Springs. There are several springs in the field to the southwest.

When Gen. Stephen Watts Kearny led his Army of the West from Fort Leavenworth, he took a trail which joined the main trail near here. Some sources put that junction a mile to the east; some say it was at Willow Springs.

Turn to the left at the marker and follow the road south a half-mile, to where it curves to the right. Continue west for nearly a mile, where the trail crosses the road just before reaching the intersection of 500N and 400 E, from northeast to southwest. Continue another 1.2 miles to Route 1039 and turn left. Proceed south .8 mile, where there is another intercept, and then .2 mile farther and turn right. A church is on the southeast corner of that intersection.

Continue west for 3.5 more miles. The trail is off on the right side of the road, sometimes by as much as .1 mile, sometimes touching it. Turn left at the intersection of 550E and 400N. There is a marker there denoting the location of the long-vanished community of Globe. The trail again bisects the intersection. This was once the town of Marion, established in 1856. The name was later changed to Globe. Continue south one mile to U.S. 56 and turn right. The buildings on that corner now are known as Globe; obviously, the town has moved.

Just 1.9 miles to the west, below a microwave relay tower, stands a stone building on the north side of the highway. This is the Simmons House, built of native limestone. Its first function was reported to be as a stage station on the Santa Fe Trail, providing room, meals, and fresh mules. Later it became simply a farmhouse. Now it stands forlorn and abandoned, windows gone, roof starting to leak.

The knob to the southwest, where the tower sits, is known locally as Simmons Point. There are faint ruts in the vicinity.

Just 2.2 miles to the west, faint ruts may be found in the field on the north side of the road, paralleling Highway 56. They continue intermittently for nearly .3 mile, where the trail crosses the highway. A DAR marker is there, along with another marker by Katharine Kelley and Amelia Betts.

OSAGE COUNTY

Proceed 8.8 miles west. About a quarter-mile to the left is the Overbrook water tower. Beneath it, atop a hill, is a grove of cedar trees, marking the location of a cemetery. Ruts of the Santa Fe Trail are visible there.

Cross an overpass one mile ahead, and go .2 mile farther. In the hollow to the right, about 200 yards distant, is a windmill atop a concrete box. This is the area of Flag Springs. The spring used by the traders, according to Glen D. Norton of Overbrook, is about 250 yards northwest of there in the same slough. Water may be obtained there to this day by digging a shallow hole.

Continue west on U.S. 56 to Santa Fe Trail High School on the left, about six miles west of Overbrook. A marker on the front lawn is the only one on the Santa Fe Trail placed by the Sons of the American Revolution.

Continue west .5 mile and turn left onto a gravel road. Proceed south nearly .2 mile, almost to the entrance gate of the Osage State Fishing Lake on the right. In the field to the east are fine ruts leading to that gate, coming over from the high school.

Return to Highway 56 and turn left. Proceed west for a little more than a mile, cross under U.S. 75 and turn immediately thereafter to the left onto the highway. Continue south slowly for .6 mile and a DAR marker will be on the right, exactly on the route of the Santa Fe Trail. On the west side of the marker the old highway comes down from the north. Continue a few yards ahead and turn very sharply to the right nearly 180 degrees and get on the old road. When opposite the marker, turn to the left onto a dirt road.

Go west for .3 mile. At times this road has been badly rutted, and other times it has been carpet-like. If the ruts are deep do not try to

The McGee-Harris Stage Station, built on the banks of 110-Mile Creek, is a stark ruin today.

keep the wheels in the ruts; place one suspension on the crown and the other on the shoulder. When crossing from one side to the other, do it at a sharp angle. Don't get more than one wheel in a rut at a time. It is not easy calling AAA from the Santa Fe Trail.

Suddenly the road will stop at a beautiful meadow, where there are two clumps of trees about seventy-five yards apart. Hiding in those trees are the ruins of two of the buildings which comprised the McGee-Harris Stage Station.

On the west boundary of the meadow is 110 Mile Creek. George Sibley called it Oak Creek in 1825 when he conducted his survey of the Santa Fe Trail. It was later renamed for its distance from the start of his survey, Fort Osage.

Susan Magoffin expressed her feelings about the trail while she was encamped here in 1846:

> Tonight is my fifth *en el campo*. Oh, this is a life I would not exchange for a good deal! There is such independence, so much free uncontaminated air, which impregnates the mind, the feelings, nay every thought, with purity. I breathe free without that oppression and uneasiness felt in the gossiping circles of a settled home.

An Oregon Trail adventurer, Fry McGee, settled here with his family, built a toll bridge, and offered accommodations to traders and stage passengers. He charged a quarter per wagon to use his bridge. By the late 1850s the Santa Fe stage stopped here twice a month.

Marc Simmons, the great chronicler of the Santa Fe Trail, reports:

> A Mr. Harris married McGee's eldest daughter, who had the unlikely name of America Puss. He built a residence and store adjacent to his in-laws and after McGee's death in 1861 operated the stage station here. A major building of stone and frame remains, apparently a residence and station. Ruins of other structures nearby may include the blacksmith shop that was part of the original complex. Traces of the trail are visible at the creek crossing about 100 yards west.

Return to U.S. 56 via the old highway and proceed two miles to the west. Turn south for one mile. The trail crosses just yards north of the corner. Turn right and drive west for three miles. During this stretch the Santa Fe Trail is along the north side of the gravel road (which soon turns to dirt), ranging from the ditch to 100 yards away. Continue to the west. Just .2 mile ahead the trail crosses to the south side of the road, to parallel it about .1 mile away. Ruts are said to be visible in parts of the last half-mile of that section. Turn left at the next corner and proceed south, cross the railroad tracks and arrive again at U.S. 56. Turn right and drive two miles into Burlingame. The highway crosses Switzler Creek almost where the trail does. The trail then loops about two blocks to the south, according to the GLO survey. U.S. 56 turns south in Burlingame but continue straight west there onto Route 31.

According to tradition the trail went smack down the middle of Route 31, or Santa Fe Street, Burlingame's main business street. Robert DuBois of Burlingame advises that the early teamsters went around the hill on the west end of the main street, to the south, and didn't head down that street until the later days of the trail, when Burlingame was well established.

Continue to the first section line road west of Burlingame. At that point the trail has looped to the northwest and is nearly a half-mile away north of Route 31, following the ridge. Continue west on 31 for almost two miles. Cross Dragoon Creek over a modern concrete bridge. The caravans crossed it over a smooth rock bottom about a half-mile to the north.

Proceed west to a point 1.1 miles west of the Dragoon Creek bridge. There is a cluster of farm buildings on the left and a DAR marker ahead on the right. Just west of the buildings is a row of trees running to the south, and far back in the field, on the west side of the trees, are the ruins of the Havana Stage Station.

For the moment at least, this is private land and permission should

After Burlingame, Kansas, was laid out, traders passed along Main Street, thus making it part of the route of the Santa Fe Trail. The photo above was made in 1879; the one below 110 years later.

be sought for exploration at the nearby farmhouse.

Walk down the west side of the trees, toward the south, for only about .1 mile. The ruins, like the McGee-Harris, are hard to see in mid-summer as the foliage obscures them. But in early spring or late fall they have a wild beauty about them. Little is known about the station today. It was part of the long-gone settlement of Havana, founded in 1858.

The energetic Heart of the Flint Hills Chapter of the Santa Fe Trail Association has plans to acquire and restore the station. This is the out-fit that has placed so many signs along the county roads, marking cross-ings of the Santa Fe Trail.

Continue west on Route 31 for another .2 mile. A turnout there is surmounted by a black tank holding highway oil. Off in the field to the right is the solitary grave of Pvt. Samuel Hunt of Kentucky, a dragoon who died here in 1835. The present marker was installed in the 1930s.

At this point the trail is in the fields south of the highway, angling down toward Soldier Creek. Intermittent traces there, faint at times, are nearly a mile long.

Proceed west on Route 31 and turn left onto a gravel road .1 mile from the turnout. Stop at the first driveway to the right. On the corner is a wire gate into the field. Pass through that gate and walk west along the north side of the fence, past a white house on the left. Cross a gully and proceed another 118 yards straight ahead. There is the crossing of Soldier Creek. No traces are visible there now, but they can be seen at times coming across the field from the northeast. (This is private land; per-mission should be obtained before hiking on it.)

Hike back to the gravel road, continue south to the next corner, and turn right onto another gravel road. Pass a low spot in the road just .1 mile to the west, climb the hill to come into view of a clearing on the right, past a stand of scrub timber. Back to the right are gaps indicating the route of the trail coming from Soldier Creek to the high ground.

Cross the Kansas Turnpike over a concrete bridge near the end of that mile, come to the T in the road .6 mile ahead and turn left. Proceed only .1 mile south and then turn back to the west again. On the right is all that remains of the once-bustling town of Wilmington. Just .4 mile ahead the road curves to the left. At that point, on the right is the Wil-mington schoolhouse. On the door is an an oval trace, where once was mounted a porcelain-enameled Santa Fe Trail sign, erected by the American Pioneer Trails Association in 1948. A DAR marker is on the right.

Here, too, was one of several markers in the shape of a wagon wheel, which marked the route of a Boy Scout hiking trail from Burlingame to Council Grove. (Scouts who would like to hike this trail may pick up a free map at the offices of the *Osage County Chronicle*, 107 Santa Fe Street in Burlingame.) Most of the markers are still in place and will be seen frequently between this point and Council Grove.

Turn south at the Wilmington School, then west again .3 mile farther. At a point 1.4 miles ahead a tall, slender water tower comes into view at a 10 o'clock direction, about a mile away. There are ruts beneath that tower. Just .4 mile ahead, the good road makes a left turn. And .4 mile from there, out in the field to the left, are some very deep ruts. This is where the trail crosses the road. Turn right .1 mile south.

Three miles ahead is the crossing of Chicken Creek. An 1888 map of Lyons County shows the trail paralleling the section line road in an absolutely straight line, just to the south.

The 1988 survey team was inspecting the area when they were approached by Ruby Hedman, who lives in the house on the north side of the road, just east of the bridge. Her grandmother came to the area via the Santa Fe Trail. She confirmed that there were ruts in the field to the south and that the wagon crossing is about where the bridge is today. She added that there was an accident in the creek in trail days when a wagon upset in the rushing water. One man was killed, but a crippled trader managed to save himself by holding onto his horse.

Proceed west .8 mile. At a T in the road, turn left. The trail passed through this intersection heading west, then turned to the southwest. Turn left and go south a half-mile. Then turn right again. There is an abandoned farmstead on the left a half-mile ahead. The trail crossed the road just east of the farm buildings, heading southwest, and there are fine traces about a quarter-mile long in that section. Proceed west the balance of that mile and turn left, onto Kansas Highway 99. The trail crosses .6 mile ahead. Proceed the balance of that mile and turn right onto a gravel road, just past the bridge over Elm Creek. Only .7 mile ahead is another trail intercept. Continue another 1.3 miles and turn left onto a good gravel road.

At .6 mile south another gravel road takes off to the right. Proceed down that road about .2 mile, to a point where it changes course to the southwest. The Santa Fe Trail comes beneath it at that point. It leaves again about a half-mile ahead, past the bridge over One Hundred Forty-two Mile (from Fort Osage) Creek. According to the GLO plats, the trail crossed right where the bridge does. A store and stage stop were here in trail days, run by Charles Withington. Proceed west 1.5 miles from the bridge, turn right, and stop. There are good ruts leading to the southwest from this place, but they cannot be reached easily from here. Turn around and head due south for two miles and turn right.

Proceed west for one mile and turn right to head north. Drive to a farmhouse on the left, a half-mile from the corner. There permission should be obtained to approach the ruts ahead. Continue the balance of that mile on a dirt road, which ends in a T. Ahead is a wire gate. Pass through it and continue north past the gate for almost a mile, afoot or in the car, to the top of a ridge. Here are ruts unbroken for a half-mile east and west, coming over from the crossing of One Hundred Forty-two Mile Creek.

Return to U.S. 56 1.5 miles south and a mile west of Allen. Turn right and proceed west 3.8 miles. Turn right onto a gravel road and proceed north for 2.2 miles. The trail crosses the gravel road there, but no ruts are discernible now. Continue north and turn left at the T in the road .2 mile ahead. One mile to the west turn left at another T and head south. Turn right into the Agnes City cemetery .4 mile ahead. Proceed as far north as possible, to the edge of the graveyard. The ruts are still another thirty to forty yards out in the field, heading due west.

Continue south .5 mile and turn right onto a blacktop road. On the left is the site of Agnes City, and not one of the original buildings of that once-booming town is left today. At a T in the road one mile to the west turn left, off the blacktop, heading south. Proceed one mile to U.S. 56 and turn right. Drive west for three miles, then turn right again.

It could have been near here where Marion Russell encountered a storm on one of her six trips over the Santa Fe Trail:

> Frightening thunder storms came up suddenly. They would sweep over us, and away they would go as suddenly as they had come. When the sky would darken and the forked lightning sent the thunder rolling, the drivers would wheel the wagons so that the mules' backs were to the storm. The men who had been walking would seek shelter with the women and children inside the wagons. The prairies would darken and then would come a mighty clap of thunder and a sheet of drenching water would fall from the skies upon us. A fine white mist would come through the tightened canvas and soon small pearl beads would glisten in mother's hair. So we would sit through wind, water, thunder, and lightning. Then, as suddenly as it had come, the storm would pass away. We would emerge then from the wagons to stretch our cramped limbs and to see the golden sun shining through the scattered clouds. Always we saw our storm, a tattered beggar, limping off across the distant hills. Looking back now it seems to me that we had a thunder storm almost every day.

There were extremes in this land. Susan Magoffin reported this experience a few miles to the east:

> Noon out on the wide Prairie. The Sun it seems is exerting himself; not a breath of air is stirring, and everything is scorching

with heat. We have no water and the animals are panting with thirst; their drivers are seeking shelter under the wagons; while mi alma [her husband] is under the carriage.

Proceed north for .6 mile. The trail comes through a farmyard on the right—a sign mounted on a post north of a utility pole, and facing north, identifies the crossing. Return to U.S. 56, and turn right, to head into Morris County.

MORRIS COUNTY

Proceed west into Morris County on U.S. 56 for four miles and turn right onto a gravel road. Drive north .2 mile and look to the right. Coming in from the east, to the creek in the foreground, are traces of the Santa Fe Trail; they extend back nearly a mile. Return to Highway 56, turn right, and continue for 2.5 miles to the town of Council Grove.

Council Grove—the very name exudes the romance of the trail to the historian. It didn't have that name when the first caravan went through. What it did have was a beautiful copse of oak, maple, walnut, ash, and hickory trees, made the more dramatic because these were virtually the only trees seen since leaving the United States.

There was also the Neosho River, a slow-flowing, clear stream. And there was grass surrounding that watercourse—acres and acres of it— the refreshing nourishment for animals beginning to jade under the work of pulling heavily-laden wagons over the prairies.

Council Grove was named by George Sibley, who here entered into a treaty with the Osage chiefs on August 10, 1825. They may not have been as bloodthirsty as the Comanches, Kiowas, or Utes, but the Osage were a troublesome bunch, and had been since the founding of St. Louis in 1764. And for no reason at all, really. All the whites really did was run them out. The Indians had no right to the land at all—check in any courthouse.

The treaty awarded $800 worth of merchandise to the head of the tribes, $300 of which was tendered immediately. The Osage in return granted Sibley permission to survey the Santa Fe Trail through their territory, and guaranteed trading caravans—Anglo or Hispanic—the right to pass unmolested along the trail and for a reasonable distance on either side, as game was sought to feed those passing through.

There is no doubt that Sibley struck a good bargain. What is unusual is that both the United States and the Osage kept the bargain.

Virtually every journalist who passed through Council Grove wrote about the sylvan setting.

Matt Field:

. . . we stood at last beneath the sombre shadow of the old trees. We rode on through the thick wood, enjoying the grateful sensa- tions occasioned by the transition from the burning heat of the prairie to the cooling shade of the grove. We reached the water— the crystal stream rushing over its white bed of pebbles. Ah! ye who in cities torture invention for new varieties of drink, to gratify your pampered palates, little can you conceive the luxury of a draught dipped with a shell, and drank upon the border of the lonely desert brook!

Gregg passed through just six years after Sibley:

Lest this imposing title [Council Grove] suggest to the reader a snug and thriving village, it should be observed that on the day of our departure from Independence we passed the last human abode upon our route; therefore, from the borders of Missouri to those of New Mexico not even an Indian settlement greeted our eyes.

When Bill Brown came through Council Grove in 1963, preparing his survey for the National Park Service, he was surprised at the lack of attention Council Grove was paying to its many historic sites. His report recommended that a numbered self-guided tour be developed. The community has done that. Proceed into Council Grove and cross the railroad tracks. Park on the west side of the old depot located there, on the right, and pick up one of those free brochures.

The first stop ought to be a couple of blocks ahead on the right, the little park with the modern shelter. That structure is over an old tree stump, all that remains of the Council Oak. Tradition has it that Sibley and the Osage chiefs were beneath this tree when the treaty was signed. The tree was felled by a storm in the 1960s; the people of Council Grove have gone to a lot of trouble to preserve what is left.

Proceed ahead another block. On the right is the Post Office Oak. There was a crevice at the base of this tree in which travelers allegedly put letters bound for whichever direction they were coming from. Folks going that way were expected to pick them up and somehow they would find their way to the addressee. Or so the legend goes.

At the corner on the right is the DAR's *Madonna of the Trail* for the state of Kansas. Just ahead is the Neosho River itself. The crossing of the Santa Fe Trail probably was a few yards to the north, but the volume of traffic, river stage, and rutting along the banks meant that the freight wagons would have entered the water wherever it was easiest, anyplace from the present bridge north.

Cross the bridge. A half-block ahead on the right is the Hays House. Newspaper accounts indicate that it probably was built in 1859 (despite the fact that the sign says 1857). Seth Hays, the first white settler in

*Malcolm Conn came to Council Grove in 1858 and built this stone store. He sold
out to Shamleffer & James in the following decade.*

*Conn's stone store looks like this today. The lighter colored rock is original; the rest
is addition.*

Council Grove, came here in 1847, took title to the land in 1857 and opened his store the following year, catering to the Santa Fe trade. It is a restaurant today, and a fine one, certainly one of the best in Kansas. Some components of the interior are original—Marc Simmons has identified a large walnut beam in the basement, the mantelpiece beam, and of course the stone walls.

Across the street, on the southeast corner of the intersection, is the Stone Store, built by Malcolm Conn in 1858. It is not on the numbered tour, but Katie Gardner has researched the Conn story thoroughly. His findings establish that the Stone Store was of great importance to the growth of Council Grove. Gardner found this account of the business climate there in the reminiscences of William Shamleffer, a later owner of the store:

> The merchant had to hustle with business customers all day, and then entertain them royally at night; for some of them came hundreds of miles to trade, and the business house had to furnish many of them with sleeping quarters, places to cook their meals, corrals in which to keep their stock, and open access to the corn cribs.
> . . . Plainsmen, hunters, trappers, wagon bosses, soldiers, bullwhackers, broncho busters, long lines of prairie schooners, and heads of horses, mules and cattle, were the attractions of the passing day. . . . In his stock were found every known variety of goods for use on the frontier, from ox yokes and repairs to cambric needles, from small boxes of pills to barrels of whisky.

Marion Russell was a small child when she, her mother, and her brother returned from Santa Fe. They had walked from Diamond Spring to Council Grove and arrived at a store, possibly the Last Chance Store but probably the Stone Store:

> I tried hard to be as brave and as uncomplaining as my mother, but the muscles in my slender thighs were twitching with fatigue when we climbed the steps of the store at Council Grove. When the grocery-man there asked me kindly if I was tired, I remember how I burst into tears and how mother had to answer him for me. We stayed that night in the home of the grocery-man where his wife put us to sleep on a great feather bed. As I dropped off to sleep that night I found myself wondering if all the beds in Heaven were not duplicates of the grocery-man's big feather one.

She was back again a few years later, now a young woman and now heading southwest:

> At Council Grove we spent the Sabbath. The grocery-man did not remember me, for I had grown tall. I wore a long dress, and

braids of brown hair were coiled coronet fashion around my head. He did remember Mother the moment that he saw her alight from the wagon, and he came with both hands outstretched to meet her. We camped by the store that night and I remember how a Kaw Indian came and traded the grocery-man a shaggy red pony for a sack of white bolted flour. While we stood watching another Kaw came and the grocery-man traded him the pony for a buffalo hide filled with yellow Indian corn.

Turn to the south around the Conn Store, proceed two blocks, cross the railroad tracks and turn left at the next corner. Proceed one block east and turn left again. Seth Hays's house is at the end of the block on the left, just south of the railroad tracks, at 201 Wood Street. Return to Main Street and continue west two blocks past the Conn store and turn right on Mission Street. Proceed north for five blocks to the Kaw Mission.

Opened in 1851 by the Methodist Episcopal Church South, it was designed to accommodate fifty students as regular boarders. School began in May of that year but was discontinued only three years later, because of the excessive cost of operation. The fact is, the Kaw Indians considered the ways of the white man degrading to the Indian character. Like most Christian missions to the Indians, it was a failure.

Proceed north to Huffaker, the street on the north side of the Mission buildings, and turn left. Proceed two blocks west and turn left atop the hill. Drive south for two more blocks and make another left turn. Proceed east two more blocks to Belfry Street and turn right for one block. On the left, out of sight from the road, is a hole in the bluff called the Hermit's Cave. Park and walk down the twelve stone steps.

Giovanni Maria Augustini, a religious mystic, lived in this cave for a short time. He approached the captain of a wagon train headed for Santa Fe, gained permission to join, and walked the entire 550 miles, and then took up residence in another cave outside Las Vegas, New Mexico, on a mountain known today as Hermit Peak.

The next street to the south is Hays. Turn west on it for just one block to Chautauqua, and then turn left toward Highway 56.

The famed Last Chance Store is on the northwest corner of Chautauqua and U.S. 56, or Main Street.

Marc Simmons advises that the Last Chance Store was erected in 1857 and later served as both a post office and a government trading post. It is now closed.

Return to the Conn Store on Main Street and turn right onto Neosho. Proceed .6 mile south to a gravel road just south of Velie Street and turn right. Proceed .8 mile. Just past a curve in the road there is an iron gate on the right leading into a field. Park just south of that gate.

Stone steps lead down to Hermit's Cave in Council Grove.

Walk up the hill on the right for about 200 yards. (It is a private property—get permission first.) Atop the knob is a monument to Fr. Juan de Padilla, priest to the Coronado expedition of 1540-42. He was martyred by the Indians somewhere in Kansas—no one knows exactly where. In all probability Susan Magoffin was on this hill in 1846:

> We struck our camp on the hill. There is a large mound just by us, from the top of which is a splendid view to be had. On one side, to the west, is a wide expanse of Prairie; as far as the eye can reach nothing but a waving sea of tall grass is to be seen. Out the other, for miles around are trees and hills. I went up onto it at sunset, and thought I had not seen, ever, a more imposing sight.

From the intersection of Main and Neosho proceed west on U.S. 56 for 5.7 miles. Turn left on a gravel road there and proceed .6 mile. The trail crosses the road just north of the farm buildings, and good ruts are in the field to the right. There, too, is an old sign marking a crossing of the Santa Fe Trail, and a new one installed in 1989 by the Flint Hills Chapter of SFTA. The ruts are out in the field to the west. Continue the balance of that mile and turn right. There is an intercept of the trail a half-mile ahead, at the half-section line. From that point proceed another 2.5 miles west. Turn left on a poor road, more dirt than gravel. Cross the railroad tracks .9 mile ahead, then turn right on a two-track, which becomes gravel in the next mile to the west. Continue five miles west of the last turn and then turn left. Just .2 mile to the south is the entrance to the Diamond Creek Ranch on the right. Turn in and ask permission to see the old Diamond of the Plains—known today as Diamond Spring.

Josiah Gregg described the spring as "a crystal fountain discharging itself into a small brook." Susan Magoffin arrived there at 2 P.M. on Sunday, June 21, 1846, to spend the night.

There was an old stone house there in Marion Russell's day, and when her caravan stopped there it was decided to break the lock and enter:

> Water tumbled from the earth as clear and sparkling as a diamond. It came in such quantity that a little stream had its source there. . . . We used that grand, old parlor [of the stone house] as a community hall. . . . It had a fireplace at one end and a pathetic old spindle-legged piano at the other. Several ladies in our party played well and one old man had a fiddle. In the evening while flames leaped on the hearth, lilting tunes would go echoing through the empty rooms. The old man would take his fiddle out of its red-lined cradle. He would nestle it under his chin. . . . The fiddle would wail like a banshee, the old piano kept on a thrumming. Flames

Diamond Spring now rises in this concrete stock tank.

lept from the hearth. Shadows danced on the stairs. . . . It has been
so long ago since we camped at Diamond Springs, and yet I think
I can hear mother's clear voice singing the ''Blue Bells of Scotland.''

Leave Diamond Spring, turn left at the gate, and proceed north 2.2
miles to U.S. 56. Turn left and go west two miles and turn left again.
The road jogs to the left for a few yards a mile to the south, then
resumes a southerly direction. There are dirt roads ahead but they are
in fairly good shape—after a rain it might be a different story. Proceed
another mile south where the road turns to the west. About .1 mile ahead
is the small bridge over Mile-and-a-Half Creek—the creeks now are
named for their distance from Diamond Spring. The trail is about .3
mile to the south at that turn, and there are ruts coming over to the
section line from Diamond Spring, which extend back to the east a third
of a mile. There are supposed to be ruts in the section to the left, also.

Continue west four miles from the last turn and turn left onto a blacktop
road. Proceed just 1.2 miles to the south. A grove of cedar trees is on
the left flanking a driveway. Just past that driveway is a DAR marker.
Turn into the driveway and enter the old Six-Mile Ranch.

On the right side of the driveway and just east of the trees along the
road is the overgrown foundation of an old stone house. Raleigh Sill,
who now owns the ranch with his wife, Bonnie, was born in an upstairs
room of that building.

Six-mile Creek was forded about where the small tree is in the foreground. The creek waters no longer flow here—it is a dry branch. The barn in the background, there in March 1988, was no longer there in June 1989.

Across the drive to the north was a log cabin, one of the buildings of the Six-Mile Stage Station. The remains of a barn are some distance to the east, and in between is the site of a stone corral. Raleigh Sill remembers when it was demolished:

> I asked mother why dad tore it down and she said it was in the way between the house and the barn. In those days anything old was junk. Dad told some people that if they would come down here and bring their crusher they could have the rock and he would help them crush it. So they did.

Sill identified the original well on the north side of the drive:

> One day my brother and I decided to clean it, hoping to find some treasure. We found only tree roots and barrel hoops. But we scrubbed it clean. It is jug-shaped and hewed from solid limestone. There is a small spring at the bottom.

Most of the stone structures, Bonnie Sill said, were built by David Waldo when his firm had the mail contract to Santa Fe. "The old stone house was torn down because the walls were going bad," she said.

The Six-Mile Crossing is now over a dry branch—the channel of the little creek has changed since trail days. It is to the left of the ranch road leading to the east, about fifty yards east of the old farm buildings. There are ruts just a few more yards to the northeast, in the pasture. Don't go on the property without permission.

MARION COUNTY

Proceed south from the Six-Mile Ranch for 2.6 miles to a stop sign and turn right. Drive west for almost five miles to U.S. Highway 77. Cross 77 and proceed .8 mile ahead to the town of Lost Springs.

The trail crossed the blacktop on the western limit of the town. Continue west for about 2.5 miles from the center of Lost Springs to the site of the spring itself. A granite DAR marker is on the left; a few yards farther is an SFTA marker pointing to the ruts in the field to the left, and on the right is an informational sign which appears to be brand new. It isn't. Fred and Virginia Shields of Lincolnville, who own the Lost Spring land, took an impossibly rusty sign, paid to have it sandblasted, then had it professionally repainted. There is a farm lane to the right, which they have opened up to allow people to get off the blacktop and out of danger while they explore the area. Shields' grandfather owned the land.

Now can be seen one of the maddening perplexities of trail research. The Kansas GLO cadastral plats show the trail looping not around Lost Spring, but around a spring in the center of the section just to the east. It then shoots down across the road and is a mile away from Lost Spring.

But it is known that the trail in fact looped around this spring, not the one to the east. An alternate route did indeed continue to the southwest, and the ruts are plain in the field across the road, heading southwest from the granite DAR marker. Evidently the surveyor made an error in 1856, an error which has been perpetuated ever since.

To find the spring, walk west across the culvert and cross the fence on the right. Hike back along the roadside ditch to the east to the bank of the creek, and then follow the creek to the northeast for seventy yards. To the right, across the creek, is a gnarled old tree. Extending from its base to the creek is a green ribbon of watercress. The Lost Spring is at the base of the tree and its waters flow beneath that cover of watercress.

Of course the spring itself is on the east bank of the creek, but it is hard to find and hard to see from there.

Donald Cress of Council Grove, possibly the most knowledgeable man about the trail in this area, said that a group of twenty Mexican traders and hired hands were lost in a blizzard trying to reach the way station which was just across the road from the spring. They were only 200 yards from the station but they didn't know that, and all perished. There is

Lost Spring rises at the base of this gnarled tree and flows into Cress Creek beneath a cover of bright green watercress.

Ruts of the Santa Fe Trail have been marked by the Heart of the Flint Hills Chapter of the Santa Fe Trail Association. This sign is at Lost Spring.

no sign of the graves today.

The branch of the trail which looped north of the road to pass by the spring joined the main trail one mile west and one mile south.

Continue west from Lost Spring. The trail loops back to the northwest to cross the road just west of the blacktop section line road 2.5 miles west of Lost Spring. Turn left at that corner. Proceed .7 mile south. A DAR marker and an SFTA rut sign are on the right. The ruts are out in the field to the right.

Proceed .3 mile south and turn right onto a good gravel road. The old Tampa cemetery is 4.8 miles west of there. It is along the right side of the road. To the west of the railroad tracks is an SFTA rut sign, pointing out the very substantial swale of the Santa Fe Trail in that cemetery. It crosses the gravel road just before reaching the Tampa intersection. Proceed ahead along the northern edge of Tampa. There is a ranch complex just west of the town on the left, and ruts may be seen on the west side of the ranch buildings. Continue west for 3.7 miles from the Tampa corner to the intersection with Kansas Highway 15 and turn left. Slow down when 1.2 miles south of that intersection, and look to the northeast. Ruts are coming up to the road at that point. They align with the shed atop the hill.

Turn right .7 mile to the south and head west. Just .3 mile ahead ruts can be seen coming to the road from the northeast. An SFTA rut marker is there. Continue just .6 mile more and turn south. (This road is an absolute monster within a day after a good rain.) Proceed 1.3 miles south and slow down. In the pasture at the left are the swales of two variants of the Santa Fe Trail as they separate, heading for different crossings of Cottonwood Creek. Green markers pinpoint the intercept .2 mile farther south on this road. A stone marker is at the end of the bushes on the right.

Cross the Cottonwood over a concrete bridge .3 mile ahead. A DAR marker is among the trees on the right, and the Cottonwood Crossing is about 100 yards northeast of there. No evidence is known to remain at the crossing.

Follow the road to the south for about a half-mile, to a gravel road coming in from the west. About twenty yards ahead is a culvert. (This road turns into a quagmire after a heavy dew.) Turn to the right just before reaching it and head out into the field. There is no road here. This is private land, and permission must be gained before entering it. It is well worth the bother.

Continue to the west toward the largest of several clumps of trees, which are perhaps a third of a mile away, then jog to the right around those trees. A few yards ahead the car will start to bounce a little—it is going over several shallow swales of the Santa Fe Trail. At this point the Durham elevator should bear due east, or ninety degrees.

To the north, less than a mile away, is the Cottonwood Crossing, also known to the traders as Cottonwood Grove. Bob Gray of McPherson, Kansas, a local expert on the trail, identifies this as the spot where Susan Magoffin sampled the wild plums:

> . . . the banks are long but not very steep; the rain has made them quite slippy, but our little light carriages passed them easy. The camp ground is on a light rise, and some three or four hundred yards down is a steep bank covered with cotton wood trees . . . Just at the water's edge are quantities of gooseberry and raspberry bushes. They were nearly rifled of their fruits by the wagoners, before I went to them. Above these . . . is a thick plumb grove—these too I missed for they are not yet ripe; however I pulled some of them only to say I had picked three kinds of fruits in one spot on Cottonwood creek.

Josiah Gregg, who camped there fifteen years before Susan, does a good job of locating the campground:

> Near twenty-five miles [from Council Grove] . . . we crossed the Cottonwood Fork of the Neosho, . . . and our camp was pitched immediately in its farther valley.

When caravans are able to cross in the evening they seldom stop on the near side of a stream—first, because if it happens to rain during the night it may become flooded and cause both detention and trouble; again, though the stream be not impassable after rain, the banks become slippery and difficult to ascend. A third and still more important reason is that, even supposing the contingency of rain does not occur, teams will rarely pull as well in cold collars, as wagoners term it—that is, when fresh geared—as in the progress of a day's travel. When a heavy pull is just at hand in the morning wagoners sometimes resort to the expedient of driving a circuit upon the prairie before venturing to take the bank.

Matt Field was delighted with Cottonwood Grove when he saw it in 1839:

> We camped here, and, after two days of sultry and weary travel we threw ourselves into the creek and laved our bodies luxuriously in the running tide. The enjoyment was a reward for the pilgrimage. We, poor, lone wanderers, deemed by our friends half crazy in leaving home, revelled there in the wilderness, and pitied, honestly pitied all who were cooped up in crowded places, totally shut out from pleasure such as ours.

Lewis Garrard, moving west in early October 1846, in the company of the famous Ceran St. Vrain, had a good-news bad-news experience here:

> Toward eleven o'clock in the morning, we arrived at Cottonwood Fork . . . One of the wagons overturned while crossing, breaking two boxes of claret. Those around had a treat most unexpectedly.
>
> We could not leave camp that day. De Lisle was under a wagon containing forty-five hundred-weight of freight, making some repairs, one wheel being off and propped up by a board, when the support gave way, and the wagon fell, confining him to the earth. . . . He was drawn from under, almost dead. He was so far recovered that the next day we traveled.

Drive back to the east to the town of Durham. From the center of town proceed south on Kansas Route 15 for 1.5 miles and turn right. Drive west for nearly two miles, to a point where the road forms a gradual curve to the south. In the middle of that curve is an underpass to the right. Turn off the road there and stop.

Leave the car and hike into the field, heading a little north of west. This is private land—get permission first, but don't fail to see this segment, for this is one of the most spectacularly eroded ruts on the Santa Fe Trail.

The heavy covered wagons started an erosion process southwest of Durham, Kansas, which has turned the old trace into an angry "blowout."

Hike for perhaps a quarter-mile (500 paces) over the sand hills. Soon a spectacular gouge in the land will come into view—the Durham blowout. The wagon wheels broke down whatever humus there happened to be in the sandy soil, and the Kansas winds took it from there, leaving a linear cavity in the earth more than a dozen feet deep and three times as wide. The eastern end of the blowout is about a mile down the trail from the last ruts described.

Most of the rut swale to the southwest has been chewed up by water, not wind, but it can be followed for more than two miles, and it is a good idea to do it if the weather is nice. It is possible for one person to drive around and meet the hikers. To drive around to see the far end of the rut segment, proceed south from the underpass and follow the road for two miles, then two miles west, and .4 mile back to the north. The swale ends on the high point of land out in the field to the northeast. An SFTA rut sign is there.

The ruts also continue across the road, heading to the southwest. Ruts are visible there for about a quarter-mile.

Return south to the corner and turn right. Drive west for just .7 mile. There the road is forced to the southwest by the railroad embankment, and the trail comes beneath the road at that point. Follow the road as it turns back to the south—the trail continues to the southwest at that point but no ruts are visible. During times of high humidity this road turns into the Great Dismal Swamp. Don't try it if it even looks like rain. Continue south for .7 mile and turn back to the right again at the section line road. An intercept is .8 mile ahead. Continue another .2 mile and turn left onto a dirt road. Proceed south .2 mile to another intercept, then another .8 mile and turn right onto a gravel road.

A trail intercept is .6 mile ahead—again, no trace. Continue for about .4 mile and turn left. Another intercept is .7 mile to the south, about .2 mile north of the tracks of the Santa Fe Railroad. A section line intersection is a few yards south of the railroad crossing.

Turn to the right at that crossing and drive one mile to the McPherson County line. The trail crosses .4 mile after the last turn—again, no trace.

At this point the configuration of rural roads rules out a direct drive along the trail intercepts, so turn right at the county line and proceed north for three miles, then turn left and drive one mile west to a blacktop road.

McPHERSON COUNTY

One mile into McPherson County turn left onto a good gravel road and drive south for 3.6 miles to the point where the Santa Fe Railroad crosses the road. Immediately past the crossing turn left onto a two-track and drive back to the east about .2 mile to the chained gate for the Jones Cemetery. This is private land. Get permission first, then park, go over the chain, and walk to the highest part of the cemetery.

There, beneath a black granite headstone and a red granite DAR marker, lies all that's left of young Ed Miller except his scalp, which was removed in 1865. Bob Gray dredged up an account written by Mollie Hoops in 1885:

> Edward Miller was a young man about eighteen years old who was familiar with the trail and was a bold and fearless rider. A Mrs. Waterman and her family were at Fuller's ranch, about twenty-five miles southwest of Turkey Creek. [Gray feels Mrs. Hoops is in error here. They were southwest of the Santa Fe Trail crossing of the Cottonwood River, at Moore's Ranch.]
>
> The Indians had raided everything up to the Waterman place and had driven off the horses and mules not picketed close to their ranch house. They made their appearance about 8 o'clock in the morning. The first knowledge the ranchers had of Indians being near was a simultaneous dash of the whole band with blood curdling yells brandishing their implements of warfare, keeping their bodies

A DAR marker stands near the headstone of Ed Miller, killed by Indians in 1864.

on the lee side of their horses while they were in a dead run, one after the other, as was their fashion. Their dazzling shields were kept in such a position as to exclude their bodies from harm.

All loose stock were stampeded and driven off. Fortunately the family was in the house at the time. After getting all the stock they could, the Indians rode on. About four miles [north]east of Waterman's, firing was heard and the Indians began circling about a horseman. There was a telescope at the ranch which was used from a lookout on the roof of the house.

They did not know it was Edward Miller, coming to tell them of the illness of their daughter and sister, but such was the case. The night was spent in fear of Indian attack.

Early the next morning a wagon train came along with an escort of soldiers from Fort Lyon, Colorado. The family was given permission to ride with them to Moore's ranch. A courier then reported that Edward Miller was missing. Now the Watermans had a clue as to who had been surrounded by the Indians.

About dark a party of four men went to Moore's ranch to spend the night. The following morning, in company with the two Waterman boys, they started out on the trail. They rode two abreast until they came to the locality where Waterman saw the circling action. Then they scattered out as they felt they would not find him in the road.

Evin Waterman loosened his reins, his horse turned to the right, out of the road, pricked up his ears, sniffed the air, and walked right up to the poor boy who was in some large weeds about fifty feet from the trail. He was shot twice with arrows, twice with spears, and his entire scalp had been taken off—only a few hairs were left around his ears. His clothing was all gone except his under drawers. He had lain in the July sun through very hot days and consequently his body was badly decomposed. The men had thoughtfully provided themselves with an extra blanket so that if they found him they could wrap him in it, but they had not thought of a shovel. Two rode back for the shovel.

Across the road from where he lay is a beautiful little elevation, perhaps a hundred feet across. When the men returned with the shovel, they made the grave and then rolled the poor boy into the blanket and carried him to his last resting place.

There he lies to this day, not a stone or anything to show that he had been doing his duty for his neighbor and for all of us.

The headstone was placed sometime between 1885 and 1906, when the DAR marker was mounted next to it

Return to the gravel road, turn left, and drive south .4 mile to U.S. Highway 56. Turn right and drive two miles west, then turn left on County Road 304, a blacktop road leading south from Canton. At .8 mile the trail crosses—a DAR marker is on the left. Turn right 1.2 miles ahead. The trail crosses from the north side of the road exactly 3.8 miles to the west. Proceed ahead another 1.2 miles and turn left. The trail has been running alongside the road to the south; no traces remain today. The crossing of Running Turkey Creek is at the intersection—the trail crossed here also. Fuller's Ranch, mentioned in the Edward Miller narrative above, is on the northeast corner of the next intersection. No traces of the trail are known to remain at the place, although Bob Gray recently found some ruts behind a barn a mile to the east.

Turn left and proceed to a small cemetery a half-mile to the south. Turn west, into the cemetery, for about thirty yards. Stop and walk about thirty yards to the right, or north. Locate the headstone for the two young Kohler brothers—Franklin, born September 20, 1855, and Benjamin, born June 12, 1864. They lived with their father in a dugout about a mile south of the cemetery. Their father was a cobbler, and on a December morning in 1874 he went to the Fuller Ranch to see if he could pick up some business.

A sudden fall of heavy, wet snow caused the roof of the dugout to collapse. The two boys, aged ten and nineteen, suffocated. It was December 5, twenty days before Christmas.

Continue south from the cemetery for 3.5 miles and turn right. Drive 5.7 miles west and turn hard left onto Kansas Highway 153. Proceed southeast along the Union Pacific Railroad for about .3 mile to a turnout for historical markers.

One of those markers was intended to designate the site of Sibley's 1825 treaty with the Kansa Indians. The trouble is, it has been picked up and moved two miles from where it should be, "so more people can see it." This is one of Bob Gray's pet peeves, and well it should be. The DAR placed that marker after a great deal of research. It was meant to mark a site of historical importance. How many people see it is secondary. It should be returned to its proper place.

To get to the correct site, return northwest to the corner and turn half-left onto County Road 445. Proceed 1.4 miles. The treaty site is off in the field to the right. (Those who would like to triangulate the site may set their compasses to 337 degrees and line up with the stacks of the refinery in McPherson, five miles to the north.)

Time to take a break. Return three miles to the east and follow the signs to I-135 northbound. Fifteen miles ahead is Smoky Hill River, Lindsborg, and its famous Old Mill Museum and Park. In Lindsborg follow the signs to the Smoky Valley Roller Mills. The museum is open from 9:30 to 5 daily April through October, and 1 to 5 on Sundays, and 1 to 5 daily from November through March. Lindsborg is a charming little town with a strong Swedish accent.

Return to the 1825 Kaw Treaty Site south of McPherson. Proceed ahead for 4.2 miles and cross the tracks of the Southern Pacific Railroad and Highway 61. The trail has made a gentle arc, coming gradually closer to this roadway. It finally crosses to the southwest through the intersection a half-mile east of the railroad crossing. At that spot it is about a half-mile to the south.

RICE COUNTY

Continue west for 1.4 miles and take an odometer reading at the section line. Then proceed ahead for 5.8 miles. The Santa Fe Trail has made a bow to the south and now has assumed a northwesterly direction to cross the road here. The section line is .2 mile ahead. Continue heading west for three miles, then turn right. Proceed north for one mile, cross the intersection, then head north for another .6 mile. On the right are the offices of the Kansas Horizon Oil Company, which owns the Santa Fe Trail property to the west. Ask permission to visit the ruts leading down to the crossing of the Little Arkansas River.

Then proceed about thirty yards ahead, turn left onto a dirt road, and drive west along the south edge of a line of trees. At .3 mile from the main road there is a fence line; turn left on the west side of that fence (there is no road as such) and proceed about 200 yards south. The ruts are straight ahead, extending from left to right, down to the crossing of the little Ark. That is the northernmost of the two branches of the trail which lead across the river.

It is very difficult to get to the crossing from this point, so return to County Road 443, drive south about .6 mile, and turn right. Proceed west for a little less than a half-mile, and just before crossing the Little Ark on a bridge, turn left on a poor dirt road. This is known today as the Cottonwood Grove Cemetery, but in trail days it was Camp Grierson.

On the west side of the dirt lane, only yards from the gravel road, there are a number of depressions in the sod. These were rifle pits for the troops. About seventy men were stationed here during the summer of 1867. An informational sign announces that George Armstrong Custer was once stationed there. Dr. Leo Oliva has a forceful commentary on that statement: ''He most certainly was not. The garrison was comprised of a company of black soldiers of the 10th U.S. Cavalry.''

Toward the end of the dirt road, again on the right, are more depressions. These once held the bodies of up to fifteen soldiers who were killed by Indians in skirmishes during the 1860s. They were later exhumed and moved to the National Cemetery at Fort Leavenworth. The site is now a privately owned picnic ground. The grave depressions do not make very good picnic benches.

Return to the gravel road, turn left, and proceed west over the Little Ark. About .2 mile ahead is a road leading to the north to a gas well. Take it for about half the distance to the well. The southernmost of the two Santa Fe Trail branches crossed here, heading a little south of due west from the river crossing. On the near bank of the river, and just south of the trail, was the stone corral.

That corral was a marvel in its day. It measured between 300 and 400 feet from east to west, and was about 200 feet wide. The sandstone walls were eight feet high and two and one-half feet thick, laid up so well, according to one visitor, ''that no light could get through.'' It was built by the first settler in the area, William D. Wheeler.

Ralph Hathaway, a Santa Fe Trail landowner who ranches west of the town of Chase, has researched the area thoroughly. He found this item in the March 23, 1861, issue of the Council Grove Press:

LITTLE ARKANSAS RANCHE

The traveling Public are respectfully informed, that the under-

signed is located on the Little Arkansas, where the great Santa Fe
road crosses the same. I always keep on Hand

PROVISIONS, GROCERIES AND LIQUORS
Also are prepared to accommodate travelers. I have several large
corrals for penning stock. Also, have built a strong and substantial
bridge across the Little Arkansas, for the accommodation of the
traveling public. W. D. Wheeler

Hathaway doubts that the great stone corral existed that early, but
he has determined that the rock was quarried about a mile west of here.
A small stone room was built into one corner of the corral. There was
a gateway at the southeast corner which allowed wagons and livestock
to enter.

Nathan A. C. Bean, who came here in the 1870s, was the first official
settler. He lived in the structure for a short time. According to Hathaway,
Bean testified that from eight to thirty wagons were camped each night
in the enclosure. Bean began selling stone from the walls shortly after
he arrived there. Eventually he sold the entire corral, every last rock,
and put the land under cultivation. Not a stone remains today, but a
local Boy Scout troop recently unearthed a cache of ox shoes and wrought
nails nearby, possibly at the site of a blacksmith shop.

Some of the stone was used to build a schoolhouse which is one mile
south and one-half mile west, but that has been stuccoed over and none
of the rock is visible today. A mile to the west of the stone corral site,
on the south side of the road, is a dramatic example of a thick stone
fence. It was probably laid up the same way the stone corral was.
Hathaway suspects that the stone came from the same quarry, which
is in the section of land across the road from the stone fence.

The river crossing to the north was distinguished by an enormous
cottonwood which, according to historian Marc Simmons, could be seen
far out on the plains. There were few other trees—the "marker cottonwood" was a landmark without a peer.

Return to the south from the road to the gas well and turn right onto
the main gravel road. Proceed .4 mile to the intersection and turn right.
A DAR marker is on the right side of the road, .2 mile to the north.
The northern branch of the trail passed just beyond it. A row of Osage
orange trees is along the left. About thirty yards past the bridge over
the Little Ark turn right into a field. This is actually only a set of tracks
along the edge of the field and can't even be called a dirt road. Don't
try this with even a four-wheel-drive vehicle if it appears muddy—it only
gets worse. Hoof it instead. Follow the northeast bank of the river along
the trees, heading a little south of east. Proceed almost a half-mile along

the edge of the field, to arrive at a low spot in the road. This is the Santa Fe Trail. Stop and hike down the trail to the right.

The marker cottonwood looms directly ahead. There is no mistaking it. Note that the trail heads right for it, then bends out of the way to the left before heading down to the creek.

Bob Gray found a rock bottom to the stream crossings in several places along here, but it is visible only in times of extremely low water. There was no such luxury in Josiah Gregg's day:

> . . . the Little Arkansas, which, although endowed with an imposing name, is only a small creek with a current but five or six yards wide. But, though small, its steep banks and miry bed annoyed us exceedingly in crossing. It is the practice upon the prairies on all such occasions for several men to go in advance with axes, spades, and mattocks and by digging the banks and erecting temporary bridges to have all in readiness by the time the wagons arrive. A bridge over a quagmire is made in a few minutes by cross-laying it with brush (willows are best, but even long grass is often employed as a substitute) and covering it with earth—across which a hundred wagons will often pass in safety.

From the marker cottonwood return to the main gravel road, turn left, and drive south to the intersection, then south for another mile and turn right onto the blacktop County Road 445. The stone schoolhouse, now in disuse, is one-half mile ahead on the right. Proceed 8.5 miles to the west. During this drive from the stone school the trail is off to the north, sweeping as close as .3 mile to the road, and as far away as 2.1 miles. Turn to the right at a gravel section line road. Proceed north for 1.6 miles.

A half-mile to the west of this point, in the line of trees, is the trail crossing of Jarvis Creek. Some Rice County trail buffs have found a substantial swale there which could well be the trail. But the crossing is of minor importance. The trader for whom the creek was named is of much greater importance. Jose Antonio Chavez was a wealthy Mexican and a veteran traveler on the Santa Fe Trail.

Chavez was en route to Independence from Santa Fe in April 1843 with five servants, two wagons, fifty-five mules, some furs, and more than $10,000 in cash. John McDaniel led a force of thugs west from Missouri with the intent of robbing Mexican wagon trains. They accosted Chavez and seven men took their share of his goods and headed back to Missouri. Eight others took Chavez down the trail a short distance and executed him.

The U.S. Dragoons apprehended ten members of the McDaniel party, who were tried. McDaniel and his brother were hanged; the others were

This immense cottonwood marks the site of the crossing of the Little Arkansas River. The trail heads right to it, then curves around to the left to cross the river.

fined and sent to jail.

The attack on Chavez took place near here—no one today knows exactly where. Jarvis Creek was named for the murdered trader—the name is an Anglo corruption of the name Chavez. Marc Simmons covered the incident well in his book, *Murder on the Santa Fe Trail* (El Paso, 1987).

Proceed north for .5 mile and turn right. Proceed back east one mile to the next intersection, stop, and look off to the northeast. Santa Fe Trail aficionados from Rice County discovered these depressions and reported them one week after *Maps of the Santa Fe Trail* had gone to the printer.

Return to the west one mile, turn right, and drive north for two miles; then turn left. Proceed five miles west to the heart of Lyons on U.S. 56.

Turn left on Kansas Highway 14 for two blocks, then right on East Lyon one block to the Coronado Quivira Museum, operated by the Rice County Historical Society. The address is 105 West Lyon Street. A wonderful stock of western books which trail pursuers need for their libraries is for sale here.

This small, elegant county museum is an outstanding testimonial to the intellect of the people of Rice County. Lyons is like many agricultural communities which endured a devastating depression during the 1980s— and "depression" is the right word, not "recession." Through it all the citizens maintained the tax and the contributions which support this institution. Many other Kansas counties continue to make the same sacrifice. They have a debt to pay to their pioneer ancestors, and a heritage to protect. They do it well. The exhibits pertain to the Santa Fe Trail, of course, but also to the Coronado expedition, and to mysterious prehistoric remains found in the area.

Proceed four miles west of Lyons on U.S. 56 and turn left at a road-side park containing a thirty-foot-high cross honoring Coronado's martyred friar, Fr. Juan de Padilla. Marc Simmons writes that there was a large Quivira Indian village in the field to the south of the park. Turn left on the gravel section line road just east of the monument and pro-ceed south for nearly a mile, where the gravel road starts to curve to the west. On the inside of that curve is Buffalo Bill's well.

This Buffalo Bill was William Mathewson, who bought a trading post founded here in 1858 or 1859 by the Beach family. The well is all that survives today. It would not even be here were it not for Arthur Hodgson and other local historians who stopped a highway crew from grading it away in a successful eleventh-hour rescue.

Proceed ahead and curve to the right to cross the bridge over Cow Creek.

From 1860 to the end of the trail days, the traders who moved west of the Little Ark knew they were in for trouble. Buffalo began to appear

Timely action by Rice County citizens saved Buffalo Bill's well from destruction. The Santa Fe Trail crossed Cow Creek to the left of the bridge in the background.

in great hordes, and the Indians who lived off them defended that resource with ferocity.

A siege by 600 Kiowas occurred here in the summer of 1864. A supply train consisting of eighty wagons, 100 men, 400 oxen, an ninety-six high-grade mules, was headed toward Fort Union from Fort Leavenworth, loaded with military supplies. They had crossed Cow Creek, evidently just a few yards south of the present bridge, and camped on the grassy plain to the west.

The Kiowa were interested primarily in the mules. So interested that they laid seige for six days. There was plenty for the traders to eat, since it was an army supply train. The water problem was solved by digging down ten feet, to find seepage water from nearby Cow Creek.

A few weeks later a similar incident occurred. A civilian detachment pulled out ahead of the military wagons and was attacked by 150 Sioux. All were scalped, but, suprisingly, two young men were found alive. One died shortly afterward, but the other, Robert McGee, lived a long life, becoming an object of curiosity, as he was believed to be the only man to live through a scalping.

The site of the crossing was pointed out to Hathaway by Herb Tappan, just a few weeks before Tappan died. His mother had pointed it out to him when he was a boy. It is very faint and small trees are now growing in the swale. During low water rocks may be found in the stream bed, aligned with the swale, which is on the west bank of the creek and can be seen from the present bridge. It is only a few yards to the south.

Josiah Gregg described the troubles of crossing Cow Creek in 1831:

. . . after digging, bridging, shouldering the wheels, with the usual accompaniment of whooping, swearing, and cracking of whips, we soon got safely across and camped in the valley beyond.

Lewis Garrard found some excitement at Cow Creek:

. . . our worthy leader approached a band of [buffalo] bulls and fired, bringing down one. It is with difficulty that buffalo can be approached, it requiring a skillful person who will not permit the keen-scented animal to get to his leeward, or in sight; for they run when a person is in view as far as a mile, and from the scent still further; so we waited, with suppressed breathing, for the report of the rifle. There lay a fine, fat, young male—ere long he was on his knees (for the hump prevents his being placed on his back) and the hide off. The men ate the liver raw, with a slight dash of *gall* by way of zest, which served a la Indian, was not very tempting to cloyed appetites; but to hungry men, not at all squeamish, raw, warm liver, with raw marrow, was quite palatable. Before the buffalo range was half traversed, I liked the novel dish pretty well.

Proceed to the west for 3.2 miles and turn left into a farmyard. Get permission to visit, then immediately turn left again to parallel the wind-break along the road. (Obviously, this is private property. The owner, Walter Sharp, is one of those wonderful people who readily grant permission to visit the ruts on his land. But don't fail to ask first.) Follow the trees for nearly 100 yards to a fence and turn right for another eighty yards to four shallow rut swales. They are about a quarter-mile long and head to the northwest.

Proceed west on the main road for .3 mile, turn right to hit Highway 56 a mile to the north. Then turn left for 2.1 miles, or .1 mile past the section line road. In the pasture on the right are two rut swales leading to the northwest, aimed toward a small metal building. Hathaway feels there were two more ruts, one on each side of the surviving swales, which have been obliterated by road work. There is a ridge between the two remaining traces.

Proceed 1.9 miles west and turn right on the Bushton-Raymond blacktop. On the left, during the turn, a sign will come into view: "Ralph's Ruts / Santa Fe Trail / ¾ mi. N." Follow those directions. A roadside parking area, installed in 1989 by the Rice County Highway Department, and a DAR marker are there. In the pasture on the right are some very prominent trail ruts, as many as seven abreast at one point. Hathaway often is credited with saving these distinct rut swales, but he modestly denies any credit: "This forty [acres] was saved from the plow because my grandfather discovered it was too sandy to become satisfactory crop ground."

Delegates to the 1987 Symposium of the Santa Fe Trail Association were greeted by this covered wagon coming down "Ralph's Ruts," west of Chase, Kansas. The land is owned by Ralph and Beth Hathaway.

About one-half mile east is the site of the Plum Buttes Massacre. (This is private land; be sure to get permission before hiking on it.) Hathaway tells the story:

> This is the farm on which my grandparents, John L. and Mary E. Hathaway, filed a homestead claim in 1878. While breaking sod on the northeast forty acres of this quarter, grandfather and his sons plowed up a pistol, a watch, pieces of hardware from burned wagons, and bits of broken ironstone china—grim evidence that some group of travelers had met with tragedy here.
>
> Prior to 1985 there was very little reliable information concerning the Plum Buttes Massacre. This account dates from 1876:
>
> ". . . a train of emigrants was broken up near the Plum Buttes in '63. . . . William McGee [a local rancher] . . . found broken and partly burned wagons, plows, barrels, tubs, boxes and earthenware; and for miles around lay scattered unworn boots and shoes, crisped by prairie fires and the scorching sun . . . denoting the place to have been the scene of a general massacre, as a row of graves was visible for some years after near this spot."

The graves mentioned were never found during the 111 years the Hathaway family has operated this farm. In 1985 a great deal of additional information on the massacre came to me from trail buff friends: Dr. Marc Simmons and trail researchers Aaron and Ethel Armstrong of Roswell, New Mexico.

Franz Huning, a Santa Fe trader, wrote that he had been bringing his mother-in-law and her teenage son to his home in Albuquerque. He was at the head of the column when a band of Cheyennes, Kiowas, and Arapahos attacked the rear of the train. They cut off the wagons in the rear, including the one occupied by his relatives, which mired in deep sand beside the trail. Wrote Huning:

> In an incredibly short time they emptied the wagons of their contents and loaded the captured mules with them. Some barrels of whiskey they set on end, stove in the heads, and set fire to them. . . .
> I saw a big crowd in one place with much noise and laughter and then a pistol shot. I knew that they were gathered around my unfortunate relatives and then that pistol shot killed the old lady. The boy having been killed at the first onset, as one of the teamsters told me.

Huning raced to Fort Zarah, about sixteen miles to the west, for military assistance and returned to the site.

Charles Christy, a government scout who returned to the scene with Huning, reported that the attack was the work of a band of "dog soldiers"—Cheyennes in a soldier society highly respected in their tribe—led by Charlie Bent, the renegade half-breed son of William Bent.

The ruts at the roadside turnout continue for another half-mile to the west. They were somewhat disturbed by oil exploration in the 1930s and do not show up clearly from the blacktop, but they are there and are plain to those hiking in the fields.

Ralph Hathaway and his family are among the most enthusiastic and selfless landowners along the trail. They deserve the courtesy of those who visit their ruts, so be sure to ask for permission.

Turn west from the Hathaway farm buildings and proceed about 1.2 miles to a section line road. Look to the left of the road ahead. The dip on the horizon is Gunsight Notch, a name attributed by Ralph Hathaway to Dave Clapsaddle of Fort Larned. Proceed ahead about .4 mile. The far side of Gunsight Notch is on the left. In the section to the right stood the Plum Buttes.

The Plum Buttes were a surprising formation. And how they were formed was surprising, as well as how they disappeared. Long before the Becknell expedition left Franklin, the relentless Kansas winds had deposited fine sand from the big bend of the Arkansas here. By the time the first wagons arrived there were three mounds of sand in this section, each about 100 feet above the level of the plain. They were there throughout trail days and came into view soon after the traders crossed Cow Creek.

Hathaway's father, who was born on the farm in 1882, told Ralph that they were still prominent when he was a child. "He told me he could see the last one from our house," Hathaway said. "It was about thirty feet tall when he was a boy."

But the winds were already taking their toll, and by the 1920s the dunes were virtually leveled. The ground is broken in this section, to be sure, but there is nothing there resembling the great Plum Buttes of the nineteenth century.

Proceed .2 west from that point and turn left onto a two-track. Bear to the right, and about seventy-five yards ahead, before reaching a little knoll, are some fine ruts, particularly on the east slope of that ridge. There is a north-south ridge toward the west end of the pasture. Trail ruts converge there to cross that ridge, and have worn the Gunsight Notch depression. The ruts continue on the west side of the ridge, excellent ones and double in places. Turn around at an oil well and head back to the road.

Proceed west .2 mile to the section line road, then turn left. The trail intersects the road .3 mile to the south, according to the GLO plats.

At least one Rice County historian advises that the DAR marker now at Ralph's Ruts was once mounted in a sandy location here. Hathaway, however, remembers seeing it at the intersection to the north. "It may have been moved from the indicated crossing to the northeast corner of the intersection, where I remember it being," Hathaway said. The marker toppled over several times, as the wind kept blowing sand away from the base. Thus, there is good reason now to leave the marker where it is, at Ralph's Ruts, rather than return it to either of the earlier locations.

Continue the balance of that mile to U.S. 56 and turn right. Five miles ahead the highway slants to the northwest, and a mile past that point it resumes a western course for a mile. There is another curve to the northwest, and a half-mile ahead, at the west city limit, is a culvert over a small creek. At this point the trail crosses the highway, headed southwest—all the way from Plum Buttes it has been north of Highway 56. The Arkansas River is only about .2 mile to the south. The great campground at the Big Bend was in what is now the southwest corner of the town of Ellinwood. That, Hathaway believes, is the place traders referred to when they spoke of the "big bend" of the Arkansas. This point is the most logical campground west of the Cow Creek crossing, eighteen miles to the east.

BARTON COUNTY

To look at the site of the Big Bend campground at Ellinwood avoid that last diagonal jog to the right—at the point where the U.S. Highway 56 slants to the northwest, a mile east of the heart of Ellinwood. Continue straight ahead on the blacktop for 1.5 miles and cross the blacktop heading south from the center of town.

Then continue west on gravel for two blocks. At that point a sand two-track takes off toward the river—it is virtually impassable in a family car. The area of the campground is straight ahead. Go no farther—turn right on South Kennedy Street and proceed north to U.S. 56 and turn left.

Proceed to the west city limit. The campground is on the left now, presently the site of a golf course.

Take an odometer reading and proceed west from the city limit. Two miles ahead on U.S. 56 the road slants back to due west. The trail ranges from .3 to .7 miles to the south, snaking along the high ground north of the river. Exactly six miles from the west edge of Ellinwood, turn left onto a blacktop road, cross the railroad tracks and at that point the road changes to gravel. Proceed .2 mile south. The county highway maps show a T in the road at that point, but a poor road continues ahead. Drive south for a little more than .1 mile and stop.

Fifty to 100 yards out in the field to the right is the site of the first Fort Zarah. It was established early in 1864 as Camp Dunlap, but the name was changed in July of that year to Fort Zarah in honor of Zarah Curtis, son of Gen. S. R. Curtis, who had been killed in an Indian battle. Bob Button, a well-known amateur archaeologist from Great Bend, was a member of the team which scientifically established the site, although no surface evidence is known to remain there today.

In February 1865 the newly-arrived Second Colorado Cavalry started work on the octagonal blockhouse, probably a copy of the blockhouse at Fort Larned. It was right on the creek bank, some 200 yards south of this site. The order to abandon this first Fort Zarah came through on April 7, 1866.

Proceed south. The road will turn into a farmyard on the left. Stop and ask permission to visit the remains of the Allison-Peacock Trading Post. To the east of the house is a metal building with wood doors. The foundation mounds of the post are just to the east of that structure, and west of the barn.

The site is near the banks of Walnut Creek, and the Santa Fe Trail crosses about at this point.

There was no building there in 1826, when a man named Broadus had an infected arm amputated here by Richard Gentry. Broadus had drawn his rifle from his wagon, muzzle first, and it fired, shattering his

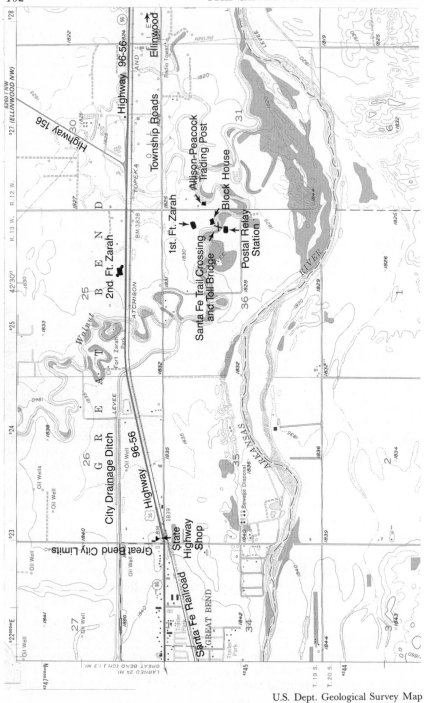

Map of Fort Zarah area by Bob Button

arm. He refused amputation until gangrene set in. Gregg described the surgery:

> Their only . . . instruments consisted of a handsaw, a butcher's knife, and a large iron bolt. The teeth of the saw being considered too coarse, they went to work and soon had a set of fine teeth filed on the back. The knife having been whetted keen and the iron bolt laid upon the fire, they commenced the operation. . . . the arm was opened round to the bone, which was almost in an instant sawed off; and with the sizzling hot iron the whole stump was so effectually seared as to close the arteries completely. Bandages were now applied and the company proceeded on their journey.

The patient survived and what was left of the arm healed rapidly. The site was the headquarters of the Allison Ranch, established in July 1855 by William Allison and Francis Booth. In September 1857 Booth developed an Excedrin headache, caused by a Mexican trader who split his skull with an ax.

That was the place Marion Russell remembered from her 1856 passage from Santa Fe to Missouri:

> When we reached Walnut Creek . . . we found that a small store, surrounded by a cluster of cabins, had been built since our passing four years before. On a level table land behind the store some Apache Indians were camping. Some of them followed us from the store to our wagon begging for the groceries we had bought from the trader. When mother refused to part with the food . . . the Indians became angry. When the wagon-master heard the loud voices he came to our assistance. A wicked-looking warrior hideously painted made a gesture as if he would lift the wagon master's scalp lock. The wagon master drew a knife and made a retaliating gesture of cutting the ugly warrior's throat from ear to ear. Muttering and sullen, the Indians moved back to the mesa. Although the wagon master laughed, he seemed a bit uneasy, especially when the trader came and reproved him for offending the Apaches.

The Indians attacked the moving caravan the next day, probably east of present Ellinwood. The train was scattered but no further damage was done.

George Peacock took over the Walnut Creek trading post in late 1858 or early 1859. George, who had a wonderful sense of humor, played a practical joke on the great Kiowa chief, Satank. The chief felt his chances of dealing with Anglos in wagon trains would be greatly enhanced if he carried a letter of recommendation from Peacock. So George agreed to write one for him.

Map by Bob Button

A model of the Allison-Peacock Trading Post has been made by Bob Button for the Barton County Museum, Great Bend.

Peacock knew that Satank couldn't read English, and George wrote a number of uncharitable references to the bearer of the letter. He probably did nothing more than tell the truth, but of course he knew what Satank expected of him.

The chief, noticing the letter wasn't working very well, evidently found someone willing to read it to him. He paid another call on George on September 9, 1860. Demonstrating that he had no sense of humor at all, he shot the trader dead.

A few weeks later the establishment was taken over by Charlie Rath, who became part-owner of a toll bridge which was built in the spring of 1863. Joseph W. Douglas took title to the place in 1867, but a party of Cheyenne and Arapaho Indians burned the place on May 19, 1868, and that was the end of the operation. The site was excavated in May 1969 by the Kansas Anthropological Association; Button was a member of the crew.

Just to the south is a mass grave on the west side of the creek, where it curves to the south. In July 1864 a wagon train carrying wagon bows and flour to Fort Union was attacked by Indians here. Archaeologists found the skeletons of eight white men buried about knee deep. The remains of two black soldiers were unearthed nearby, from a separate grave somewhat more shallow but almost adjacent to the white grave. The site is about 100 yards south of the farmhouse.

Return north, then head west on the gravel road for exactly a half-mile, and then turn south for .3 mile. Cross Walnut Creek on an iron bridge and drive another .2 mile south. The road turns left there. Drive east for .4 mile and park just before reaching the farmyard on the right. A postal relay station stood about fifty yards from the bank of Walnut Creek, due north of the road. A log-strewn depression leads from the high ground down to the very steep bank of the creek, heading a little east of due north. Somewhere in the bed of the creek are the stubs of the log pilings which once held Charlie Rath's long-gone bridge.

Backtrack to Highway 56 and head west. The site of the second Fort Zarah is .4 mile to the west. Slight depressions a few dozen yards out in the field north of the highway mark the building site.

The second version, started in June 1866, included a sandstone structure with a tin roof.

Just before crossing Walnut Creek the trail split—one branch closely followed the bank of the Arkansas and the other followed the creek, to cross about where the highway bridge does. The road on the higher ground joined the highway at the bridge and proceeded along or under U.S. 56 for one mile to the eastern limit of the present city of Great Bend.

At that point the highway assumes a due-west course, but the Santa Fe Railroad continues a southwestward slant. So did the trail, probably

The second Fort Zarah, located just north of present U.S. Highway 56, was sketched in 1864.

beneath the tracks. Continue into Great Bend for 1.5 miles to Main Street. Turn south for a half-mile, crossing the railroad tracks and the Arkansas River along the way. The Barton County Museum is on the right.

This splendid little museum has everything a local museum should have. But it has something else—a stunning archaelogical display. Button and his colleagues have carefully modeled the two forts, and mounted those models in artistically-designed cases. These amateurs exhibit a degree of professionalism which could be envied by any formally trained archaeologist.

The artifacts the Fort Zarah archaeologists found at the site of the Allison-Peacock Trading Post and the two Fort Zarahs are integrated into those displays. The history of those dramatic sites is presented with great skill and sensitivity.

Proceed north across the Arkansas River bridge. At the Garvey elevator, just before reaching the railroad tracks, turn left on an unmarked street known locally as Railroad Avenue. Drive .4 mile west, turn right, cross the tracks, and immediately turn left again, still on Railroad Avenue. Continue west another 2.1 miles and join Highway 56 headed southwest.

PAWNEE COUNTY

Only about .3 mile ahead the trail crosses the highway from south to north. It continues to parallel the highway, about a quarter-mile to the right. There will be a diagonal intersection 4.5 miles ahead at the town of Dundee. A half-mile north of there the Santa Fe Trail split again into "wet" and "dry" routes. The two remained apart for seventy-five miles.

Ride with Susan Magoffin on July 10, 1846, to a point a few miles west of Great Bend:

> . . . traveled well till 6 o'clock [P.M.] when a very hard thunder storm came up and detained us *in the road* till after eight. A thunder storm at sunset on the Prairie is a sublime and awing scene indeed. The vivid and forked lightning quickly succeeded by the hoarse growling thunder impresses one most deeply of his own weakness and the magnanimity of his God. With nothing before or near us in sight, save the wide expanse of Prairie resembling most fully in the pale light of the moon, as she occasionally appeared from under a murky cloud and between the vivid lightning, the wide sea. There was no object near higher than our own wagons, and how easy would it have been for one of them to be struck and consume the whole crowd, for with it was a high wind, sufficient to counteract the effects of the drenching rain.

It probably was near here that Marion Russell, then age seven, came upon a "tall ramshackle house." She thought it was abandoned until the party saw some men lounging in the shade, who "seemed sullen and taciturn." The men in the wagon train gained permission to draw water from the well, however. As they were resting, a woman came from the house.

> I shall always remember the hopeless look of longing in her eyes as she talked to us. . . . she asked mother to stay with her until her expected baby was born.

When that didn't work the woman asked to ride along with the caravan to Kansas City. "I am in danger here," she said. "I cannot tell you about it. My husband would kill me." One of the lounging men then arose and headed toward the woman, who promptly returned toward the house. Mrs. Sloan, Marion's mother, reported the incident to the wagon master, who then approached the man and offered to take the pregnant woman along. The answer was a steady flow of curses.

Four years later, Marion and her mother were headed back to Santa Fe.

> When we drew near the place we realized that this time it actually was deserted. No sullen men loafed in shade there. Empty windows stared at us . . . It was [her brother] Will who discovered the grave by the wire fence half-hidden by tumble weeds. A bit of weather beaten board with letters printed upon it told the meager story. "Sarah Grace Austin and infant daughter. October 24th 1856."

Pawnee Rock was a favorite haunt for hostile Indians. Dozens of traders met their demise here.

No one today knows where that site is.

About four more miles southwest on U.S. 56 Pawnee Rock, or what's left of it, will come into view on the right. Follow the sign and turn hard to the right onto the Erlich Highway. Follow it north about a half-mile to Pawnee Rock. It is in a small roadside park. Circle up behind it, almost to the top, and park. A circular stair leads from the top to a concrete observation pavilion atop the formation. The observation platform, according to George Elmore, is nearly as high as the rock before quarrying started. Elmore, a native of Larned, is a knowledgeable historian on the National Park Service staff at Fort Larned.

Elmore said that much of the rock was quarried away for building the Santa Fe Railroad and more for construction of homes in the area. The ground below is filled with unmarked and now invisible graves. The rock, according to many of the travelers who passed this way, was a place of ambush.

It was also an autograph rock. Quoting Susan Magoffin:

> We went up and while *mi alma* [her husband] with his gun and pistols kept watch, for the wily Indian may always be apprehended here, it is a good lurking place and they are ever ready to fall upon any unfortunate trader behind his company. . . . I cut my name,

Clay Ward

Covered wagons crossed Ash Creek west of Pawnee Rock, and Susan Magoffin's carriage upset at this point.

among the many hundreds inscribed on the rock and many of whom I knew.

It was July 4, 1846.

Through it can no longer be seen from this vantage point, Fort Larned bears 240 degrees, some fourteen miles west-southwest.

A little to the left of that sightline a white dome is in view about seven miles to the southwest, at the Larned airport. The dry route of the Santa Fe Trail follows in that direction from a point between Pawnee Rock and Highway 56. The wet route is about two miles to the southeast, heading for the south part of the city of Larned.

Return to the highway and turn right, around an old stone building. That rock was quarried from Pawnee Rock.

Follow the highway only a half-mile southwest of Pawnee Rock, slant to the right on a blacktop road and head west for 4.4 miles. Turn left and drive south for two miles; then turn right for .3 mile to a sign marking the crossing of Ash Creek. Both banks of the creek have been reworked for agricultural purposes, obliterating fine cut-downs on both banks made by the traders.

This is the spot where Susan Magoffin got in trouble:

No water in the creek and the crossing pretty good only a tolerably steep bank on the first [north] side of it. . . . The bank though a little steep was smooth and there could be no difficulty in riding down it.—However, we had made up our minds always to walk down such places in case of accident, and before we got to it *mi alma* hallowed "woe" . . . but as there was no motion made by the driver to that effect, he repeated it several times and with much vehemence. We had now reached the very verge of the cliff and seeing it a good way and apparently less dangerous than jumping out as we were, he said "go on." The word was scarcely from his lips, ere we were whirled completely over with a perfect crash. . . . I was considerably stunned at first and could not stand on my feet. *Mi alma* . . . carried me in his arms to a shade tree, almost entirely without my knowledge, and rubbing my face and hands with whiskey soon brought me entire to myself.

Susan Magoffin was not a complainer, and she felt her injuries were negligible. However, the child she didn't yet know she was carrying was lost at Bent's Fort a month later, the miscarriage possibly due to the accident here at the Ash Creek Crossing.

Across the road from the crossing was a major campground. Many glass shards have been culled from the site.

Proceed west for .7 mile and turn left. Just .5 mile south the trail crossed. A half-mile down the trail is another split. The road continuing to the west goes to Fort Larned. The branch leading southwest joins that route just south of Fort Larned. The wet route, meanwhile, is on the right-of-way of U.S. 56. Continue ahead two more miles and slant to the right on U.S. 56. In a half-mile the road will turn due west for another half-mile. At that point U.S. 56 turns south and Kansas Highway 156 proceeds due west. Take 156 straight ahead.

About two miles ahead turn left on a blacktop road. Just .3 miles to the south is the Larned Cemetery. A chain link fence is on the east boundary of the cemetery. Beneath that fence and in the cemetery, in an area about thirty yards north of the stop sign, are shallow impressions of the Santa Fe Trail—the center one of the three roads heading to the southwest. Return to 156 and turn left. Proceed west for .6 mile and turn left into the Santa Fe Trail Center.

Old Fort Larned was abandoned on July 13, 1878, and sold to agricultural interests in 1884, but after World War II Pawnee County residents recognized its great historical value. The Fort Larned Historical Society was founded in 1957 to develop the site and open it as a tourist attraction. Not long after it was taken over, the society realized that the responsibility for restoring the fort rightfully belonged to the federal government.

The National Park Service took it over in 1966. That, however, left

The Santa Fe Trail Center, near Larned, Kansas, is one of the finest museums along the trail. This is one of the outdoor exhibits.

the Fort Larned Historical Society with no place to exhibit its own collections. Through massive donations from the citizens of the county and city of Larned, the Santa Fe Trail Center was built. It opened in 1974 and serves not only as an area museum, but as a library and archive. Handsome exhibits are on the western portion of the twenty-five-acre tract, including a sod house, limestone cooling house, a Santa Fe Railroad depot, windmills, a country schoolhouse, and a pioneer dugout patterned after one excavated in Ness County, Kansas, in the 1870s.

The energetic Ruth Olson directs the center's professional staff, which hosts a three-day seminar on the Santa Fe Trail in the spring of even-numbered years.

Return to Highway 156 and turn left. Go one-half mile west to the next intersection and turn left on Highway 264. Proceed south another mile to the grounds of the Larned State Hospital. Turn right at the end of the highway. Now it is necessary to get permission from the hospital before leaving the paved road. Just .2 mile to the west turn off the road onto a two-track which leads up to a parking area beneath the water tower. Walk to the west to the brink of the bluff and look down and to the left. There is the Pawnee Fork. A DAR marker is approximately where the covered wagons forded the stream. The Fort Larned flag may be seen five miles to the west.

Return to the hospital drive and continue the loop road to the southwest. Turn right past a small red brick building onto a dirt road leading west. Cross a concrete bridge. It is narrow and looks rickety, but it is sturdy. There is a Y in the road just past the bridge. Bear left. In the field on the right is the site of Boyd's Ranch. That was no Girl Scout camp. An 1875 census showed five unattached women in residence. The entrance room was a saloon; the assignation cribs lined the hallway to the rear.

Return to Highway 264. Proceed one-half mile north and turn left. This is a dead-end road which passes a real Girl Scout camp, Camp Pawnee. Just .7 mile from the turn is the quarry from which sandstone for the new Fort Larned blockhouse was taken. This is adjacent to the quarry used in 1867-68 by the army to build Fort Larned. The road turns left there. Proceed south about 100 yards and turn right on an ungraded dirt road. Drive ahead about fifty yards. On the left, according to tradition, is the site of "Camp on Pawnee Fork," established October 22, 1859. This was an attempt to control the growing Indian attacks on the travelers using the Santa Fe Trail, and also to protect the mail station erected there by Waldo Hall & Co., mail contractors. The installation was no more than a number of dugouts for the troops. The name soon was changed to Camp Alert. The site was subjected to a formal archaeologal dig, but archaeologists were unable to uncover any military

Fort Larned was a ranch from 1884, six years after its abandonment by the army, until 1957.

The stone buildings at Fort Larned have been completely restored by the National Park Service.

artifacts dating to the period. For that reason, Elmore has his doubts about the authenticity of the site. However, occupation was very brief; not many artifacts would have been left as evidence. The garrison moved to the site of present Fort Larned in June 1860.

Return to Highway 264, follow it back to the north to 156, and turn left. Proceed west for 3.6 miles and turn left into the parking lot for Fort Larned. This is one of the great jewels of the National Park Service. There would be a lot less crabbing about taxes on April 15 if more people could visit this place on April 14.

The first buildings here were of adobe, an unfortunate decision. The orders came through in 1866 for more permanent buildings of stone, and by 1868 most of the construction was completed. The stone military buildings at Fort Larned looked much the same as they do today. Every building on the site has been carefully restored and furnished to that period. The only stone building known to have been destroyed was the blockhouse; that was reconstructed in 1987-88.

But the buildings aren't static exhibits. Elmore and the rest of Superintendent Jack Arnold's staff stage programs frequently to illustrate daily life at the post.

Perhaps the most fascinating aspect of the Fort Larned visit is the self-guided Fort Larned History Trail. In taking this tour the imaginative visitor may see buildings which have been gone for more than a century. The site of the first adobe barracks has been located and is pointed out. So is the first post cemetery. Sixty-six bodies were moved to the Fort Leavenworth cemetery after the post's abandonment; now it is believed about forty bodies may remain in unmarked graves.

The oxbow which was once a part of the Pawnee Fork is visible, as is the site of the stables and corral. The site of the mail station can be seen, along with traces of the beef corral. Then the visitor walks out onto the prairie, where the Santa Fe Trail has been mowed for easy walking, and a myriad of native prairie grasses and prairie wildflowers enrich the landscape on the hike back to the fort's buildings. The trail may be covered at a leisurely pace in a half-hour. It could be the most memorable and poignant half-hour spent on the Santa Fe Trail.

Return to Highway 156, turn left, and proceed .3 mile west to the first intersection. Turn left there and drive south for four miles.

At a stop sign, turn right and drive a mile west, then turn to the left. Just .9 mile ahead is a turnout on the east side of the road. Park there and hike the path a few dozen yards to an elevated wood viewing platform. Climb the stairs to the top of the structure and look toward the left. There, coming down from Fort Larned, are five distinct sets of ruts heading toward the junction with the wet road. Many buffalo wallows are also there, where bison would roll in dust or mud to relieve the at-

Six distinct swales lead down to Coon Creek, west of Garfield, Kansas.

tacks from biting flies.

Continue south 2.8 more miles to Highway 56 in Garfield and slant to the right, or southwest. The junction of the wet route and the Garfield road is about a quarter-mile to the southeast. At this point, the dry route is four miles to the northwest.

Proceed southwest for 1.1 miles and pull off the road to the right onto a two-track, proceed ahead a few yards and park by a small clump of trees. To the west a concrete bridge carries the highway over Coon Creek. This is private land, so first get permission. Then walk to the west (the road goes southwest) to where the land starts to slope down to the bank of the creek and then walk north. During this little hike, about fifty yards, five or six swales will be encountered. They are more evident in the spring, while the vegetation is dormant. There are matching swales on the west bank.

Proceed twelve miles to the southwest. U.S. 183, which had been with 56 to this point, leaves it in the town of Kinsley. Follow 183 south for a few blocks to the intersection with U.S. 50, and there turn left. Drive three miles east and cross the bridge over the Arkansas River. Just .3

mile ahead is a historical marker describing the Battle of Coon Creek.

Some 140 soldiers went up against 200 Comanches and Osages on June 8, 1848. After the fight the soldiers were astounded to see a stately woman dressed in elegant tribal regalia passing among the defeated Indians giving directions on the disposition of the wounded. The Americans thought she was a Comanche queen. Since then it has been speculated that this person was of an entirely different type—a homosexual, possibly a transvestite, who was deemed to have excellent communication with the spirit world. Dr. Melburn D. Thurman, the noted Plains Indian ethnologist, said that scholars are only now coming to understand the mystical role of the *berdache* in Comanche society.

Return to Kinsley. Highways 56 and 50 join about a mile west of the center of town. Take an odometer reading there. Drive to the southwest on both highways for twelve miles. A blacktop sectionline road there slants to a due south direction. Turn left there. (The road is a few yards east of the bridge over Little Coon Creek and less than a mile east of the little town of Bellefont.)

Drive south for exactly three miles. That is an intercept of the dry route of the Santa Fe Trail. Another half-mile ahead is a T in the road— turn left. Proceed back east only for .6 mile and take the curve back to the right. Ten miles farther is the intercept of the wet route of the old trail, which goes precisely through that intersection.

Continue south for another mile, where the blacktop is forced by the Arkansas River to turn to the west. A half-mile ahead the blacktop curves to the south to cross the river, but don't take it—continue on ahead on a gravel road. Just 2.5 miles west of there turn left onto a dirt road. This is a "tractor" road—it is rarely mowed. By midsummer the weeds can be three feet tall. It is not for low-slung cars. Continue south for .3 mile. The road ends at a steel gate there. Stop. This is private land—it will be necessary to get permission before visiting the Black Pool.

FORD COUNTY

Hike or drive to the west onto the prairie for about .4 mile—gentle indentations of the trail will be all along the way. They start out in the field a few yards west of the end of the dirt road and lead past the north side of the Black Pool, continuing on for perhaps a mile. This, of course, is the wet route.

The Black Pool is a pond and spring at the bottom of an arroyo in the pasture. Walking toward it the visitor will find a rock on which has been incised "Black Pool U.S. Post 1843." The inscription, which certainly appears to be old, is surrounded by a rectangular border. Beyond it the pasture land falls away and the visitor can stare into what appears

The Black Pool lies at the bottom of this ravine. Tracks of the Santa Fe Trail are nearby.

to be a small pond at the bottom of an arroyo. It is extremely deep, and has a dark coloration due to the underlying strata of black shale.

Around it are hundreds of names cut into the rocks. Most of them seem to be from the post-trail era. The curious part is that so far not a single diary reference or reminiscence has come to light mentioning the Black Pool.

Return to the gravel road and resume the westerly direction. A dirt section line leads off to the right a mile to the west. Continue west for another half-mile. One branch of the wet route crosses here heading northwest, and about fifty yards out in the pasture to the right, it assumes a bearing of due west. One rut swale is about ten yards wide and as much as three feet deep. It begins about at this point, just past the house on the right. (The pasture is private land.) A half-mile ahead there is a windmill on the right side of the road; the ruts head toward it and disappear just before reaching it.

Continue to the west for 1.5 miles and the road becomes blacktop. Highway 154 is another half-mile ahead—turn right and follow it northwest for about .3 mile. The trail to the lower crossing of the Cimarron Cutoff intersects the highway here, heading for the Arkansas .4 mile south-southwest. Here, on the west bank of Mulberry Creek, a few early traders left the main trail to cross the Jornada to Lower Cimarron Spring. Most, however, stayed on the north bank of the Arkansas for many more days.

Kansas State Historical Society

Fort Dodge in 1879

One mile ahead the wet road comes beneath the highway and stays there all the way to Dodge City. Just 8.6 miles ahead is a DAR marker on the right. It is about here where the dry and wet roads merged.

Proceed another .8 mile northwest and turn left at the main gate of Fort Dodge, onto Sheridan Street. Named for Gen. Grenville M. Dodge, the fort was established on April 10, 1865, to house military escorts for the wagon trains wending through increasingly hostile Indian country. Construction started with a few dugouts with sod roofs. Soon these were replaced with sod—two still stand, now handsomely faced with cut stone.

One block inside the entrance turn right onto Custer Street. The building on the inside corner, numbered 226, is a two-story double house which was used as officers' quarters. Next to it is the original commanding officer's quarters—a red-roofed, white two-story stone structure with a front porch supported by columns. George A. Custer passed through the area on the way to one of his campaigns, but Dr. Leo Oliva has discovered that Custer was never part of the post garrison.

Fort Dodge was the southern terminus of the Fort Hays-Fort Dodge Road, which carried an enormous amount of traffic from the Union Pacific railroad at present Hays, Kansas, to this point, from 1867 to 1872, when the Santa Fe Railroad reached Dodge City. The fort played a major role in the winter campaign of 1868-69.

Proceed ahead one block. On the right, at the corner of Garfield and Custer, is Pershing Barracks, built in 1867 as the post hospital. Turn left for a block, then left again back to Sheridan, and make another left turn toward the gate. On the right are old stone houses believed to have been a part of the original fort.

The garrison at the fort did its job without much fanfare, and as the years passed the Indian depredations along the Santa Fe Trail increased. Many military men felt the only way to end the carnage was to starve the Indian to death. Gen. Philip Henry Sheridan addressed a hearing of the Texas Legislature in 1875:

> . . . [destroy] the Indians' commissary. For the sake of lasting peace, let them [the buffalo hunters] kill, skin, and sell until they have exterminated the buffalo. Then your prairies will be covered with speckled cattle and festive cowboys.

That, essentially, is exactly what happened. By 1882 Fort Dodge was shuttered and much of the reservation land was sold off. Congress turned the remainder of the post over to the state of Kansas. In 1890 it became the Kansas State Soldiers' Home, and it serves that function today.

Proceed west on Highway 154 for three miles to the east edge of Dodge City. Betty Braddock and Noel Ary, director and assistant director, respectively, of the Kansas Heritage Center, like to call attention to the stupendous mural girdling the building of the High Plains Dressed Beef Company, on the right. Continue following the highway until it reaches First Avenue.

Turn right there, cross the tracks, and pass the beautiful old Santa Fe depot on the right. It is in the shape of an L. Turn into the parking lot on the north side of the depot, drive to the east and turn right around the short leg of the L, drive to the tracks and turn left.

Santa Fe Park is on the east side of the depot. A stone tablet marks the site of the 100th meridian. To the easterners that was a wall. It also was their notion of the western limit of cultivatable land. South of the Arkansas River (in the southern part of Dodge City), the 100th meridian marked the official boundary between the United States and Mexico, until 1848.

The street along the north side of the Santa Fe depot is Wyatt Earp Boulevard. Return to the west and turn right on Fifth Street, to enter the parking lot of the Boot Hill Museum and Dodge's historic Front Street. There is a charge for admission, gained through the visitor center.

It appears to be an old hotel, and a visitor must pass through this building to get to "Front Street," a row of false-front buildings depicting Dodge in the cowtown days. A professionally produced sound-slide presentation is in a small theater in the building.

V. James Sherer, executive director of the museum, has gained accreditation for the museum through the American Association of Museums. Boot Hill Museum was founded in 1947. The reconstructions along Front Street are identical in appearance to those which lined

Dodge City's original Front Street in 1876. Those buildings, which were a block south and two blocks east, burned in 1885.

The cowtown days are recalled each evening by daily simulated gunfights, a popular attraction for tourists. This is followed by a show in the simulation of the Long Branch Saloon.

This sort of activity attracts the kind of dollars it takes to fund the serious work. Of primary interest to the Santa Fe Trail partisan is the 143-acre tract west of town, which is owned by the Boot Hill Museum. There are plans now to develop it into a real trail experience, where visitors may be able to hike in the ruts, as a means of preservation. Horseback and wagon rides in the ruts are also being considered. Certainly some sort of active use is necessary, as those ruts are inexorably fading away.

Wyatt Earp Boulevard is U.S. 50. Continue west and take an odometer reading at the traffic light at 14th and Earp. At 2.1 miles take a left onto a blacktop road. Cross the tracks and proceed south for .1 mile. Turn right and drive west just .3 mile.

The site of Fort Mann lies across the road at this point. That fort was established in April 1847 as a post midway between Fort Leavenworth and Santa Fe. It was actually a quartermaster wagon repair station, where stock could also be replaced.

Lewis Garrard stopped here on his way east, and decided to stay a few months to make some extra money as a hired hand.

> The fort was simply four log houses, connected by angles of timber framework, in which were cut loopholes for the cannon and small arms. In diameter the fort was about sixty feet. The walls were twenty in hight.

Fort Mann was abandoned in 1848.

Return to Highway 50 and turn left. One mile to the west, on the right side of the highway, is a white stone obelisk commemorating Forts Mann and Atkinson, plus The Caches.

The Caches, one, two, or even more, were jug-shaped holes dug in 1822-23 by the trading party led by James Baird and Samuel Chambers. The two leaders, who had been imprisoned in Chihuahua years before because of an illegal expedition to Santa Fe, found their luck holding true to form here when they were blasted by a ferocious blizzard. Their livestock promptly froze to death and they were stranded for three months. Baird and Chambers had to protect their goods while they went ahead to Taos to replace the livestock. They cached their goods here. The openings were only wide enough to admit their packs. They must have been a dozen or more feet deep, and perhaps a dozen feet in diameter at the base to hold the trade goods.

Baird and Chambers returned the following spring, found the merchandise intact, went on to Santa Fe with it, and made a handsome profit. The holes remained, of course. And they were noted by countless traders plying the old road to Santa Fe. Probably the narrow opening would have been enlarged by the weather, and much of the overburden would have caved into the holes, leaving two large depressions in the earth. No descriptions of the holes in later years survive today.

The Caches were located somewhere near the farm buildings northwest of the obelisk, according to the legend on the marker. They were filled in several decades ago, and no one has been found today who can cite the precise location.

Susan Magoffin was still hurting from her spill at Ash Creek, an indication that internal injuries were not healing. Yet, that remarkable woman still wrote in her diary almost every night. She described The Caches and their history, then commented on their location:

> They are situated about a quarter of a mile from the River, on rather an elevated piece of ground, and within a hundred yards of the road, which runs at present between them and the river. They are quite as noted as any point on the road and few travellers pass without visiting them. I was rather too much of an invalid, though, to go nearer than the road.

The site of Fort Atkinson is due south of The Caches, about a quarter-mile south of the highway. It was established as Camp MacKay on August 8, 1850, to minimize Indian problems in the area. It failed in its mission. The fort was built entirely of sod, and nothing is known to remain at the site today. It was abandoned October 2, 1854.

There are no less than six crossings of the Arkansas River in the next twenty-five miles—all designated as "Middle Cimarron crossing." The first is due south of the site of Fort Atkinson, probably a half-mile from the highway. The Santa Fe Trail is beneath or within a few yards of Highway 50 for many miles to the west.

From this point proceed west on the highway for 1.9 miles. There is a rock outcropping on the right. That was the Point of Rocks, the first of four sites bearing that name on the Santa Fe Trail. To widen this highway, the Point of Rocks was blasted to smithereens. Not in the 1950s, when preservation was unheard of, but in the 1980s.

The road to the second crossing leaves the highway 1.1 miles ahead—the actual crossing being about .9 mile southwest of the section line road at that point.

Just 3.3 miles past that point, or 9.3 miles west of 14th and Earp, is a DAR marker, a turnout, and a sign heralding the great rut swales west of Dodge City which are owned by the Boot Hill Museum. The main

Kansas Department of Commerce

Ruts of the Santa Fe Trail west of Dodge City are on a 143-acre tract owned by the Boot Hill Museum. This photo, taken in 1956, shows the Soule Canal cutting through the swales. U.S. Highway 56 is at left.

route is under the highway, according to the Kansas GLO survey. These ruts are a "dry" road, used when the Arkansas River had risen to soak the original trail.

Park, walk through the turnstile and a short distance farther to the granite monument in the corner of the field, on which appears a National Historic Landmark marker dated 1966.

On the way from the turnstile to the monument four faint rut swales are crossed. They are bearing about 295 degrees, or west-northwest. They proceed in the same direction for a little less than a half-mile, then turn sharply to the south, where they cross the highway and disappear in the cultivated valley.

Deeper ruts are several yards farther north, and they are much easier to see. There are many braided swales there across a distance of about .7 mile, where they were wiped out by the construction of the Soule Canal in the 1880s. They are also heading west-northwest and take a gradual curve to the southwest about a half-mile ahead. All the swales enter the tract from the highway, about .3 mile east of the turnout, to head northwestward.

The museum plans to remove the fence in the fall of 1989. Then all of the swales may be easily reached by the public.

GRAY COUNTY

Drive to the Gray County line marker, which is 1.1 miles from the turnstile. Between .2 and .3 mile ahead the great rut swales curve into the highway, as they head toward the river.

The Middle Cimarron crossings continue in the town of Cimarron, which is eight miles to the west. Kansas Highway 23, Main Street, crosses 50 in the center of town. Turn left there and proceed south. A half-mile ahead is Cimarron Crossing Park. Turn in, to the right, and stop at one of the most elegant granite markers on the Santa Fe Trail. Here is incised a map showing the Mountain Branch and the Cimarron Cutoff, plus a description of the two routes.

A bridge carries Route 23 over the Arkansas River. There is no precise spot where the wagons crossed. As is the case all along the river, the trains crossed where it happened to be easiest on that particular day. It might have been upstream or down, as far as a mile or more, but Louise Barry, the noted Kansas historian, assembled plenty of evidence to indicate that the major crossing was one mile west of the present town.

Return to U.S. Highway 50, take an odometer reading, and turn left. Drive west for 2.6 miles. At that point the trail leaves the highway abruptly in a northerly direction, then bends to the west to intersect the highway six miles ahead. However, 5.9 miles from Route 23 in Cimarron is another intercept, just .1 mile east of the center of the town of Ingalls. The trail at that point is a mile to the north, and some wagons would have left it there to head south-southwest to a crossing of the Arkansas River exactly one mile south-southwest of the highway.

Continue northwest from Ingalls for 2.6 miles. Here the trail comes into the highway from the east, loops quickly to the north side, then back to the southwest again. At this point close the windows and turn the air conditioner on "max" (or at least shut down all fresh air intakes). The smelliest feed lot on Planet Earth is about a mile ahead on the left.

Here the Santa Fe Trail is a quarter-mile to the left. Southbound wagons would have left it there and crossed the river, heading southwest, about a mile from the highway. This was a major crossing site. No ruts are known to be visible there, but there are some good, sharp creases farther south, on the ranch of Dale Eichenauer and for some distance to the north.

It is a good thirty miles out of the way, but a visit with Dale is recommended. Backtrack 3.5 miles to the town of Ingalls and turn right. In the heart of town, in front of the depot-museum, is a DAR marker. It was once up on the highway, but it had fallen over and some folks felt that it might be stolen from there. So they moved it here, across the street from another DAR marker. It ought to be returned to the proper place.

As Paul Bentrup has wisely noted, people have been playing Chinese checkers with these markers for decades, and a concerted effort ought to be made to return them all to their original sites.

Take an odometer reading here. Proceed southwest for 1.5 miles, where the highway curves half-left. Continue south 4.7 miles from that curve; that's where the blacktop ends. A section line road is .1 mile ahead. Keep going south for one more mile; then turn right. Proceed west on gravel for seven more miles and turn right. The Eichenauer ranch is .7 mile to the north, on the right (east) side of the road.

Dale has some good ruts in his land, leading northeast to the Ingalls feed lot. He took a pair of bronze welding rods and held them straight in front of him as he walked down the trail ruts one day. Suddenly the rods crossed; he was unable to hold them parallel. He came back the other way. The same thing happened. He returned to the barn for a spade. Three and one-half feet down he was into a char-filled pit. Up came rusted old wagon parts, then an ox chain eight feet long. And then one ten feet long. Dale readily shows the chains to visitors. He will hand the divining rods to the disbelieving, too, and ask them to hold them parallel as they walk over a metal plate.

Return south to the first gravel road and turn back east for two miles. There is a good gravel road heading due north at this point. Take it back to the highway, a distance of nearly ten miles.

FINNEY COUNTY

Turn left on U.S. 50 and drive west for six miles to Pierceville. Turn left on the blacktop (take an odometer reading upon leaving the highway), cross the Santa Fe tracks on the south side of town, and turn right immediately on Mansfield Road, a gravel road paralleling the railroad. Proceed three miles and stop at a turnout on the left, labeled ''Weldon Outdoor Classroom.'' The formation on the right is known as Point of Rocks. The acreage to the left is believed by Paul Bentrup to be the site of the Pawnee Fort.

The area is owned by Jim and Hazel Weldon Tancayo, who live on this same road a half-mile west of Pierceville. Hazel's parents encouraged schoolchildren to come to Pawnee Fort to learn—not just history but ecology as well. That tradition has been carried on by Jim and Hazel. They encourage visitors, but it is only polite to ask first if there are plans to leave the public road.

The Santa Fe Trail is beneath the railroad for all this distance from Pierceville (and in fact all the way to Garden City).

Paul Bentrup believes that it was here, or within a mile or two of here, that Sister Mary Alphonsa Thompson was buried. That, and its

The Point of Rocks west of Pierceville, Kansas, is believed to be also the site of Pawnee Fort.

twentieth-century aftermath, constitute one of the most gripping stories of the Santa Fe Trail.

Sister Alphonsa was one of five nuns accompanying Bishop Jean Bautista Lamy, first bishop of Santa Fe, to his see city. They left St. Louis June 10, 1867. The caravan, by this time consisting of 180 ox-drawn wagons, was attacked by Indians at dusk on July 17. That siege lasted three hours.

A second attack occurred at 10 A.M. July 22. That night it became evident that Sr. Alphonsa was ill. Her condition worsened and by 6 P.M. the following day the bishop "assisted her for death," according to an account by Sister M. Kotska Gauthreaux, who was along on the journey.

The caravan continued to move at 10 A.M. on July 24, but stopped within minutes, out of respect for the dying religious. She died at 10:46 that morning and was buried at 1 P.M.

John Geatley was with the caravan; he dug the grave. This is his account, considerably at variance. However, it was written in 1927, sixty years after the fact:

> On the 22nd, late in the evening, the Indians attacked our party, and our train was hurried into corral. . . .
>
> July 23rd. We were passing the day in camp at Cimmaron Crossing, where it had been decided to ford the river. The detail of cavalry

*John Geatley buried Sr. Alfonsa and
wrote an account of it sixty years after the
fact.*

with some of our horsemen were out scouting and reported a large
body of Indians north, apparently moving south. The boy, wounded
by the Indians yesterday, died about noon. He was baptized by one
of the priests of the Bishop's party. Poor boy, his father was with
him. . . .

July 24. Moved on early, . . . Two wagons, a dozen yokes of oxen
to each, were now ready to ford. The water is not deep, about two
feet, but the heavy wagons sink in the sand to the wheel hubs and
even deeper if not kept moving continually. . . . That evening, the
young nun that had assisted in nursing the patients was prostrate,
not with cholera, as she appeared deathly pale in her coffin, . . .

July 25th. Moved as usual and at noon, encamped some ten miles
farther west. Preparations were made at once to bury the dead sister.
The extension boards of some of the wagon beds were used and
a clumsy coffin made. . . .

It will be understood that the dear Sister was buried two days
travel west of Cimmeron Crossing near the river, a quarter of a mile
or more from the highway north of the Arkansas River.

Paul Bentrup, a wizard on the Santa Fe Trail in this part of Kansas,
advises that the Lamy train eventually crossed the swollen river near
Bent's Old Fort, on the Mountain Branch.

A famous picture is associated with this incident. It shows two weep-

Sisters of Loretto

This photo, long believed to have been made at the time of the burial of Sr. Mary Alfonsa Thompson in 1867, actually was taken during a reenactment in 1902.

ing Sisters kneeling at the grave, with the rest of the entourage in the background. A second photo supposedly taken at the same time shows the dead Sister, her two companions, and Bishop Lamy looking into the camera. Or actually, his face—it has been pasted over someone else's body. The head of Father J. M. Coudert, assistant to Lamy's vicar general, was pasted over another body.

Investigation by The Patrice Press disclosed that both photographs were taken in mid-October 1902, during celebration of the golden anniversary of the arrival of the Sisters of Loretto in Santa Fe. The reenactment took place just outside of Santa Fe.

In the meantime, the search continues for the nun's grave. It is hoped that some of the readers of this book will take some extra time during their journey over the Santa Fe Trail to assist in the search. Check in at the fine Finney County Museum, in Fineup Park, in the southeast corner of Garden City.

The record of another burial near here has survived. Louise Barry's monumental *The Beginning of the West* offers this quote from a member of Kearny's Army of the West:

> On the 22d [of July 1846] passed "Pawnee Fort," an old decayed stockade (Sgt. Augustus Leslie who died this day was buried on the 23d four miles above it.)

William W. Salisbury's 1859 journal also reported that he saw a dead Indian interred up under the shelving rocks at Point of Rocks. The body

Sisters of Loretto

This grotesque photo is a montage on which the face of Bishop Jean Baptiste Lamy was pasted over the person impersonating him during the reenactment.

had been dug up by wolves, and "some of his bones mocasins blanket bow and arrows were in sight. camped on the flats 20 miles."

The site of Pawnee Fort is believed to be on the north bank of the Arkansas River near here. Jesse Scott, Jr., a trail historian from Garden City, translated the data from the Sibley survey to place it in this vicinity. The Sibley party camped there September 23-24, 1825. The parallel of latitude shot by the party passes through the Point of Rocks.

Lewis Garrard passed Pawnee Fort on September 24, 1846:

> . . . a grove of timber in which a war party of Pawnees, some years before, fortified themselves when besieged by a hostile tribe. Nothing now remains but a few crumbling logs to mark the site of this Indian bulwark.

Katherine Powell, identified by Paul Bentrup as an expert on Finney County history, has written that the area had a substantial Indian population:

> Indians were there for sure. An account published in the Garden City *Herald* on May 13, 1893, reported that an Indian medal given by President Martin Van Buren in 1837 had been found there.

. . . [The medal was found] sticking up out of the ground "as bright as when it came from the mint."

Continue ahead on the gravel road along the Santa Fe tracks. Just 3.2 to the northwest a gravel road intersects heading due north. Faintly visible ruts are just to the east of that road on the Foulks ranch. This, of course, is private property, and the ruts usually are heavily overgrown and difficult to see. Just 5.5 miles from Point of Rocks turn right onto Farmland Road, on the east edge of Garden City. All the way from Point of Rocks the trail has been under the gravel road or the Santa Fe tracks.

KEARNY COUNTY

Follow Farmland .9 mile north to the intersection with U.S. 50 and turn left. Follow Highway 50 west, about thirteen miles west of the northwest edge of Garden City. The trail is off to the south from 1.5 miles to .3 miles, riding the left bank of the Arkansas River.

Take an odometer reading opposite the Deerfield water tower. About 2.5 miles west of Deerfield is the first of two bridges over ditches—they are about a half-mile apart. Pull into a turnout on the right side of the highway just past the second bridge.

There is a historical sign identifying the ruts given by Paul Bentrup to the Kearny County Museum. They are known as Charlie's Ruts, named for Bentrup's father, who refused to plow them because of their historical value. Several swales come over the rise to the northeast, heading down to the low area east of the historical sign.

Bentrup has installed a mailbox next to the sign, in which he keeps a register of visitors, brochures on the Santa Fe Trail Association, and other material to enrich the experience of the visitor.

Proceed one more mile on the highway—that is where the trail crosses again, to the north side. In another mile it crosses back to the south and stays there through Lakin. At a point one mile southwest of the last intercept, or one mile northeast of the heart of Lakin, the trail is about .2 mile south of the highway. Here some wagons turned due south to cross the Arkansas 1.7 miles farther south.

On the west edge of Lakin turn south on Bopp Road for .8 mile, then turn right at a T in the road to proceed along the north side of the railroad tracks. Take an odometer reading at the T. Now the trail is along the right side of that road.

Just 1.3 miles ahead is a split in the trail, the northern branch going straight west for two miles before slanting back to the tracks. The other branch stays alongside the road. At 3.8 miles ahead the last of the wagons headed for the Cimarron left the main trail and crossed the Arkansas

Paul Bentrup stands at the foot of "Charlie's Ruts," named for his father, which he donated to the Kearny County Museum.

River a mile to the south.

However, just 3.4 miles west of Bopp Road turn half-right onto another gravel road.

Cross a canal and turn left immediately on a rutted two-track. This is private property—please get permission before driving farther. Take another odometer reading here. Cross a cattle guard. A Y is a few yards ahead. Bear left. Snake around a hill and pass to the left of a windmill. Continue to drive across the top of the hills, which are often ablaze with wildflowers of many varieties.

Pass a gas well identified as Beymer A No. 2. Another .2 mile is Indian Mound. It is 1.3 miles from the canal. Walk the rest of the way to the summit and look to the east. About a mile away is the site of the Upper Cimarron Crossing. It passed over long-disappeared Chouteau's Island. To the west is the Mountain Branch. The two don't join again until Watrous, New Mexico, is reached. (The Aubry Cutoff, which begins some miles to the west, connected the Mountain Branch with the Cimarron Cutoff.)

Maj. Bennet Riley was here in the spring of 1829 with four companies of the Sixth Infantry to guard a caravan on the way to Santa Fe. The escort ended here, while the traders went into the Jornada, Mexican territory, alone. Gregg tells the story:

Indian Mound is believed to have been much higher than it is now. It is gradually eroding into the landscape.

Bennet Riley

Harper's Magazine *published this sketch, entitled "Fording the Arkansas River,"* *in 1862.*

They had hardly advanced six or seven miles when a startling incident occurred which made them wish once more for the company of the gallant Major and his well-disciplined troops. A vanguard of three men riding a few hundred yards ahead had just dismounted for the purpose of satisfying their thirst when a band of Kiowas, one of the most savage tribes that infest the western prairies, rushed upon them from the immense hillocks of sand which lay scattered in all directions. The three men sprang upon their animals, but two only who had horses were enabled to make their escape to the wagons; the third, a Mr. Lamme, who was unfortunately mounted upon a mule, was overtaken, slain, and scalped before any one could come to his assistance. Somewhat alarmed at the boldness of the Indians, the traders dispatched an express to Major Riley, who immediately ordered his tents to be struck; and such was the rapidity of his movements that when he appeared before the anxious caravan every one was lost in astonishment. The reinforcement having arrived in the night, the enemy could have obtained no knowledge of the fact and would no doubt have renewed the attack in the morning, when they would have received a wholesome lesson from the troops, had not the reveille been sounded through mistake, at which they precipitately retreated.

The island was named for Auguste P. Chouteau, whose party of about twenty trappers held off a force of 200 Indians here long before the Santa Fe Trail was opened. George Sibley's party left the river here on September 27, 1825, headed for Taos. Here, a twenty-eight-mule train of Jones-Russell Co. was destroyed by a prairie fire, supposedly set by Pawnees. The teamsters escaped by crossing the river.

The caravans crossed the east end of the island. They skirted the west side of Clear Lake, and then traveled in the dry bed of Bear Creek.

Surveyor Joseph Brown, with the Sibley expedition, wrote this about the area:

> Crossing of the Arkansas just below the bend of the river at the lower end of a small island, with a few trees. At this place there are no banks on either side to hinder waggons. The crossing is very oblique, landing on the south side a quarter of a mile above the entrance on this side. The river is here very shallow, not more than knee deep in a low stage of the water. The bed of the river is altogether sand, and it is unsafe to stand long on one place with a waggon, or it may sink into the sand. After passing a few wet places just beyond the river, the road is again very good up to Chouteau's Island. Keep out from the river or there will be sand to pass.
>
> At Chouteau's Island the road leaves the river altogether. Many things unite to mark this place so strongly that the traveler will not mistake it. It is the largest island to timber on the river, and on the south side of the river with some cottonwood trees. On the north side of the river the hills approach tolerably nigh and on [one] of them is a sort of mound, conspicuous at some miles distance, and a little eastward of it in a bottom of some timber, perhaps a quarter of a mile from the river.

FINDING THE CIMARRON CUTOFF

KANSAS

Return to Lakin and turn right on Kansas Highway 25. (Lakin uses their streets as storm water conduits—that means big dips in the gutters, so cross at a slow speed.)

Proceed south, crossing first the Santa Fe railroad tracks and then the Arkansas River. The cutoff crosses the river about 3.5 miles to the west-southwest.

Hobart E. Stocking, the last generation's scholar and cartographer of the Santa Fe Trail, described the caravans' preparation for the trip through the Jornada:

> . . . a day of rest, filling of water kegs and cooking food for the next two days. Traverse of *La Jornada* usually began in late afternoon and continued until midnight. Sometimes by then the slightest dew dampened the sparse grass and given opportunity and moist herbage even a very thirsty ox would graze for a time and rest as long as allowed. After two or three hours they were under way again. By mid-morning, Lower Cimarron Spring was in sight and the Jornada behind. East-bound wagons with lighter loads might leave Lower Spring when the sun was three or four palm-widths above the western horizon and traveling through the night in one uninterrupted plod, reach Upper Crossing with the sun.

About 2.5 miles south of the bridge over the Arkansas the highway curves to the southwest. At that point the cutoff is three miles to the west. At ten miles from the bridge the highway curves back to the south, and there the trail is only a few yards to the west. Each minute the automobile moves, it covers a distance that it took the caravans almost an hour to traverse.

The Jornada of today would not be recognized by the traders. Where once there was nothing but bitter desert, there now are lush, green fields

The location of the Lower Cimarron Spring, known later as Wagon Bed Spring, was confirmed during the 1988 expedition by the National Park Service.

of wheat and other crops. Powerful engines bring water to the sprinklers from the Ogallala aquifer, nearly 200 feet below. And someday, perhaps fifteen years from now, that water table will be too far below to tap economically, and it will all be the Jornada once again—this time for keeps.

The center of Ulysses, Kansas, is 23.4 miles from the bridge. U.S. Highway 160 is along the south edge of town. Turn left there and drive back east almost a half-mile, to the Grant County Museum. The street address is 300 Oklahoma. It is well worth a visit.

Return to Kansas Highway 25 and turn south. Eight miles south of Ulysses, past the Mesa Petroleum plant, the highway curves to the southeast. Don't curve with it; proceed straight ahead on the blacktop for 2.7 miles. At that point the better road turns to the west—don't turn with it either. Keep going straight south on a good gravel road and follow it as it curves to the southeast. Just .6 mile from the blacktop turn right onto a dirt road. Pass through a cattle guard and follow that road for about a mile, directly to Wagon Bed Spring. Along the way, and to the right of the road for the first quarter-mile, are the ruts of the Cimarron Cutoff coming southwest from the middle crossings (at Cimarron and Ingalls). They are so faint that only the most skillful rutwatcher can tell where they are.

However, a few hundred yards east of the spring there are some fine, deep ruts. They are on private land.

Arrive at a fenced enclosure, walk through the gate, and proceed about twenty yards to a hole in the ground.

Here at Wagon Bed Spring is a classic example of the good an outfit such as the Santa Fe Trail Association can do. A few members of SFTA, headed by Fern Bessire, Ed Lewis, and Ron and Karla French, got together to form a chapter of the association. The new Wagon Bed Spring chapter contacted officials of the Grant County Highway Department, who cheerfully bladed the road leading to the spring. It curves a little, and maybe it would need some cuts and fills to be declared an interstate, but it will do the job. When the weather is dry it is great. That means that two or three days out of each summer it isn't great.

The chapter also persuaded the Minter-Wilson Company to drill a well at the spring. No charge. They asked Mesa Petroleum to provide the material for a low pipe fence, a less obtrusive barrier than the original wire fence. Cattle must be kept from the site. No charge for the fence.

Members have found an old wagon bed, and soon it will be in place in the spring, once again keeping the mud away from the water. Until early travelers placed a wagon bed there, (a local newspaper account indicates it happened in 1847), the place was known as Lower Spring.

Karla French, who is a fifth grade teacher at Hickok Elementary School in Ulysses, arranged for two school buses to take the new road to Wagon Bed Spring. Thus, the youngsters had a first-hand look and feel for the Santa Fe Trail. It is a lesson in geography they probably will carry with them all their lives.

It is almost certain that the traders coming through the Jornada from Chouteau's Island did not get to the Wagon Bed Spring. They would have hit the Cimarron about five miles southwest of there, but good springs flowed both east and west of Wagon Bed in trail days.

Return to the blacktop, go three miles north to the Mesa plant, and turn hard right onto Highway 25. Just 2.8 miles ahead is the bridge over the Cimarron, dry these many years. Another 1.3 miles ahead is a roadside park and three historical markers. One commemorates the spring and another cites passage of the Mormon Battalion through the area in 1846. The third deals with the death of the great mountain man, Jedediah S. Smith, who was killed by Indians near here.

From the markers proceed fourteen miles south to the intersection with U.S. 56 northeast of Hugoton. Follow 56 through Hugoton and to the southwest. The cutoff remains on the north bank of the Cimarron, about ten miles away and paralleling 56.

Twenty-four miles from Hugoton the traveler has a decision to make. By continuing eighteen more miles to the offices of the U.S. Forest Service in Elkhart, one may pick up a detailed map of the Cimarron National

Highway 56 parallels the Santa Fe Trail from Kansas City to the New Mexico border, running next to the Cimarron Cutoff most of the way.

Grassland, which will also provide the precise route of the trail. That costs $2 and is well worth it. Available free is an auto tour guide of the grassland, but it is too sketchy for accurate guidance. The Forest Service office is on the east side of U.S. Highway 56, less than a mile northeast of Elkhart.

Or, turn right here, at Wilburton. Drive north on a gravel road for 5.4 miles to a crossing of the Cimarron River. Proceed ahead another .3 mile and note the gravel road leading to the left. Continue ahead for nearly a mile. On the right is a DAR marker. On the left is a stile. This is the point where the Santa Fe Trail crosses the Wilburton Road. It is a good place for a short hike down the ruts—the U.S. Forest Service encourages this. Cattle range in this land but so far there has been no conflict. There are ruts for nearly a mile to the northeast; this is also Forest Service land.

This was the heart of the Dust Bowl of the 1930s. Farms by the hundreds were abandoned as ranchers surrendered to the blowing sand and dust. The federal government bought the ranches, reseeded, and hoped to reclaim the land. It was a long, agonizing process, but now the National Grasslands are productive and support livestock under carefully regulated programs.

The Cimarron River in Kansas rarely flows above its bed. But this is a rare occasion. After the wet summer of 1989 it had a strong current north of Wilburton.

Miles of ruts of the Santa Fe Trail can be found in the Cimarron National Grassland. These are north of Wilburton, Kansas.

Return about a mile and turn right on the gravel road .3 mile north of the bridge. Take an odometer reading there. Proceed west for .5 mile, where the trail may be seen emerging from a gravel pit on the right side of the road. Continue west another two miles—more ruts are near the windmill.

Drive on west to a point exactly 3.5 miles from the Wilburton Road. Cross a yellow cattleguard. Exactly .3 mile ahead is a rutted two-track coming to the gravel road from the left. Turn there and drive toward the Cimarron River for just .1 mile to a fenced area on the left—the graves of Madge Irene and Perry Merle Brite. They lived about six miles up the Cimarron in a thirteen-room house on the Point Rocks Ranch, at Point of Rocks.

Early in the morning following the heavy rains of April 30, 1914, Mrs. Nora Brite noticed murky water spreading beyond the banks of the Cimarron. Soon it had risen enough to threaten her chickens and she rushed out to get them. Before she could return to her home, a devastating wall of water swept her off her feet. Gasping, she splashed toward the house, but as she opened the door, another wall of water struck, throwing her inside and across the room.

Her three-year-old daughter, Perry Merle, was asleep in the bedroom and drowned. An older daughter, Madge Irene, age eleven, was upstairs screaming for help. Her father, Perry C. Brite, who had just raced up

The grave marker for Madge and Perry Brite, drowned in the great flood of the Cimarron in May 1914.

to the ranch house, called to her to jump out the window.

Just as she jumped, and as her father was waiting to catch her, another huge wave hit them. Both went down and were separated.

Madge's body was not recovered until after the waters had started to recede. The two children were buried on the 81 Ranch, below the Brite home, in caskets made from the sideboards of old wagons.

Continue ahead to Kansas Highway 27, north of Elkhart. Note the road which continues west across the highway, but don't go there yet. Turn to the right. Drive north for a half-mile and turn left, following the signs to the U.S. Forest Service overlook.

Here is a good view of the Cimarron River, which is usually bone dry. But it's there just the same, usually flowing through sand several feet below the surface. During trail days, and in fact until 1940, few trees grew along the Cimarron. Now protected from fire, a lush growth of cottonwoods, willow, and tamarack grow there.

Return to the road a half-mile to the south and turn right. Drive west for 1.8 miles. There will be a cattleguard on the right. Turn there, and a few feet ahead bear right at a Y in the road. Several pools of the Middle Spring are on the right, and the Forest Service has provided picnic tables for the site. Beavers occasionally dam the little streams which peter out in the grassland.

Follow the road as it loops back to the cattle guard and turn west again. Proceed about .3 mile farther—in the valley to the left are several deep

These pools of the Middle Spring, near Point of Rocks, were formed behind beaver dams.

rut swales of the Cimarron Cutoff, heading toward the Point of Rocks. Another .6 mile farther is a Y in the road. Bear left and climb the Point of Rocks.

Down below is as fine a view of the Cimarron River as it is possible to get. The trail went about midway between the base of the Point of Rocks and the Cimarron River, then continued southwest along the bank.

Return to Kansas Highway 27 and drive south to Elkhart. The new Morton County Museum is on the east side of the highway, on the northeast edge of Elkhart. By all means stop and see their fourteen-foot tipi, a covered wagon hooked up to life-size horses, a half-dugout, and many other artifacts representing the hardships of carving out a life on the open prairies. This small county has also had two Olympic medalists— runners Glenn Cunningham and Thane Baker. Other exhibits commemorate the feats of these Elkhart athletes. This museum is a splendid effort by the citizens of the county to preserve the past for future generations.

OKLAHOMA PANHANDLE

In Elkhart turn to the southwest on U.S. 56 and pass into the state of Oklahoma. Take an odometer reading at the state line, and proceed twenty-four miles to Keyes. If would be great if this book could guide

The main Point of Rocks in Kansas is a striking formation when viewed from above.

A road now leads to the top of Point of Rocks, where a splendid view of the Cimarron River may be gained.

the traveler to the Willow Bar, the crossing of the Cimarron. One would have to turn right, opposite the end of Oklahoma Highway 171, and proceed 12.8 miles to the bridge over the Cimarron. Then one would have to drive .3 ahead to where the trail intercepts. There is no trace there. Another .4 mile ahead the blacktop curves right and a gravel road takes off to the left. Willow Bar is about four miles down that road.

But there is a problem. About .1 mile ahead is the gate to a ranch— even the road is private land. The foreman of that ranch, who has been all over the land for decades, can pin the Willow Bar crossing down to only about a mile and one-half because of the wanderings of the Cimarron down through the years. Furthermore, it cannot be reached with a family car. It can't be reached with a jeep. The area is accessible only by horseback. And the rancher would rather people not ask—he has a tough time keeping up with things as it is; there is no time to be escorting visitors to a nebulous place like Willow Bar. So don't go. Keep driving southwest for fifteen miles on U.S. 56 from Keyes to Boise (rhymes with Joyce) City.

The members of the Santa Fe Trail Association who live in the Panhandle have devised a plan which will ease the chore of the visitor in gaining permission to visit the historic Santa Fe Trail sites in the area, all of which are on private land. There is a circle drive around the courthouse. Follow it until reaching a brightly painted caboose, the headquarters of the Boise City Chamber of Commerce. Contact Joan Walton there, (405) 544-3344. She will have the latest information on the sites and the receptivity of the owners to visitors. She is eager to help, so don't hesitate to contact her.

Turn right at the courthouse in Boise City onto Highways 287 and 385 northbound. Just 9.3 miles to the north there is a turnout on the left where the highway crosses the route of the Santa Fe Trail; a marker there commemorates the role of Joseph C. Brown, surveyor for the Sibley survey group of 1825. Wolf Mountain is less than a mile away, to the northeast. Another short branch of the trail passed to the north of Wolf Mountain.

About the only way to see Flag Springs is to drive or hike the Santa Fe Trail in from the marker on the highway. It is 1.75 miles on a west-southwest sight line, bearing 260 degrees. This is private land, so get permission first. Because of the pressures of ranching it is rare when the owner can take time to provide the necessary escort for visitors. It is a half-hour hike but well worth it if permission can be gained. About a mile to the west the trail veers to the southwest of the great rock pile by Flag Springs. When 1.7 miles from the highway, the rock pile will be bearing 335 degrees, or north-northwest. Turn in that direction onto a two-track ranch road. It is only a half-mile away.

The traveler is walking in the footsteps of Josiah Gregg, who wrote

An earthen dam has impounded the output of Flag Springs, but it is still a sylvan spot.

this on June 30, 1831:

> . . . the Upper Spring . . . is a small fountain breaking into a
> ravine that declines toward the Cimarron some three or four miles
> to the north. The scarcity of water in these desert regions gives to
> every little spring an importance which, of course, in more favored
> countries it would not enjoy. We halted at noon on the brook below
> and then branched off towards the waters of the Canadian, in an
> average direction of about thirty degrees south of west. As the wagon-
> road passes upon the adjacent ridge a quarter of a mile to the south
> of this spring, some of us, to procure a draught of its refreshing
> water, pursued a path along the ravine, winding through dense
> thickets of underbrush matted with green-briers and grape-vines,
> which, with the wild-currant and plum-bushes, were all bent under
> their unripe fruit. The wildness of this place, with its towering cliffs,
> craggy spurs, and deep-cut crevices, became doubly impressive to
> us as we reflected that we were in the very midst of savage haunts.
> . . . After regaling ourselves with a draught of the delicious beverage
> which gushed from the pure fountain, we ascended the rugged
> heights and now rejoined the caravan half a mile beyond.

An earthen dam at Flag Springs now impounds a small body of water,
but the springs (there are several) still flow wild and free. At the base
of one side of the rock pile is an abandoned, roofless cabin made of poured

Autograph Rock, a towering rock wall on the ranch of Dan and Carol Sharp, holds hundreds of inscriptions by trail traders.

concrete.

There is a problem with all this. Rancher and Santa Fe Trail enthusiast Dan Sharp recently talked to an elderly man who, in his youth, "cowboyed" with old men who knew about the Upper Spring. The man said it wasn't Flag Spring at all, but another spring which popped up in Trujillo Arroyo, which is eight miles up the trail to the northeast, or about a quarter-mile south of the Cimarron today. It doesn't fit Gregg's description, of course, but the river could have moved in the ensuing 160 years.

Return to Boise City and turn right onto state route 325. Proceed west for five miles and turn right onto a blacktop road. Four miles to the north turn left onto a gravel road, drive two miles west, and curve with the road to the north.

Drive about a mile and one-half north, cross a cattle guard, and the road will start twisting and turning, mostly to the northwest. The road becomes very hairy at the cattle guard, with drifting dust and fine sand. It may be impassable in a family car. Follow it for about two miles, to the ranch of Dan and Carol Sharp. Be sure to check with the chamber of commerce first. The Sharps are true trail enthusiasts, and if they are not too engrossed in the business of making a living, they often escort visitors to the nearby Autograph Rock.

Cold Spring rises in this stone spring house on the Buck Sharp Ranch. The rock ledge behind it contains inscriptions from many trail travelers.

The rock is covered with the signatures of hundreds of traders, many of whom signed in several times as they plied the old road to Santa Fe.

Turn back to the south for two miles, to an intersection a half-mile past the point where the road straightens out in a due south course. Then turn left and drive east for three miles.

Turn left again and drive north for 3.2 miles. The Santa Fe Trail crosses at this point. Proceed another .6 mile north and the road curves to head northwest for nearly one mile.

Just as it starts to resume a northerly course a dirt road leads to the left—take it. The road ends at Buck Sharp's ranch. Again, this is private land, so permission must be gained before visiting the Cold Spring. Buck Sharp is Dan Sharp's father, and Dan requests that permission be gained from him before visiting his father's place. The spring rises in an old stone building to the right of the ranch house. Dozens of names are incised in the rock walls, but the building was erected after the Santa Fe Trail fell into disuse. Behind it is a low rock ledge called Inscription Rock. This is another register of the traders, and some of these names are of people who took the Santa Fe Trail to get to the California gold rush in 1849.

Return to the Y in the road, backtrack that mile to the east and again turn south. This time drive 7.7 miles to intersect Route 325, known locally as the Kenton Road. Turn right and proceed eleven miles west. Take the gradual curve to the right and proceed north for 3.6 miles. A turnout

The foundations of Camp Nichols, strictly off limits for ground exploration, are much more evident from the air.

and historical marker are on the left. There are sharp ruts on both sides of the highway, but this is private land so don't go hiking without permission. Return to the south, but at the point where 325 makes its gradual curve back to the east, don't. Continue straight ahead on gravel for a mile, then turn right on the blacktop. Drive to the west for five miles to the hamlet of Wheeless and stop right there.

The remains of Kit Carson's Camp Nichols are exactly three miles from here, on a sight line of 324 degrees. Those who go there without permission are endangering themselves in two ways. First, the owner is liable to run them in for trespassing. Second, members of the Santa Fe Trail Association are liable to fill them with buckshot, for this is one of the most delicate situations on the trail.

The rancher operates shorthanded—there never is enough time to do the work demanded on this 13,000-acre spread. Excessive calls for permission are irritating, and more than once there has been a threat to close the property to everyone.

The only chance of seeing the ruin is by contacting any of several members of the Santa Fe Trail Association who live in the area. They have been maintaining good personal relations with the new owner. Perhaps the situation will be less tense in the future, but for now, hands off.

Camp Nichols today is nothing but a foundation ruin, but it was heaven to Marion Russell in 1865. She had married Lt. Richard Russell at Fort Union in February of that year. In May Col. Kit Carson ordered him to assist in the building of Camp Nichols. Carson told her it would be unsafe for her there in the first weeks of the camp's short life.

When he saw the tears that were gathering he said, ''Little Maid

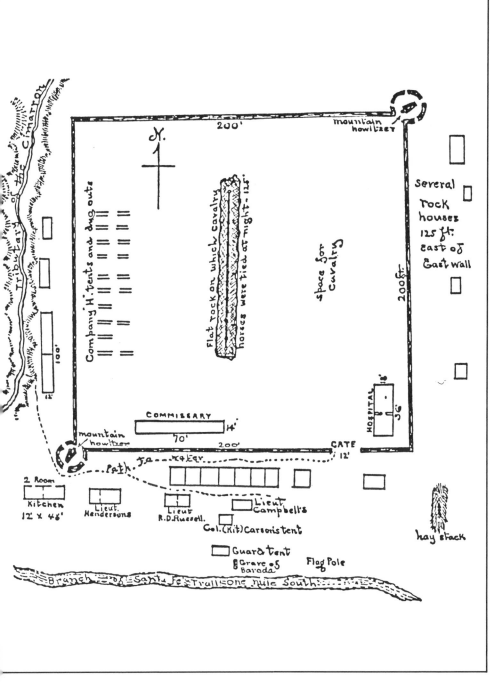

This plat of Camp Nichols was drawn by Marion Russell.

National Archives

Kit Carson

Marion, believe me I will take you out to Camp Nickols as soon
as it is safe for you there.'' Years later I was to go to the ruins of
Fort Union and find the little roofless room where Colonel Carson
had stood that May day refusing me the one thing on earth that
I wanted.

By mid-June her wish came true; Marion accompanied her husband
to Camp Nichols.

> When we reached Camp Nickols no house had yet been finished.
> Several hundred army tents were being used as quarters. Colonel
> Carson had a tent erected next to his own for Richard and me. . . .
> One night a great thunderstorm came up. I had never known
> the wind to blow so hard. It came fitfully and in a circular motion.
> At intervals the lightning would tear jagged holes in the black sky
> and our tent would be illuminated with an unearthly blue light.
> Suddenly our tent pole buckled. I hid my head under Richard's
> arm and did not hear Colonel Carson calling. Richard was trying
> to find his clothing when the Colonel's cry changed suddenly into
> a roar of rage. His tent had fallen down upon him. Richard had
> to call out the Corporal of the guards to get the Colonel extricated.

Marion Russell returned to the site in 1928 in her middle 70s. She
then drew a map of the Camp Nichols she remembered, which is
reproduced here. Her measurements were checked four years later and
found to be accurate. Through the use of that map it is possible to stand
on the site of the tents of the Russells and Kit Carson. Construction

began on a stone house for the Russells shortly after their arrival, and that site, too, can be identified.

Drive four miles on ahead, to the west, from Wheeless. There is Mexhoma. That consists of one church and one house—the home of David and Shirley Hutchison. Enthusiastic trail supporters, they invite travelers to stop and get specific directions on trail sites. They frequently escort visitors. One of their favorite spots is a half-mile farther west, where the ruts of the Santa Fe Trail cross the road. Immediately after crossing they turn straight west and parallel the highway on the left, all the way to the next corner, which is the New Mexico state line.

The trail now strikes to the southwest. Jog to the left for one-third mile at the New Mexico border, and then turn right.

NEW MEXICO

Proceed west for two miles on New Mexico Route 410. At this point the road makes a sharp curve to the right. There, at the T, turn left, on Route 406. Look to the northeast. Out in the field are the ruts of the Santa Fe Trail, heading toward a cut in the horizon.

Look to the southwest. There is the peculiar twin-peaked mountain known as Rabbit Ear—a trail landmark from the beginning. Continue west for 1.3 miles and follow the highway as it makes a gradual curve to the south. Another 1.1 miles ahead and the highway crosses the North Canadian River, known locally as Corrumpa Creek, and in trail days as Louse Creek. Just .8 mile ahead is a marker for McNees Crossing, and about 100 feet north of the marker is a fine steel gate. Open it and drive in. Then close the gate behind you. Head toward the windmill. When there, look about 100 yards to the southeast to the American Legion marker. It commemorates the Independence Day celebration held here by members of a 100-wagon caravan in 1831. Once at the marker, McNees Crossing will be obvious. Billie Mock, the landowner, is one of the nicest people on the Santa Fe Trail. So be nice to him—keep the gate closed so his cattle don't get out.

To the east of the crossing the two branches of the trail come together— they had parted about 1.5 miles southeast of Camp Nichols. The creek usually is dry, but in the spring it is sufficiently shallow to allow visitors to wade across. The stream bed at this point is rock.

In 1828 two young men heading back to the states went ahead of their caravan, arrived here, and decided to take a nap on the banks of the creek. One was Daniel Monroe, and the other was a son of Samuel G. McNees—the boy's first name is lost to history.

Members of the caravan found McNees dead and Monroe mortally wounded. They had been shot with their own guns by Indians. McNees

Visitors are welcome to walk through the ranch of Billie Mock to view McNees Crossing. Don't forget to close the gate!

was buried here—the grave has long been lost. Monroe was carried to the Cimarron, where he died and was buried.

Josiah Gregg tells what happened next:

> Just as the funeral ceremonies were about to be concluded six or seven Indians appeared on the opposite side of the Cimarron. Some of the party proposed inviting them to a parley, while the rest, burning for revenge, evinced a desire to fire upon them at once. It is more than probable, however, that the Indians were not only innocent but ignorant of the outrage that had been committed, or they would hardly have ventured to approach the caravan. Being quick of perception, they very soon saw the belligerent attitude assumed by some of the company and therefore wheeled round and attempted to escape. One shot was fired, which wounded a horse and brought the Indian to the ground, when he was instantly riddled with balls! Almost simultaneously another discharge of several guns followed by which all the rest were either killed or mortally wounded except one, who escaped to bear to his tribe the news of their dreadful catastrophe!

Gregg then reports that the surviving tribesmen dogged the caravan and robbed it of nearly 1,000 head of horses and mules at the Arkansas

There are striking ruts on the Kiowa National Grassland, north of Clayton, New Mexico.

River. They killed other traders along the trail in repeated acts of revenge. These incidents prompted the call for armed escorts, which resulted in the expedition led by Maj. Bennet Riley in 1829.

Proceed 3.3 miles south on Route 406. There the road turns to the west. Follow it for exactly three miles, to the point where it turns back to the south. Just as that curve is about to be completed, there is a Y in the road. Bear to the right, leaving Route 406 for a gravel road headed straight west. Continue west for exactly three miles, and the road curves to the right. Follow it north for another mile, and curve with it to the left. Proceed west about .1 mile and stop.

Now the traveler is in the Kiowa National Grasslands. The Department of Agriculture encourages citizen participation in the Santa Fe Trail experience, so climb over the fence on the right side of the road, walk straight north for a few dozen yards and arrive at some of the finest eroded ruts of the Santa Fe Trail. One may walk to the southwest for about a half-mile, to the point where the ruts cross the road. They continue on the other side for countless miles, but some stretches are not quite as deeply eroded as this rut. Across the deeply eroded cut are three more swales.

Proceed west 3.2 miles from the last corner. William C. Wheatley, veteran state senator from Clayton, feels that this is the spot where George Sibley sketched the panorama of several landmarks of the Santa Fe Trail for his report to Congress.

On the left is Rabbit Ear Mountain. Moving to the right is Mount Dora, without any distinguishing features at all. Then Round Mound, known today as Mount Clayton. Ahead and slightly to the right of the road is the great symmetrical peak, Sierra Grande, snow-capped when Sibley saw it on October 11, 1825, (he called it ''The White Top Mount-tain'') but bare most of the summer. And finally, somewhat more to the right, is Capulin Mountain. If the day is hazy, Capulin will not be in view.

Turn left at that point and head directly toward the west peak of Rab-bit Ear. Exactly one mile ahead cross Alamos Creek at the bottom of a draw—it was known as Turkey Creek in trail days. It usually is dry. Drive ahead another .4 mile and turn left on a very rough two-track. (This is private land—get permission first.) Follow that two-track for about a mile to the east, passing a stone corral along the way. That was the sheep corral of the old Eklund Ranch. The road follows the south bank of Turkey Creek. The creek will curve to the right, as does the two-track, and a few hundred yards ahead the ruts may be seen coming down from the east toward a stone bed in the creek. They cross there, heading west.

Work back to the gravel road and resume a southerly course. About two and one-half miles ahead the road curves to the west. Drive west for 1.2 miles and turn left—this will be New Mexico Route 370. It starts out gravel and eventually becomes a blacktop road. Continue south for five miles—at this point the west peak of Rabbit Ear is about 1.5 miles due east.

Keep on driving south for another eight miles to Clayton. Highway 370 will end at U.S. Highways 64-87. Turn left there and drive to the traffic light in Clayton.

The old Eklund Hotel is on the right, just past the light. The dining room of the old building has been restored to approximate its original appearance—it is a fine restaurant today. The hotel has yet to be restored. It was built by Carl Eklund, a fabulously successful Clayton rancher who operated it after the Santa Fe Trail had fallen into disuse.

Turn left at the light and take Highway 56 eastbound in Clayton. (This is one of those towns that uses its street system to channel storm water. Hence there are deep dips at some of the intersections. Cross them at

Rabbit Ear Mountain

William E. Brown

The covered wagons would have crossed Turkey Creek about at this point.

The Rabbit Ears Creek campground had it all: a broad level dish for camping, live water nearby, plus plenty of grass for the livestock. The trail ran along the ridge in the background. The ruts are still there.

more than twenty-five miles an hour and a normal sedan could become a convertible.)

At 1.6 miles from the electric signal in Clayton the highway crosses the deep swale of an early trail, visible on both sides of the road. Sue Richardson, a Santa Fe Trail enthusiast who operates the Meadowlark KOA Kampground in Clayton, believes these are the ruts of the Kenton freight route, active at the turn of the century.

But she then points to Gregg's statement, that earlier caravans passed to the south of Rabbit Ear, and advises that this set of ruts could have been made initially by Santa Fe traders prior to 1831.

Return to the traffic light in Clayton and turn right on U.S. Highways 64-87. Follow this route west for eighteen miles to the sign announcing the town of Mt. Dora. Trouble is, there is no Mt. Dora. Mount Dora, at 6,290 feet, is two miles to the northeast of there, and it is no more distinctive here than it was when viewed from the Cimarron Cutoff.

Turn right onto a gravel road a few yards beyond the Mt. Dora sign, cross the railroad tracks, and drive north 3.2 miles to the ranch of Imogene Thoma. The Rabbit Ears Creek campground is about 2.5 miles to the northeast, on the bank of Rabbit Ears Creek. It is difficult to find, and without help from someone on the ranch it will be impossible. Do not

Round Mound

try it without permission.

Those lucky enough to see the campground will be thrilled by it. It is a broad dish in the valley, perhaps a half-mile in diameter. On the southeast edge flows Rabbit Ears Creek. On the ridge to the north is the Santa Fe Trail—the ruts up there are clean and sharp. Beyond the tracks are the foundation ruins of two structures—possibly buildings from a stage station.

Proceed another 2.2 miles north and turn to the left on a good gravel road. Proceed west for seven miles to the town of Grenville, population twenty-one. The road turns left there to cross the Santa Fe tracks and U.S. Highways 64-87. Continue south on the unimproved New Mexico Highway 453 for 2.5 miles from the highway, heading directly toward Round Mound.

The road curves to the right there—the trail is less and a half-mile south at that point. (Round Mound is one mile south.) Proceed two miles west and the road turns to the left again. The intercept with the trail is 1.3 miles south of the point where the road straightens out.

Continue south on gravel for 16.6 more miles to U.S. Highway 56 and turn right. Drive 29.4 miles to the west, noting the great bulk of Sierra Grande twenty-five miles north and the wall of the Sangre de Cristos due west. At that point there is a state roadside park park on the right. Stop there and read the inscription on the marker, then backtrack a few

Josiah Gregg made this sketch of one of his caravans headed toward Santa Fe, while he was seated atop Round Mound.

The Point of Rocks in New Mexico, owned by Pete and Faye Gaines.

yards to the gravel road marked C52 and turn left. Just 6.4 miles ahead cross the last of three cattle guards. Then proceed ahead to a point between .1 and .2 miles north. There the broad swale of the Santa Fe Trail may be seen on both sides of the road, aligned in an east-west direction.

Proceed less than .3 mile ahead to the next corner and turn right onto another gravel road. Drive two miles east and turn left for a little less than a mile, to the end of the road, the ranch of Garrett (Pete) and Faye Gaines.

Stop to ask permission to visit the Point of Rocks. Both Pete and Faye are usually eager to share their love of the place, but sometimes the demands of the ranch prohibit sociability.

If permission is given, the first stop ought to be in the small fenced field to the east of the ranch house. In that field is a pile of flag rock. Two of those stones are pieces of a headstone, that of Isaac Allen, who died in 1848. The stone is face down, to control weathering. A "historian" from Las Vegas was caught digging in the grave—in his haste to depart he dropped the headstone and broke it. No other record of the death of an Isaac Allen here has been found.

In the rise of the great rock pile behind the ranch house is a concrete well—it houses the spring which attracted the caravans to Point of Rocks. Here is the description left by Josiah Gregg in 1831:

> . . . we soon passed the Point of Rocks, as a diminutive spur projecting from the north is called, at the foot of which springs a charming little fount of water. This is but thirty or forty miles from the principal mountains, along whose border similar detached ridges and hills are frequently to be seen.

This spring supplies the potable water for the ranch. The windmill pumps bad water from 160 feet below, which is used to water the lawn.

On the west side of the road, in the plain below the Point of Rocks, are eleven graves, all marked with small piles of flag rock, most with a small bush growing out the top. One bears 280 degrees from the windmill, about 500 yards away. Three others are perfectly aligned with it, bearing slightly to the north of west. Seven others are scattered about.

Two American traders were the first to be killed by Indians. A party of Mexican traders then came through and also were butchered by the Indians. A caravan passed the carnage later and discovered that wolves had torn into the victims, scattering body parts over the plain. They were buried where they were found.

There are a number of tipi rings in the plain—rather difficult to see, but they are there.

The mouth of Youngblood Canyon is in the northwest corner of the plain. Pete Gaines said the canyon was named for Charlie Youngblood,

Most of the graves at Point of Rocks seem identical—a few pieces of flag rock and a single bush growing over the grave.

Faye Gaines points out the site of Youngblood Canyon to Dr. Jere Krakow of the National Park Service. Her husband, Pete, waits in the pickup to escort the study group to the graves at Point of Rocks.

In the distance, just to the right of the roof of this abandoned building, is the point of the mesa around which the trader wagons rolled. On the other side of the mesa is the Rock Crossing of the Cimarron. There are good ruts between the old building and the mesa.

"who trapped the last of the lobo wolves from this area." He also said that the next canyon over was a hideout for Black Jack Ketcham, the desperado who is credited with robbing almost as many trains as Jesse James is.

Ketcham took a shotgun blast in the right arm during his last train robbery. He was apprehended and taken to Trinidad, where his arm was amputated. Then he was removed to the Clayton jail. There the good people nursed him back to health before they hanged him. The long recuperative period agreed with Black Jack. The food wasn't good but there was a lot of it and he put on a few excess pounds. When the trap was sprung the weight was too much for his neck, and his head popped off. It rolled in the dust beneath the scaffold. Merchants in Clayton have photos of the execution in their store windows. Others are in the saloon of the Eklund Hotel.

There is a mystery in the ramparts of Point of Rocks. Sharp eyes will be able to discern fortifications up there—stone fences waist-high, reaching across gaps in the rocks. Nobody knows who did it, when, or why. No shell casings or other artifacts have been found behind the walls.

Frequently eagles may be seen soaring over the great rock pile.

Return to the highway and turn right. Just 10.2 miles to the west the road makes a shallow turn to the northwest. At that point the trail is a little over a mile north. Three miles from there it heads back to the west and a mile farther on the trail crosses the road.

On the left is an abandoned rock house. Trail ruts may be seen south of the highway about 100 yards west of that building. Sight over the house to the southwest. About two miles away a mesa ends—the trail crossed the flat land and bent around the south slope of the mesa, to head for the Rock Crossing of the Canadian.

Continue three more miles to the highway bridge over the Canadian River. Just past the bridge are the old buildings for the Dos Rios Ranch. The Rock Crossing of the Canadian is two miles south of there.

Dos Rios is owned by Sue and Dr. Joe Knowles. Knowles left a thriving medical practice in Texas to raise longhorns through holistic ranching techniques. No one exits from a field the same way it was entered, so no new trails will be cut. All ranching activity is natural, and ecologically beneficial. Joe Knowles uses his land with great skill. Those who can talk him into dropping his ranching duties to escort them to the Rock Crossing are lucky indeed. Next to impossible to find without an escort, the Rock Crossing is two miles to the south, but there are no roads.

The crossing itself is amazing. The trail comes around that mesa, crosses the rock bottom over only a few inches of clear water, then pulls the gentle rise on the west bank. It splits out in the field to the west, the northern branch being an extension of the military road from Granada, Colorado, to Fort Union. The branch to the south heads for Watrous and Santa Fe.

Gregg describes it:

> . . . having descended from the table-plain, we reached the principal branch of the Canadian River, which is here but a rippling brook hardly a dozen paces in width, though eighty miles from its source in the mountains to the north. The bottom being of solid rock, this ford is appropriately called by the Ciboleros El Vado de Piedras. The banks are very low and easy to ascend. The stream is called Rio Colorado by the Mexicans, and is known among Americans by its literal translation of Red River. This circumstance perhaps gave rise to the belief that it was the head branch of our main stream of this name: but the nearest waters of the legitimate Red River of Natchitoches are still a hundred miles to the south of this road.

To the north, the Canadian has a bottom of soft sand from this point almost to the Colorado border. A few dozen yards to the south the river enters a deep rock gorge which extends almost unbroken for nearly 100 miles. Thus, the rock crossing was fortuitous indeed. It would have been worth a detour of many miles to the traders; yet, it is right on the logical line of the trail. Becknell apparently took his first wagons below that rock

Top: Dr. Leo Oliva finds the Rock Crossing of the Canadian to be easy going. Bottom: A few yards downstream it would be impossible to cross with a covered wagon, and very difficult even with a pack train.

canyon. It is not known who first discovered it.

It is recommended that visitors not even ask to see the crossing for it means taking a good three hours out of the day of Joe or Sue Knowles.

Proceed 5.9 more miles to the west to the town of Springer and turn south onto Interstate Highway 25. A little more than ten miles to the south, at the hamlet of Colmor, the military road crosses the highway. The ruts are barely visible out in the range to the east.

But something is now visible on the southwestern horizon—the unmistakable form of Wagon Mound—clearly the most remarkable of the formations along the Santa Fe Trail. Proceed to the Wagon Mound exit, turn left, and follow the main road for .8 mile to a pair of cemeteries on the right. Turn in between them.

For all its fame, the celebrated trail journalists wrote little about Wagon Mound. Susan Magoffin refers to it as if she had seen it, but she couldn't have. On the day of her diary entry she was climbing Raton Pass from the north. Josiah Gregg sailed right by it without writing a word.

But after May 7, 1850, the site had a terrifying aspect to travelers. On that day Jicarilla Apaches slaughtered ten white men accompanying a mail wagon to Santa Fe. On May 19 a wagon train bound for Independence came upon the scene, as reported in *Journal of the West* (April 1989) by Marc Simmons:

> Parts of bodies were scattered about, eaten by wolves and ravens. Two corpses, those of a large man and a middle-sized man, were inside the wagon. They had not been devoured. The mail bags, cut open, were found on a hilltop . . . about a mile away. As many as possible of the windblown letters and papers were collected, and the entire caravan immediately turned back, fearful that the Indians might be watching the trail.

The attacking party evidently numbered more than 100 warriors. The location of the mass grave is unknown, but there has been speculation that it might have been the start of the present Santa Clara Cemetery, at the northern base of Wagon Mound.

Return to I-25, take an odometer reading, and drive to the southwest. The ruts have been wiped out for the first mile or so, but about 1.9 miles south there are deep traces starting to the east of the highway, just west of the Santa Fe Railroad tracks. They continue for about .9 mile, then cross the highway exactly five miles from the town of Wagon Mound; however, another branch stays to the east almost to Watrous.

Meantime, the military road which branched away west of the Rock Crossing is a dozen miles away to the northwest, heading down to Fort Union.

A rest stop is twelve miles south of Wagon Mound. Two miles from

No sight is more impressive along the Santa Fe Trail than the Wagon Mound.

The mud ranch of Sam Watrous now is the adobe palace of Barbara Doolittle.

there, and off into the land to the right, is a stretch of ruts estimated by Marc Simmons to be eight miles long.

Continue on I-25 to the town of Watrous, 20.3 miles southwest of Wagon Mound. Take Exit 366 onto New Mexico Highway 161 (and old U.S. 85) heading east. Proceed south .7 mile, and on the left will be the Doolittle Ranch. The building is in the form of a quadrangle with a court-yard in the center. The northwest corner is the original home and store of Samuel Watrous. It has been altered only to comfortably accommodate modern living. Other structures as old as 1849 were in terrible condition and had to be removed. The Doolittle family duplicated the original adobe structures, working from the 1940 drawings of the Historic American Buildings Survey, in completing the quadrangle—a terribly expensive technique but the right way to do it. Today the interior is the ultimate in residential design. The building even has a large natatorium.

Proceed south .1 mile on Highway 161 and stop at the bridge over the Mora. It is possible to hike down the bed of the Mora for about .2 mile (getting permission first, of course) to the confluence with Sapello Creek. That is ''La Junta''—the name this area bore until Sam Watrous showed up and the railroad needed a name different from that of the Colorado town.

Continue south for .7 mile and turn right, onto the second gravel road which comes to the highway. That leads to the old, picturesque town of Watrous. The buildings are very old, some dating to the last days of the trail. Pass the old Protestant church on the right and drive to a T in the road. On the right is the deserted Watrous School, a WPA project. Turn to the left and drive south, passing the abandoned Masonic

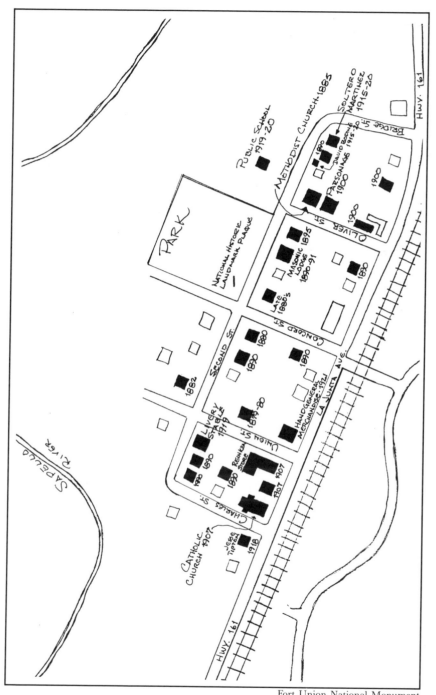

Fort Union National Monument

The entire town of Watrous has been declared a National Historic Landmark.

The Sapello Stage Station is little altered from trail days.

hall on the left. Two more blocks ahead turn left and return to Highway 161.

Continue south for .8 mile to the next interchange, pass beneath I-25, cross the Sapello, and follow the road as it turns back to the north. Turn left .3 mile ahead onto a gravel road. Ahead .2 mile is a long ranch house. That is the old Sapello stage station, used by the Barlow and Sanderson Stage Company. The exterior of the building has been altered slightly by an application of stucco and the addition of a front porch, facing the road.

The ruts of the Santa Fe Trail are out in the field to the right of the gravel road, just past the station. They are heading toward Sapello Creek. The Cimarron Cutoff united with the Mountain Branch before the crossing, just north of the stage station. Therefore, this is the end of the Cimarron Cutoff.

Ruts of the Mountain Branch of the Santa Fe Trail are shown to the north of the Sapello station. They merged with those of the Cimarron Cutoff just north of Sapello Creek and west of the stage station.

FINDING THE TRAIL IN NEW MEXICO

WATROUS TO SANTA FE

Travelers with plenty of time and film may want to take a side trip to Mora. If so, leave the Sapello stage station, turn left, and continue west on New Mexico Highway 161, following the Mora River, for fifteen miles to the intersection with New Mexico Highway 518. Turn right there onto New Mexico Highway 518 for 3.1 miles. At that point 518 will curve to the left, but bear to the right onto New Mexico Highway 442. Follow it only a few yards, and on the left is the ruin of Vincente Romero's La Cueva Mill. Just to the east is the two-story adobe home of Romero, whose 33,000-acre ranch was headquartered there. He came to the area in the early 1850s. Romero's ranching innovations and irrigation techniques later became world famous. Return to Highway 518 and continue 8.3 more miles to Mora.

The Taos Revolt of early 1847 spread to Mora quickly. Shortly after Gov. Charles Bent was murdered in Taos, a band of New Mexicans killed eight Americans escorting a wagon train. In retribution, the U.S. Army brought up some heavy artillery and flattened the town.

Eight years later Ceran St. Vrain came to town. He had been a one-third partner with the Bent brothers in the Bent's Fort operation and was a highly respected businessman who had the confidence of both the Americans and the Mexicans.

At the center of Mora turn right onto Route 434. Head north for one block and cross the Mora River. Just past it on the left is St. Vrain's mill, which probably dates to the 1860s. To see his home, return to 518 and turn right, and stop. The long adobe house is on the left at that point. It is private property.

Those with still more time may want to visit Taos. Follow 518 back to La Cueva and turn left on 442. Follow it for twenty-one miles to Ocate and turn left on New Mexico Highway 120. This is the old mule track to Taos, the one taken by Sibley in 1825. Follow it for sixteen miles to

Vincente Romero's mill at La Cueva

Ceran St. Vrain left the Bent partnership and moved to Mora, where he built this mill.

Black Lake and turn right on New Mexico Highway 434. Continue north through the ski resort of Angel Fire to U.S. Highway 64. Turn left and follow that highway west for twenty-one miles to Taos.

There are three attractions that make a Taos visit worthwhile. The most important is the home of Charles Bent. He was murdered in that house. Then there is the home of Kit Carson, and finally, Carson's grave.

Those who would rather not take that time could return all the way to Las Vegas via Highway 518. A New Mexico historical sign is 19.2 miles south of Mora at a turnout on the left side of the road. (Unfortunately, it is facing south. It calls attention to Hermit Peak, about seven miles west of there. It is the mountain with a U-shaped dip in an otherwise flat top. Marc Simmons tells the story of the hermit who once lived in the Council Grove cave in his *Following the Santa Fe Trail:*

> The peak is named in honor of Giovanni Maria Augustini (or Agostini), the hermit. He arrived in Las Vegas in 1863 with a freight caravan of the Romeros, who with the Bacas were one of the two leading merchant families of [Las Vegas]. Augustini reputedly performed a number of cures and miracles, but the crowds he was attracting caused him to flee to the flat-topped mountain fourteen miles west of Las Vegas and take up the hermit's life once more. He remained there three years and then headed for southern New Mexico where he was murdered in the Organ Mountains near Las Cruces in 1867. A few pilgrims from the Las Vegas area still climb Hermit's Peak to visit a shrine honoring Augustini.

In Las Vegas, stop at the traffic light at Mills, which is 28.4 miles from Mora. Turn right and follow the signs to the Plaza. Turn left about a mile away onto Hot Springs and follow it for about a mile to the Plaza.

Las Vegas (the meadows) was named for the flat land watered by the Gallinas River. This was a favored camping place for the traders, where the nourishing grasses could prepare the livestock for the last big push over Glorieta Pass to Santa Fe.

Circle the Plaza. (It is one-way counter-clockwise.) On the far side of the circle is a long one-story building, numbered 210-218. That is said to be the building Gen. Stephen Watts Kearny climbed to deliver his proclamation to the Mexicans on August 15, 1846, announcing that they were now under the flag of the United States.

Kearny, it will be recalled, marched here from Fort Leavenworth. He camped east of the Plaza—Simmons feels the campground probably was on the site of Highlands University—before marching to the plaza. He and the alcalde used a ladder to mount the building and address the citizens from the rooftop. The one-story adobe building is the only one on the plaza to predate the Mexican War.

Library of Congress

Gen. Stephen Watts Kearny

Next door west, numbered 220, is the celebrated Los Artesanos Book Shop, run by Diana and Joe Stein. This shop has a remarkable collection of western Americana, including many scarce volumes on the Santa Fe Trail.

Two doors farther west, numbered 230, is the Plaza Hotel, a skillfully restored showplace of Las Vegas. Construction on the hotel began in 1880, after the arrival of the Santa Fe Railroad. It was said to be the most elegant hotel in the territory. In 1982-83 the Plaza Associates meticulously rehabbed the building, which has since become an object of civic pride. Unfortunately, a stay there cannot be recommended.

The dining room, however, is elegantly appointed. The lounge is fun for those who like their music very loud.

Drive back toward I-25 on National Avenue. This is the route the traders used coming from the east. One branch of the Santa Fe Trail paralleled the route of I-25 just to the east, but another cut across, making the ruts about to be viewed, and headed into the heart of town over present National Avenue.

At Main Street turn right for a block, then left on Grand to pass over I-25. Take an odometer reading and get on the highway headed north. Drive exactly 1.3 miles from Grand, pull far over on the right shoulder, turn on the clickers and stop. Look to the right. Headed right for the plaza is a wide, eroded swale of the Santa Fe Trail.

Continue north to the next interchange and get back on the highway headed south. Take the next exit and turn left on Grand once more.

Drive south on Grand for 1.4 miles to I-25. Just before reaching the ramp to I-25, angle to the left and proceed under the highway. About a block ahead turn right onto the east service road. A branch of the trail which bypasses Las Vegas continues down the east side of the highway,

Spectacular remains of the Santa Fe Trail east of Las Vegas, as viewed from I-25

about one-third mile away. The other branches are headed south-southwest out of Las Vegas toward Kearny Gap.

One mile from the last turn the road will curve to the west and pass over the interstate, heading toward Kearny Gap. Continue west for about one mile and pass through the gap, as did the Army of the West in 1846. About .3 mile farther the traveler will be abreast of an abandoned steel bridge about fifty yards to the left of the road. Marc Simmons found the remains of the Kearny Gap stage station a few dozen yards southeast of there. Nothing is left but a portion of a stone wall, but it is easy to see from the road.

Return to the I-25 overpass and turn right onto an access road on the east side of the highway. Proceed south and west for 4.3 miles, to the next I-25 interchange. The alternate trail, which avoided Las Vegas, is still off to the east a few hundred yards. After making the broad curve to the west, the highway passes through Puerto del Sur, or South Portal. So did the trail. The Santa Rosa interchange is just a mile to the west— leave the highway there, and turn right. That road will immediately curve back to the east to parallel the highway.

Then it turns sharply to the left, changes to a dirt road, and heads toward Puertocita Pedregosa, "the little rocky gate." Follow that road generally westward for 2.3 miles. Along the way the ruts from the Puerto del Sur branch will be on the left, headed toward the road. After the Ojitos Frios ranch road is passed, a road coming south from Kearny Gap will pop into view on the right.

The canyon through the Puertocita is .6 mile long, and the road exits onto a broad plain. There on the left are a maze of badly eroded cuts in the land—many of which probably were started by wagon wheels. After leaving the gap the ruts turn to head toward the Tecolote Mesa to the south.

Return to the interstate and head south. One branch of the trail will be next to the highway; the one which went through the Puertocita will be off to the west about a mile—both heading for Tecolote. Proceed 4.1 miles to the Tecolote interchange and leave the highway again. Turn right to cross a cattle guard and then turn left. This is the main branch of the Santa Fe Trail. It leads to the Tecolote plaza.

Richard Russell, tired of the rigors of army life, resigned his commission in 1866 and moved with his wife Marion to Tecolote. They erected a large rock building on the plaza. In front was the store; five dwelling rooms were in the rear.

> Tecolote, like all New Mexico towns, was just a collection of low adobe houses and narrow crooked streets. It was thriving and prosperous and we felt we would do well there. . . . The store was wide and spacious. Its low ceiling was crossed by massive beams. The

This old church is the centerpiece of Tecolote.

long shelves were piled high with everything under the sun. There were implements, feed, food, household furnishings, clothing, saddles, bridles, harness and Navajo blankets.

The couple struggled with the Tecolote economy until 1871, when they left for the San Luis Valley of southern Colorado.

Drive behind the Tecolote church. There are the remains of a stone corral which once was part of the stage station complex. Return to the front of the church, which is the center of Tecolote. Turn right .1 mile ahead and drive to a little foot bridge which crosses Tecolote Creek. Below it and to the left is a gentle slope, the approximate site of the crossing of the Santa Fe Trail.

Return to the service road and turn right. Proceed a half-mile ahead, cross a cattle guard and then angle half-right, to head due west on a red dirt road. Less than .2 mile ahead turn left on an even more primitive road. Drive a few yards to the south and the road gradually improves to become a poor blacktop—that is where the route of the trail goes beneath the road. This road is terrible, so take it slowly. A gate is just .8 mile ahead. Turn around there and return to the service road alongside I-25.

Susan Magoffin was shocked at the women of this area:

> The women slap about with their arms and necks bare, perhaps their bosoms exposed (and they are none of the prettiest or whitest) if they are about to cross the little creek that is near all the villages, regardless of those about them, they pull their dresses, which in the first place but little more than cover their calves—up above their knees and paddle through the water like ducks, sloshing and spattering everything about them.
>
> And it is repulsive to see the children running about perfectly naked, or if they have on a chimese it is in such ribbands it had better be off at once. I am strained to keep my veil drawn closely over my face all the time to protect my blushes. . . .
>
> Tonight our camp is among the pine trees at the foot of a mountain [Starvation Peak], with no other camp near us.

Proceed 4.7 miles to the south and turn left to cross over the highway. Here the trail is on the far side. Continue west on the service road. The impressive bulk of Starvation Peak, once known as Bernal Mountain, dominates the skyline.

Now the trail, and the highway, are starting a long, gradual curve to the right known today as the ''fishhook,'' for the way it crosses the Sangre de Cristo to get to Santa Fe.

Drive 3.2 miles to the west. Deeply eroded ruts will be in view on both sides of the road. Just .9 mile from that point turn right and cross under

National Archives

Starvation Peak dominates the little settlement of Bernal. This photograph was made in 1939.

I-25. Head due west on the north service road. Three miles ahead turn left on New Mexico Highway 3. Proceed .4 mile to the underpass and drive beneath I-25. Proceed 2.2 miles to the old town of San Miguel, passing through Ribera along the way.

This historic old town of San Miguel, thoroughly Hispanic to this day, was the primary outlier of Mexican Santa Fe. It was here that Becknell and his companions were taken by the soldiers who met them somewhere to the north. In the summer of 1841, a ragtag band of "'Texians,'" determined to add New Mexico to their infant Lone Star empire, were apprehended by soldiers from the army of Governor Manuel Armijo and sent in chains to Chihuahua.

There was no Las Vegas in 1831, so Josiah Gregg found San Miguel to be the first Mexican settlement on his road to Santa Fe:

> This consists of irregular clusters of mud-wall huts and is situated in the fertile valley of Rio Pecos, a silvery little river which ripples from the snowy mountains of Santa Fe—from which city this frontier village is nearly fifty miles to the southeast. The road makes this great southern bend to find a pass-way through the . . . mountains

Museum of New Mexico

Manuel Armijo

. . . which from this point south is cut up into detached ridges and table-plains.

The church, of course, was and is the center of San Miguel, and community life revolved about it. The first settlers came to the town before the turn of the nineteenth century, and construction on the church began in 1805. Matt Field described it when it was only thirty-four years old:

> There were no seats of any kind in the church, and the worshippers were all either standing or kneeling. The mud walls were whitewashed, and a few wretched daubs of paintings, actually frightful to look at, were fastened up, some to rude frames, others hanging in rags with no frame at all. Among these was one piece of rotten canvas, with a little paint still lingering in it, but so completely demolished by time that it was impossible to discover what could have been the subject of the design of the artist. . . . In a recess at one side of the altar, stood two men, one playing a fiddle and the other a guitar, and on these instruments the musicians seemed to be studying what kind of an extravagant and fantastic discord they could make. . . . These musicians composed not only the church choir but also the ball room orchestra, and it may be supposed that they felt a necessity of making as broad a distinction as possible between the dancing and the sacred music.

Outside, the front of the church features a bell and an assembly of pipe fittings made into a rosary. In an elevated tract at the rear of the building is an ancient graveyard, totally devoid of vegetation.

The Pecos River flows just to the east of the town. The ford is about a block east of the church, probably about where the bridge is today. Matt Field described it:

The church of San Miguel is believed to be the oldest parish church in continuous use along the Santa Fe Trail.

Crossing the Pecos was tough business.

A beautiful crystal stream rushes through this town, at no part
more than four feet in depth, and so clear that the white pebbles
can be seen glittering at the bottom and skipping along with the
force of the current.

Return to southbound I-25 via New Mexico Highway 3. Proceed 2.4
miles west to the San Jose—San Juan interchange, turn right to backtrack
.7 mile and cross under the highway to San Jose. The old church in the
center of the plaza was built after the trail became defunct, but most
of the buildings surrounding the plaza do date to trail days. The town
could well have been named Fort San Jose, for the buildings around the
square indeed formed a fortification against Indian attack, even before
the trail was opened.

A dirt road leaves the plaza heading southeast. Follow it for .3 mile
to a steel bridge over the Pecos. Veer right at the approach, toward the
abutments of a long-disappeared bridge. Marc Simmons feels the crossing
may have been here. It was a secondary crossing of the Pecos which
avoided the two-mile swing to the south. However, as Simmons says,
the approach was more difficult. No tracks remain, but there are good
ruts leading down to San Miguel, indicating that crossing was preferred.

Return to I-25, take an odometer reading, and proceed to the west.
Punta de la Mesa de San Jose is exactly 1.3 miles southwest of here. That
is the point where the great Glorieta Mesa begins. The trail, highway,
and railroad will parallel this formation all the way through Glorieta
Pass and down to Cañoncito. The gradients leading to the top of the
mesa are very steep; the valley is level and forms an ideal passageway.

Just 1.2 miles from the interchange the trails from San Miguel and
San Jose mesh, then cross the highway. Leave the highway at the Rowe
exit, 11.3 miles west of the Highway 3 interchange. Along the way the
trail will be off to the right, between the highway and the Pecos River,
less than a mile to the northeast. Drive north on New Mexico Highway
63, toward the Pecos National Monument. After traveling one mile look
to the left—intermittent ruts of the Santa Fe Trail are between this road
and I-25, over a distance of about a mile.

The headquarters buildings of the Forked Lightning Ranch, owned
by actress Greer Garson Fogelson, are on the right side of Highway 63,
3.4 miles from the Rowe interchange. The structure was built of adobe
bricks scavenged from the nearby mission complex by Martin Kozlowski,
probably in the 1850s. The ranch buildings are on private property, of
course.

A few yards to the north the highway crosses a bridge over the branch
of Kozlowski's Spring, which is on the bank of the creek to the right
of the highway.

The ranch is doubly historic, for it was here that the Union Army

National Archives

Ruins of the Pecos church were sketched in 1848.

was headquartered in March 1862, during the Battle of Glorieta Pass. Proceed northwest for a half-mile to the Pecos National Monument. Here is the story of one of the Southwest's earliest civilizations, told through the science of archaeology. The National Park Service has not incorporated much information on the Santa Fe Trail in their interpretation of the site. A new wing on the visitors' center focuses on the trail. That was a development that came more than two centuries after the grandeur that was Pecos.

Tour the visitors' center first. This was funded largely by grants from E. E. Fogelson and Greer Garson. The NPS has done its usual splendid job of interpretation here. A pathway leads from there to the church and convento ruins—an easy drive or a short walk. A hiking trail 1.2 miles long winds through the excavations and takes about an hour and one-half. It is time well spent.

The Pecos pueblo once was home to 2,000 Pueblo Indians. All that remains today are several grass-covered mounds north of the church. For years historians were puzzled by early accounts of the church, surviving from the early 1600s, which describe it as being "large, splendid, magnificent, and of unusual design." Yet, the ruins indicated a structure of normal size, although the convento was much larger than would be needed for a church of those dimensions.

In 1967 archaeologists found stone foundations and burned adobe wall fragments under and near the remains of the later building, indicating that the earlier structure was nearly 170 feet long, ninety feet wide at the transept, and thirty-nine feet wide at the nave.

The Pecos church ruin is a dramatic sight today.

That church and the convento were built in the 1620s and destroyed by fire set by the Indians sixty years later, in a revolt engineered by Pueblos who wanted to return to the old ways. The Church prevailed, and the more modest building was erected in the early 1700s.

After the reconquest a ceremonial kiva in the convento area was filled in. It had been dug shortly after the revolt. Archaeologists excavated it and it now may be examined by visitors.

The Pueblo population declined sharply in the 1770s. Drought, disease, famine, and internecine wars coupled with white encroachment doomed Pecos Pueblo, and, according to the NPS literature, the last of the Indians left here in 1838.

Matt Field was here in 1839, however, and spent the night in the abandoned church, which was still largely intact. Here he found a man "bent nearly double with age, and his long silken hair, white with the snow of ninety winters, renders him an object of deep interest to the contemplative traveller." The old man related the story of "the sacred fire" to Field. Susan Magoffin picked up the same story on August 29, 1846:

> It created sad thoughts when I found myself riding almost heedlessly over the work of these once mighty people. There perhaps was pride, power and wealth, carried to its utter most limit, for here tis said the great Montezuma once lived, though tis probably a false tradition . . .
>
> I am told by persons who saw it, that tis only within some two or three years since it was inhabited by one family only, the last of a once numerous populations. These continued to keep alive "Montazuma's fire," till it was accidentally extinguished, and they abandoned the place, believing that *Fate* had turned her hand against them. This fire, which was kept in vaults under ground, now almost entirely filled in by the falling ruins, was believed to have been kindled by the king himself, and their ancestors were told to keep it burning till he returned, which he certainly would, to redeem them, and it has been continued down to this time, or within a few years.

Marc Simmons has found ruts of the Santa Fe Trail across a field behind the park headquarters in an area normally not open to the public.

Continue north for 1.5 miles to the center of the town of Pecos, and turn left on New Mexico Highway 150. At 2.3 miles from that point there are trail ruts on the left side of the road. Drive 2.4 miles farther to the west and stop at a small stuccoed adobe building on the right—all that remains of the once-extensive Pigeon's Ranch headquarters structure. This is the principal site of the Battle of Glorieta Pass.

That fight, according to historian Leo E. Oliva, was the single most

Gen. H. H. Sibley, CSA   *Col. John M. Chivington*

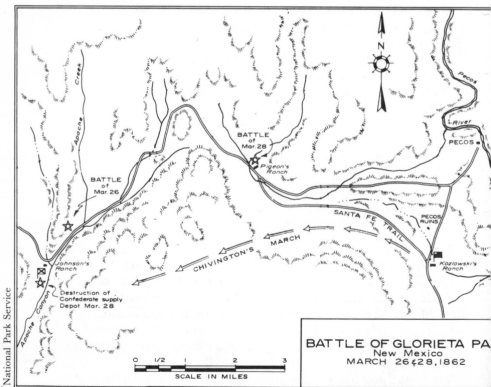

There was no shortage of hucksterism at Pigeon's Ranch in 1939. The bus is on the main highway to Kansas City.

important western battle of the Civil War. Gen. H. H. Sibley sought to lead his Confederate forces north to capture Santa Fe and Fort Union. Having done so, there is a good chance he could have taken Denver and California, too. Most important, he would have the flow of gold from both Colorado and California for Confederate use. Certainly he wouldn't want for supplies—Fort Union's depot contained $300,000 in stores.

With Santa Fe in his pocket, Sibley's forces, under Maj. Charles L. Pyron, marched down the Santa Fe Trail to intercept the Union forces marching in from Fort Union. They camped on the night of March 25 at Johnson's Ranch, near Apache Canyon. The Union troops, commanded by Col. John P. Slough, camped at Bernal Spring.

Slough sent a force ahead for a first strike, under command of Maj. John M. Chivington. He crossed Glorieta Pass and was entering Apache Canyon when he first contacted the Rebel forces, on March 26, 1862. Chivington and his 418-man scouting party encountered Pyron's smaller detachment, which was routed. Chivington didn't press his advantage, as it was nearing sundown.

He instead withdrew to Pigeon's Ranch to spend the night. There wasn't enough water there, so he pulled back to Kozlowski's. Thus ended the Battle of Apache Canyon, prelude to the larger Battle of Glorieta Pass.

Confederate reinforcements marched quickly to Johnson's Ranch, arriving at 3 A.M., and Col. William R. Scurry took command. The next morning the Union forces moved back toward Pigeon's, and were surprised by Rebel artillery—a quiet advance had been made during the night-long truce.

The battle raged much of the day, and the Union forces were driven

Pigeon's Ranch today

This obscure little bridge played a dramatic role in the Battle of Apache Canyon, prelude to the greater Battle of Glorieta Pass.

back to Kozlowski's.

Simmons reports that the ranch building at Pigeon's served as a hospital briefly during the battle, and "bodies of dead soldiers were stacked to the ceiling in one room."

The master stroke of the battle came when Col. Slough sent Chivington with a small force through the formidable mountains, away from the Santa Fe Trail, to try to gain the enemy's rear. He crested a hill above Johnson's Ranch and spotted the Confederate supply train. It consisted of seventy-three wagons, 500 to 600 horses and mules, and a handful of men guarding it. The Union force attacked quickly and burned the wagons. No longer with any supplies, Scurry knew he was whipped. The Confederate forces retreated to the Rio Grande and the Union in the West never again was seriously threatened.

In the winter of 1988-89 two large holes were gouged in the adobe walls of this remaining building of Pigeon's Ranch, evidently by treasure-seeking vandals. Marc Simmons said that Spanish colonists sometimes hid their valuables in the walls of their buildings. This structure is of much later vintage and would not have yielded any treasure. The damage to the walls, twenty-two inches thick, was repaired promptly.

Continue west one mile to the Glorieta interchange of I-25, cross over the highway, and follow the old highway to the right. Pass through the little town of Glorieta, and immediately beyond there will be deeply eroded scars on the left, on the far side of a fence—probably started by wagon wheels. Drive a short distance to the end of the road, turn around, and return to the interchange.

Take I-25 toward Santa Fe and take exit 297 at Valencia. Take an odometer reading and turn left to pass beneath the interstate—then turn right onto an old highway continuing to the west, paralleling the interstate. Stop at 1.1 miles from the interchange. They aren't easily seen, but across the road are two wood fenceposts forming a gate of sorts. Pass between them and take the footpath which is at right angles to the road. Where the path tends to turn to the right, descending to the floor of the canyon, turn left, and walk about 100 yards to view an old, wood-floored bridge with both approaches missing.

This is the bridge over Apache Canyon, built by the army in the 1850s. Marc Simmons feels it would have been used by covered wagons in the last years of the trail. Here the first conflict of the Battle of Glorieta Pass occurred. During the Battle of Apache Canyon the fleeing Rebels crossed over the bridge, then dismantled it. The pursuing Union horsemen didn't hesitate a moment—they jumped the canyon one at a time. All but one of them made it.

The floor of the bridge undoubtedly has been replaced several times, but the foundation certainly is the original.

Backtrack to the interstate and take it to the west. Exit at number 294, Cañoncito at Apache Canyon. At the stop sign make a 180-degree turn to the right. Proceed ahead .1 mile to a picturesque church. The road proceeds ahead a block and curves to the left, to arrive at a gate and a "no trespassing" sign. On the left is the site of Johnson's Ranch.

This is the spot where Chivington's men won the Battle of Glorieta Pass. The Confederate supply wagons were massed here, guarded by only a few Rebel soldiers. The Union force descended from the hill above the present interstate, routed the guard, and destroyed the entire supply base. The war in the West was over.

Return to the U-turn by the interstate, but instead of remounting the highway continue on to the southwest. Just 3.2 miles ahead turn hard right onto a gravel road labeled "Apache Ridge." At 1.3 miles ahead there is a Y in the road—bear right. Ruts may be seen here, on both sides of the road—one set will be crossed .1 mile ahead. Make a U-turn here and return .1 mile. Turn hard right to go down the Lone Pine Spur. Ruts will be seen the right side of the road .1 mile from the turn, about 100 yards long.

Return to Apache Ridge Road and turn right. Drive down to the stop sign, then turn right on the paved road, heading northwest. Off to the right are the Sierra Negro hills, and the trail is behind them. Turn right onto the graveled Santa Fe County Road 67C, 3.5 miles ahead. Just .9 mile ahead the trail comes beneath the road. There is a Y there—bear left. Continue another 1.5 miles and very faint trail ruts will be off to the left.

Drive another 1.9 miles toward Santa Fe. A golf course will be on the left. A deep swale of the Santa Fe Trail used to go through the grounds and proceeded on through the new subdivision to the northwest. Now all the ruts are gone. Marc Simmons feels this is the site of the famous sketch of the caravan entering Santa Fe.

Despite their growing excitement at nearing the old city, the traders would have halted a few miles back for some hasty ablutions. Some would have been without a bath for weeks; many had gone as long without a shave or haircut. Then the wagons would roll again. Gregg talked about the arrival:

> . . . wagon after wagon was seen pouring down the last declivity at about a mile distance from the city. . . . the riders grew more and more merry and obstreperous as they descended towards the city.
>
> The arrival produced a great deal of bustle and excitement among the natives. *"Los Americanos!"*—*"Los carros!"*—*"La entrada de caravana!"* were to be heard in every direction; and crowds of women and boys flocked around to see the new-comers; . . . [The traders] had spent

National Archives

The highway through Apache Canyon was a dirt road in November 1912. This photo was made by T. W. Wilby.

Johnson's Ranch

It was a joyful moment when the traders caught their first view of Santa Fe.

the previous morning in rubbing up; and now they were prepared, with clean faces, sleek-combed hair, and their choicest Sunday suit to meet the fair eyes of glistening black that were sure to stare at them as they passed.

Return to the blacktop, Old Santa Fe Trail, and drive north and west for two miles to the Santa Fe museum complex. Here are: the Wheelwright Museum of the American Indian, Museum of Indian Art and Culture, and the Museum of International Folk Art. Follow Old Santa Fe Trail to its intersection with Old Pecos Trail and bear right. Follow Old Pecos Trail (the old Santa Fe Trail) down toward the plaza, but stop at De Vargas Street, just before crossing the nearly dry Santa Fe River. On the right is the towering Chapel of San Miguel. Park and tour the building.

Many dates are given for the building of this church, from 1610 to 1640. There is no doubt that it is the oldest Christian church in the United States. The caravans of the Santa Fe Trail passed by the front door, from the first expedition of William Becknell to the last days of the trail.

The Christian Brothers conduct individual tours of the structure; they are well worth the while of the traveler.

Continue north on Old Pecos Trail for two more blocks and jog to the left. On the right is the famed La Fonda Hotel, the most historic inn on the Santa Fe Trail. It was rebuilt in the 1920s.

Diagonally across the street is the plaza, the end of the Santa Fe Trail. It was laid out in 1610, when Santa Fe was founded. Here the goods were unloaded and sold to eager buyers at many times the original cost.

San Miguel Mission, in Santa Fe, is believed to have been built in 1621.

Abert's Report *carried this sketch of Santa Fe in 1846. Fort Marcy is shown on the bluff in the background.*

When the market appeared to be saturated the traders continued on down the Rio Grande to Chihuahua. Spend some time here; reflect on the excitement which prevailed here for the sixty years of activity of the Santa Fe Trail.

Facing the plaza on the north is the Palace of the Governors, constructed in 1610 by the first governor, Pedro de Peralta. To this day, Indians and New Mexicans lounge under the broad portico to sell their wares. The palace is home to the Museum of New Mexico, a haven for both scholars and tourists. There is a modest admission charge.

Marc Simmons's *Following the Santa Fe Trail* contains a detailed description of Santa Fe sites related to the history of the Santa Fe Trail, together with highly detailed maps.

The sight which greeted the traders was, in one way, apalling. The streets were alive with goats, chickens, dogs, pigs, and other livestock. There was dirt everywhere—the very buildings, of course, were made of mud. The narrow roads, seldom more than ten or twelve feet wide, were composed of a fine red dust, with nothing to hold it down but an abundance of fecal matter.

But there were joys, too—the legendary young women of Santa Fe had never heard of Queen Victoria. They picked out a man they wanted and they were off and running. Not many traders resisted; not many wanted to. They'd come a long way from Old Franklin. One twentieth-century writer wondered why the traders ever left Santa Fe.

Marion Russell writes of her entrance to the city:

Palace of the Governors

We crossed a water ditch where half-naked children stood unashamed and unfrozen to watch us. Then we passed through a great wooden gateway that arched high above us. We moved along narrow alley-like streets past iron-barred windows. We were among a scattering of low, square-cornered adobe houses. We saw a church with two cupolas. Mexicans, Indians, and half-breeds shouldered by us. We saw strings of red peppers drying, and brown babies asleep by old adobe walls.

Our caravan wriggled through donkeys, goats and Mexican chickens. We came to the plaza and found there a man, a tall man, leaning on a long rifle. He had a neck like a turkey, red and wrinkled, but he was the boss of the plaza. We went where he told us. Under his guidance, wagon after wagon fell into place. Dogs barked at us. Big-eyed children stared at us. Black-shawled women smiled shyly at us. We were in Santa Fe. Because bedlam seemed let loose, mother did not let Will and me out of the wagon until the mules were unhitched and led from the plaza.

As darkness deepened Santa Fe threw off her lassitude. Lights glowed in saloons and pool-halls and in the Fonda, a great mud-walled inn. As soon as our freight was delivered at the customs house, our drivers began eagerly to sign up and draw their wages. They washed their faces and combed their hair. Pierre even drew the comb through his choppy mustache. . . . From a dance hall came the tinkle of guitar and mandolin, a *baile* was forming.

State Historical Society of Missouri

The cathedral at Santa Fe

Museum of New Mexico

*The Elsberg-Amberg wagon train is shown arriving at the Palace of the Governors
in October 1861.*

National Park Service

Mounds of earth at Fort Marcy were more evident when this photo was taken in 1958 than they are today.

Matt Field remembered his arrival:

> The sun was just setting when we rode into the large square of Santa Fe and shook hands with the American store keepers. Here we were after our two months pilgrimage, arrived at last in the strange place to which our wild love of novelty had led us, and as we gazed round upon a race of beings, . . . we saw the dark eyed Señoritas peep at us from door and casement, and from beneath their shawls, worn like hoods, a buoyant excitement tingled through our veins more delightful than the exhilaration of the wine bowl.

The street on the east side of the Plaza is Washington. Turn north on Washington for .5 mile to Artist Road. Turn right on Artist and drive .3 mile to Prince—Artist becomes Hyde Park along the way. Then turn right at a T, proceed ahead to the first turn to the left, and stop. The point ahead and to the right is Fort Marcy.

Construction of a blockhouse was ordered by General Kearny shortly after his arrival in Santa Fe in 1846. It was built on this hill overlooking the plaza. Santa Fe never came under the expected Mexican counterattack, so it was never used. The mounds of earth here are all that remain.

Susan Magoffin saw it on September 23, 1846:

> . . . we commenced winding our way through the clogged streets of Santa Fe; first we found ourselves inspecting the artillery, arranged in two rows on one side of an outer street—from this we wound our way along . . . [and] ascended a long and rather steep hill, on

the summit of which stands fort Marcey, sole master of the entire plain below. It is the most perfect view I ever saw. Not only every house in the city can be torn by the artillery to attoms, but the wide plain beyond is exposed to the fullest view—and far beyond this still are the majestic mountains some of which we passed in coming in. The Fort occupies some two acres of ground, has double walls built of adobes, the space between being filled with stones and mortar.

Return to Washington and turn left. Follow it south for only two blocks to Paseo de Peralta, and turn right. Follow that street west for several blocks to Guadalupe Street and bear to the right. Proceed northwest on Guadalupe for .3 mile and turn right into the National Cemetery.

Proceed to the second cross street and turn right. Drive south to the first yellow water hydrant on the left, about midway down the row of graves. Park and walk forward three more paces, or two rows of headstones, from the hydrant, turn left and proceed five rows into the cemetery. There is the grave of Gov. Charles Bent.

Kearny named Bent the territorial governor immediately after the American occupation in 1846. He ruled from his home in Taos, but not for long. Early in a mid-January morning in 1847, tumult exploded around Bent's home. Attacking Pueblos were tearing his house apart in their rush to kill him. He was wounded with arrows, yet still tried to reason with them. They threw him to the floor and scalped him with a bowstring while he was still alive.

He died while they were mutilating his body. Then they pillaged the town. The revolution spread, along with unspeakable atrocities. But Charles Bent was a revered man among the Americans; it didn't take long to round up the ringleaders, both Mexicans and Pueblos. Lewis Garrard was in Taos and watched as the supreme penalty was exacted:

> Bidding each other *"adios,"* with a hope of meeting in Heaven, at word from the sheriff the mules were started, and the wagon drawn from under the tree. No fall was given, and their feet remained on the board till the ropes drew taut. The bodies swayed back and forth, and, coming in contact with each other, convulsive shudders shook their frames; the muscles, contracting, would relax, and again contract, and the bodies writhed most horribly.

They were cut down after forty minutes, and the book closed on the Taos Revolt. Charles Bent, a gentle man, would not have been pleased.

The great scout and trader, Francis X. Aubry, lies in the next cemetery to the south, but nobody knows exactly where. His headstone has been missing for decades.

FINDING THE MOUNTAIN BRANCH

FORT UNION TO RATON

Scholars agree that there were fully as many New Mexican traders on the Santa Fe Trail as there were Americans. They quickly saw the revenues the Anglos were taking from the pent-up demand for such goods as calico, hardware, pots and pans, needles, and knives. They were taking back to Missouri vast loads of furs and pouches full of silver. Not many Yankees could have resisted bragging about 2,000-percent profits.

For the New Mexican traders, the Santa Fe Trail stretched from Santa Fe to Missouri, rather than the other way around. That is the route along which the visitor will be directed in the return toward Missouri on the Mountain Branch of the Santa Fe Trail.

The first eighty miles are the easiest. Get on I-25 eastbound and return to the Watrous exit, number 364. Turn left on New Mexico Highway 161. Turn left onto a gravel road a half-mile ahead and once again pass the Sapello Stage Station. Continue southwest on that road for .3 mile. There is a large rock corral on the right, backed by a modern metal shed. The rock corral was built to contain the beef cattle for the Fort Union garrison. Here at the Sapello there was an abundance of good grass and live water. There wasn't much of either at the fort.

Return to the interstate and drive north to the next exit, number 366, marked for Fort Union. Turn left and drive northwest on Highway 161, a fine paved road leading only to the fort, eight miles away. But, only one mile from the interstate, turn left on a gravel road and drive .5 mile west to Tiptonville.

Tiptonville today is uninhabited, but the buildings are in use by ranchers. (This is private land, but the road is public.) The place was named for William Tipton, Sam Watrous's son-in-law, who came here late in trail years. Two variants of the Mountain Branch joined here. One to the left went to the early Fort Union (1851-63) and the other to the latest fort (1863-91). They bracketed the present-day highway. Con-

The remains of the Fort Union beef corral on Sapello Creek

Some of the buildings at Tiptonville are still in use.

The stark ruin of the old Fort Union arsenal comes into view of today's motorist prior to reaching the main fort. This installation was abandoned during the Civil War because of its indefensible position, beneath the bluff.

tinue ahead. Tipton's ruined two-story house is on the left. It burned in 1957. Other ruined structures are on both sides of the road. The road will arrive at a T—turn right and drive .1 mile to intersect the blacktop to Fort Union and turn left.

The Mountain Branch coming south from the old fort is nearly a mile to the west, but the deep swale of the main track is on the right at this point—it is visible cutting through the ridge. From here to the fort, remnants of the trail will be in view from time to time on the right side of the road.

A shallow pond, rimmed in white, is .6 mile ahead on the right. During times of drought it is dry. But when it is wet, according to Fort Union superintendent Harry C. Myers, that pond attracts many varieties of birds and animals.

Another mile and one-half ahead is a second pond, which is never dry. These are *Los Pozos*. On the night of August 12, 1846, long before the fort came into being, Gen. Kearny and his troops camped around these ponds.

On taking the final curve up to Fort Union, look to the left. Far out in the field are the ruins of the old fort and arsenal. This site is not open to the public. A sign ahead describes the ruin. Proceed ahead to the visitor center and park.

Fort Union was founded in August 1851 by Lt. Col. Edwin V. Sumner, as a means of defense against marauding Indians. The location was near "La Junta," the junction of the Mountain Branch and Cimarron Cutoff of the Santa Fe Trail, and also near the junction of the Mora and Sapello rivers. This is the site which came into view a mile before reaching the

National Park Servi

The repair shops at the mechanics' corral at Fort Union

visitor's center. It is in the valley to the west.

From these locations, operations were conducted against the Jicarilla Apaches, Utes, Kiowas, and Comanches—all raiders of the plains north and east of the fort.

But that Fort Union could not have held against a concerted attack. So Col. Edward R. S. Canby, in charge of federal forces at the outbreak of the Civil War, ordered construction of a second Fort Union, called the "Star Fort."

Shaped of earth in the form of a six-pointed star, that fort never saw action, thanks to the strategy of Chivington at the Battle of Glorieta Pass. The threat gone, the Star Fort was abandoned in 1863. Today the outline is clearly visible in mounds of earth near the visitor center.

Construction began immediately on the third Fort Union, the fort which is the centerpiece of the splendid National Park Service display today.

The free NPS brochure on Fort Union describes it well:

National Archives

The depot quartermaster's office at Fort Union, shown in September 1866

This sprawling installation, which took 6 years to complete, was the most extensive in the territory. It included not only a military post, with all its attendant structures, but a separate quartermaster depot with warehouses, corrals, shops, offices, and quarters. The supply function overshadowed that of the military and employed far more men, mostly civilians. An ordnance depot was erected on the site of the old log fort at the western edge of the valley, rounding out the complex. . . .

Peace [came] to the southern plains in the spring of 1875, albeit on the white man's terms. Though Fort Union's involvement in the Indian wars had come to an end, its garrison occasionally helped to track down outlaws, quell mob violence, and mediate feuds. . . . By 1891 the fort had outlived its usefulness and was abandoned.

The remains of Fort Union were given to the people of the United States in a munificent gesture by the owners of the Fort Union Ranch, which lies to the northeast. All that remains today are the brick fireplace towers and fragments of adobe walls. The National Park Service has worked to stabilize the stark ruin ever since it took title, and it appears as if the techniques have been successful.

But visitors are cautioned against climbing on anything—thick mud walls could well collapse under additional weight.

The ruts of the Mountain Branch are a few yards to the east of the hospital ruin, and visitors are encouraged to hike on them. That variant cut across the plain to intercept the Cimarron Cutoff north of Coyote Creek, about four miles northeast of the main junction. The main stem of the Mountain Branch, however, cut between the hospital and the rest

Fort Union Hospital in the 1870s

of the buildings, heading due south to Tiptonville and Sapello Creek. The road is no longer visible at that point.

The park service brochure includes a hiking trail which leads through the ruins. Fort Union visitors are encouraged to take it, and split up, so they can be alone. When the hot summer winds lace through those ragged walls, when nothing is in sight but the haunting adobe fragments—then the mystique comes through.

It was here, in the summer of 1864, that Marion Sloan met the man she would marry, Lt. Richard D. Russell.

> I was rounding a corner rather suddenly, my green veil streaming out behind me. The wind was blowing my hair in my eyes and I was trying to keep my long skirts where they belonged when suddenly he stood before me. That was the moment the whole wide world stood still. My tall, young lieutenant stood and smiled at me while I struggled with my skirts, veil and hair. Then on he marched with his company, taking my ignorant young heart right along with him.

She returned to Fort Union at the age of eighty-nine, in 1934:

> I found crumbling walls and tottering chimneys. Here and there a tottering adobe wall where once a mighty howitzer had stood. Great rooms stood roofless, their whitewashed walls open to the sky. Wild gourd vines grew inside the officers' quarters. Rabbits scurried before my questing feet. The little guard house alone stood intact, mute witness of the punishment inflicted there. The Stars and Stripes was gone. Among a heap of rubble I found the ruins of the little

Only the brick fireplaces remain to mark the row of officers' quarters at Fort Union.

chapel where I had stood—a demure, little bride in a velvet cape—
and heard a preacher say, "That which God hath joined together
let no man put asunder." I found the ruins of my little home where
Colonel Carson once had stood beneath a hanging lamp. I heard
or seemed to hear again his kindly voice, "Little Maid Marion,
you cannot go [to Camp Nichols with Russell]. I promised your
mother to take good care of you."

It is not possible to cut through the Fort Union Ranch lands to follow
the trail to the north. Therefore, return to I-25 and drive north twenty-
one miles to Wagon Mound, exit and drive west on New Mexico Highway
120. The trail crosses the highway at mile marker 25. Drive 13.7 miles
and there will be a mailbox on the right labeled "Mora Ranch." A dirt
lane leads about 1.6 miles north, almost to the south edge of Apache Mesa.

A small wood bridge leads over Ocate Creek. Ruts of the trail are a
few yards to the south of there—hard to see from the south side but very
evident from the north. This is the approximate location of the Ocate
Crossing. From here the Mountain Branch turned abruptly east for nearly
three miles to skirt the point of the mesa, then doubled back to the northwest toward Rayado. (This land is private, and so is the lane for that
matter, but there should be no trouble so long as the visitor doesn't leave
the car.)

This little wood bridge spans Ocate Creek. The dark line beyond it marks the eroded swale of the Mountain Branch.

Josiah Gregg was saddened here, where he

> . . . encountered a very sudden bereavement in the death of Mr. Langham, one of our most respected proprietors. This gentleman was known to be in weak health, but no fears were entertained for his safety. . . . he was seized with a fit of apoplexy and expired instantly. As we had not the means of giving the deceased a decent burial, we were compelled to consign him to the earth in a shroud of blankets. A grave was accordingly dug on an elevated spot near the north bank of the creek, and on the morning of the 13th [of April, 1838], ere the sun had risen in the east, the mortal remains of this most worthy man and valued friend were deposited in their last abode, without a tomb-stone to consecrate the spot, or an epitaph to commemorate his virtues.

Susan Magoffin evidently climbed to the top of Apache Mesa:

> At the top I found a thicket of pine trees, and fearing lest a hungry bruen might be lurking in them, or a *tiger cat* . . . I did not dare venture farther, but returned to camp.

Rayado is only thirteen miles to the north, but it is impossible to get there over the trail. So return to I-25 and drive twenty-four miles north to Springer, take the first of two exits, and follow the road to the heart of town. Turn left onto New Mexico Highway 21. Drive west for 21.3 miles, where the road turns abruptly to the north. Drive 1.5 miles ahead, and look to the left. For most of the last mile into Rayado, ruts of the

New Mexico Historical Society
Maxwell's mansion on the Cimarron

Mountain Branch are on the left side of the road, only a few yards away.
   The first building on the left was once home for Kit Carson. Now owned by the Philmont Scout Ranch of the Boy Scouts of America, the home was "restored" many years ago, to the point where it bears no resemblance to the house Carson knew.
   The big house on the left, across the road from the church, includes remnants of the house once lived in by Lucian Maxwell. Maxwell inherited the Beaubien-Miranda grant, probably the largest land grant in America. It encompassed 1,714,764 acres in southeast Colorado and northeast New Mexico. Maxwell built here about 1850. He moved to a sprawling mansion in Cimarron later in the 1850s.
   Take an odometer reading and continue north out of Rayado on Highway 21. Just outside of town the highway makes a sharp curve to the left. At that point look to the northwest—the Mountain Branch may be seen coming down to the highway. At 3.1 miles from Rayado eroded ruts appear on the right side of the road. Just 1.7 miles from there are more ruts, this time on the left.
   Just 5.4 miles north of Rayado is one of the most striking bed-and-breakfast inns in America—Casa del Gavilan ("House of the Hawk"). It was built in the early 1900s by J. J. Nairn, whose Congoleum-Nairn organization had a corner on America's floor-covering market. It is now part of the vast UU-Bar Ranch, which includes sixty sections of land from the Cimarron to Ocate Creek.
   Continue ahead on this twisting road for .3 mile and pull over to the right in a turnout. This is high above the famous Philmont Scout Ranch, on the right.
   The wagons came down this grade too, just inside the present highway. There has been a great deal of erosion, of course, but traces of the

Casa del Gavilan, an elegant 1908 ranch building south of Cimarron, now is a bed and breakfast establishment.

Mountain Branch are still visible winding down to the valley below. Some of them may be seen .3 mile ahead.

The Philmont museum is .4 mile ahead on the right side of the road. It is a good place to visit, with exhibits which should bring pleasant memories to men who were once Boy Scouts.

Continue ahead for 3.4 miles—intermittent, deeply-eroded ruts may be seen from time to time on both sides of the road. The old town of Cimarron is just .8 mile ahead. Cimarron is bisected by the Cimarron River—not the same one followed by the Cimarron Cutoff. The older part of town is entered first, when driving up from the south.

Simmons has an excellent tour guide and map of Cimarron in his *Following the Santa Fe Trail*—it should be studied before leaving the town. The old Colfax County jail is the first significant building on the right. The rock structure with a tin roof was built in 1872. On the near corner of the intersection ahead, on the left, is Swink's gambling hall, a place with a notorious reputation earned in the last days of the trail.

Turn left at that intersection and drive west for one block. On the right is the Old Aztec Mill, operated by Maxwell from 1864 to 1870. Most of the machinery is still there, intact. The structure now is used to display the exhibits of the Cimarron Historical Society, and is worth a visit.

Return to Route 21 and turn left. On the right is the St. James Hotel, erected in 1873 as a saloon. Hotel literature claims that twenty-six men were ventilated by gunfire within those walls—there are still bulletholes

Lucien Maxwell's Old Aztec Mill, Cimarron

in the ceiling of the main dining room. It was restored in 1985 by Ed and Pat Sitzberger and now ranks as one of the most charming hotels in New Mexico. The tours are free. The rooms definitely are not.

Facing the hotel on the north was the great mansion of Lucien Maxwell, built in 1864. The front of the building looked east, toward the town plaza in the next block. The house burned in 1885.

Cross the Cimarron River and drive north to the stop sign at U.S. Highway 64. Take an odometer reading and turn right. There are ruts three miles out of town, about one-third mile out in the plain to the west. At 12.3 miles from Cimarron is a sign for the Dawson road. Proceed a half-mile ahead. There are more ruts on the left, some .6 mile out into the flat.

Thirteen miles from there is the junction with Highway 445, known locally as Hoxie Junction. Somewhere near here the Mountain Branch split—one variant led down to Maxwell, and the main trail continued to Cimarron.

Proceed 32.5 miles northwest of Cimarron to an overpass crossing above the Santa Fe railroad tracks. Take another odometer reading there. (That bridge should be used as a checkpoint—minute error can build in odometers over such a long stretch.) Continue ahead exactly 2.3 miles, carefully cross the highway to the turnout on the left, and park.

Walk to the north a few yards from the midpoint of that turnout and sight to the southwest. There is a linear mound there, perhaps twenty feet high. That is an abandoned railroad grade. Sight to the right of there, over the trees lining the little Canadian River. Due west from this point, or 270 degrees, and out in the flat, is a tiny, irregularly shaped mass. That is a standing adobe shard, all that remains of the once-famed Clifton House. In the summer field glasses are mandatory, as the fragment is about the same shape as the scrub cedar and other plants in the vicinity.

This is private land—get permission before leaving the highway. It takes roughly twenty minutes to walk to the site of Clifton House, and is well worth the trip. Hike to the right of the railroad embankment, then cut due west to cross the Canadian at the narrowest place. It is shallow and can be waded. A good broad jumper could vault it. Then a short distance to the west is the adobe fragment, suddenly grown considerably. It is ten to thirteen feet tall, depending on which side the viewer stands, and perhaps five or six feet wide.

Clifton House was built in the late 1860s by Tom Stockton, at the point where the Barlow and Sanderson Stage crossed the Canadian River. It closed after the railroad came through, and burned six years later.

Now the last portion of adobe is melting into the earth—in a few more years nothing will be left but the foundation.

Clifton House was a three-story emporium built for the convenience of the Santa Fe traders. It stood on the banks of the Canadian River, about a day's drive south of Raton.

This single shard of adobe is all that remains from the Clifton House.

Proceed .3 mile ahead and turn left onto I-25. Drive five miles north into the city of Raton and leave the highway at Exit 452. Turn left there and proceed west on Highway 72. The road turns right, where it is called Guadalupe Street, but it is still Highway 72. Continue driving toward the business district. Turn right onto Second Street. Drive to a "dead end" sign and keep on going on a gravel road (now Railroad Avenue) for less than a block, to a residence on the right marked 545 Railroad, and stop. The Santa Fe Railroad is on the left. A small sign identifies this place as Willow Spring. That name is also incorporated into the ornate metal gates. It is the home of Willie and Mary Gaskin.

If the Gaskins have time, they escort visitors down their driveway to a concrete patio area near the back door of their home. There, beneath a round concrete cap, flows Willow Spring. This was the site of the Willow Spring Stage Station and Ranch. The clear, cold spring water is forced onto the lawn and that spot is a lush showplace.

This was a favorite watering place for the traders, and in the late 1800s the Santa Fe Railroad published a stereograph of the spring, to encourage settlement along their line.

Backtrack to North First Street, go through an underpass, and turn right on Second Street. Proceed about three blocks to the right to Moulton Avenue and turn left. Follow Moulton to a T and turn left on Hill Street. Within a block the climb begins. This is the old road over Raton Pass. Just .7 mile ahead is a breathtaking view of this beautiful city, and, over the housetops, the broad valley of the Canadian. About three miles ahead is the old New Mexico Welcome Center, abandoned for many years. Continue ahead for another .8 mile, where further progress is barred by a fence and dozens of enormous boulders. The drive back down is as much fun as the one going back up. This is one of the alternates of the Santa Fe Trail. The main Mountain Branch came over the pass very close to the route taken by I-25 today.

Return to I-25 and drive north for 6.2 miles to the Colorado border and Raton Pass.

TRINIDAD TO LAKIN, KANSAS

At the Colorado state line, the summit of Raton Pass, Wah-to-yah comes into view. Those are the majestic Spanish Peaks, long a landmark for southbound trail travelers on the Mountain Branch. A careful scan of the valley to the left while about 1.5 miles north of the border will yield a fleeting glimpse of the buildings of the Wootton Ranch. Leave the highway at Exit 2, two miles north of the summit. To proceed to the wagon road over the pass it will be necessary to get permission from the owner of the ranch. Contact Mark Gardner, administrator of the

Willie and Mary Gaskin use the outflow of Willow Spring to water their lawn.

Willow Spring Ranch, about 1880

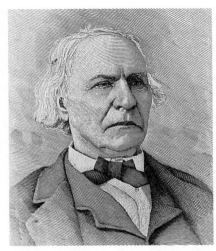

Uncle Dick Wootton

Pioneer Museum in Trinidad, (719) 846-7217.

The southbound service road, on the west side of I-25, is the Santa Fe Trail, and it proceeds only a few yards to a steel gate barring farther progress. The gate will be open only if permission to enter has been gained.

The Wootton Ranch buildings are .2 mile south of the gate. Behind the handsome mobile home is a one-story adobe building, all that remains of the great house built there in the 1870s by Richens Lacy ("Uncle Dick") Wootton. He was a mountain man, Indian fighter, and trapper of great ability, on a par with the Bent brothers as a pioneer of the old West.

He had a rich career in the Rocky Mountain West. His biography, *Uncle Dick Wootton,* only recently went out of print. The last publication was by the Bison Books division of the University of Nebraska Press. It is filled with Uncle Dick's stories of his life in the West, but none measure up to the one told by the ranch owner. It was told to him by a former owner, who was acquainted with Uncle Dick.

One day some men were approaching the toll gate and noticed a wisp of smoke where there shouldn't have been any. Uncle Dick's roof was afire. They rushed to his door, and all the men helped carry buckets of water from the creek to the house, eventually getting the blaze extinguished. Uncle Dick thanked them profusely. They turned to go through the toll gate. He held out his hand: "Ain't you boys forgetting something?"

Susan Magoffin would have been near here on the night of August 13, 1846, the first of her five days of transit over the rocky, tortuous mule path:

Mark L. Gardner Collection

The Wootton ranch in May 1881, from a stereograph card photographed by George C. Bennett

Colorado Historical Society

The Wootton house prior to its devastating fire

> Came to camp . . . at Sun Set, and just at the entrance of what
> is called the "Raton," a difficult pass of fifteen miles through the
> Mountains.
>
> Our tent is stretched on the top of a high hill, at the foot and
> on the sides of which I have been rambling accompanied by our
> faithful [dog] Ring, who all the while kept strict watch for *Indians,*
> *bear, panther, wolves* &c., and would not even leave my side as if con-
> scious I had no other protector at hand

Marion Russell remembered her passage over the Raton:

> Breaking camp while it was still early, our cavalcade began the
> steep and tortuous ascent of the Raton Pass. Today [the 1930s] we
> glide easily over hairpin curves that in 1860 meant broken axles and
> crippled horses. The trail was a faint wheel mark winding in and
> out over fallen trees and huge boulders. . . . Our horses were jaded
> and tired, six of our wagons had broken axles.

Uncle Dick built a massive two-story home here of adobe; the one-
story addition on the site today was added later. The big house burned
in 1890 but was rebuilt on the remaining walls in 1908. This rebuilt home
was demolished in 1980, with the exception of this small adobe structure,
and the debris was hauled away about 1980.

Here, too, was the gate for Uncle Dick's toll road, which he improved
and opened in 1865.

Ahead on the left is a great two-story adobe barn said to have been
built by the Wootton Land and Fuel Company, which included finan-
cier J. P. Morgan among its backers, in the early 1900s. Mark Gardner
recently found a stereograph published by the Santa Fe Railroad, taken
from above the house toward the old barn. At that time, probably in
the 1880s, there definitely was a one-story barn on the same site. Gardner has examined the structure—he found no evidence that it ever was
a one-story building.

Another gate is abreast of the barn. The Santa Fe Trail is believed
to be the same as the present dirt road. Continue past that gate for .7
mile. On the left is the grave of Cruz Torrez.

Torrez was a corporal in the U.S. Army. He recently had had three
privates bound and gagged for misbehavior at a fandango, and they were
itching for revenge. They had stopped at Wootton's place:

> They left at an early hour, going in an opposite direction from
> their camp, and I closed my doors soon after for the night. They
> had not been gone more than half an hour when I heard them talk-
> ing, not far from my house, and a few seconds later I heard the
> half-surpressed cry of a man who had, I was satisfied, received his

The remains of the Wootton house were leveled in 1980.

Mark Gardner stands in the doorway of the one-story structure which stands today at the Wootton site.

The two-story Wootton barn

Grave of Cruz Torrez

The Santa Fe eliminated the switchbacks atop Raton Pass by construction of this long tunnel.

death blow. I had gone to bed, and lay for a minute or two thinking whether I should get up and go to the rescue of the man whose cry I had heard, or insure my own safety by remaining where I was.

A little reflection convinced me that the murderers were undoubtedly watching my house to prevent any interference with the carrying out of their plot and that if I ventured out I should only endanger my own life . . .

In the morning . . . I found the dead body of the corporal stretched across Raton Creek not more than a hundred yards from my house. As I surmised, he had been struck with a heavy club or stone, and it was at that time that I heard him cry out. After that his brains had been beaten out and the body left where I found it.

The men were quickly apprehended and two of them were hanged. The third was the lookout—the man who indeed stood by Uncle Dick's door ready to do him in, too, should he interfere with their scheme.

Drive .8 mile ahead, where the road ends at the Santa Fe Railroad. To the right is the north portal of the tunnel which the railroad cut beneath Raton Pass to eliminate costly switchbacks. Unfortunately, the cut eliminated all trace of the wagon road over the pass at that point.

It is possible to hike several miles of the high country, and south of the tunnel intermittent ruts are visible along the west side of the tracks

The Santa Fe Railroad had to cross Raton Pass through an elaborate system of switchbacks.

The Spanish Peaks

Fisher's Peak, formerly Raton Mountain, towers over Trinidad.

for more than two miles.

Especially noteworthy is the view of the snow-capped Spanish Peaks, which are even more impressive here than when viewed from I-25.

(A pleasant alternative is to take Amtrak over the pass, either from Trinidad or Raton. It takes about an hour—that's one big hill—and is very inexpensive. It also delivers some fine views of the Wootton Ranch.)

Return to I-25 and continue north nine miles to Trinidad, passing Fisher's Peak, originally called Raton Peak, on the right as the approach is made. Take Exit 14A, marked for Colorado Highway 12, headed west.

After some false starts in business, Marion and Richard Russell decided to establish a ranch near the Stonewall, a unique rock formation thirty-eight miles up the Purgatoire River from Trinidad. Marion describes her first trip to their Eden:

> Mid-afternoon on the second day of our travel, we saw the great Stone Wall rising from the blue mists at its feet. Behind it, with all its towers and turrets, rose the white-capped Sangre de Cristo Mountains. The Sangre de Christo, meaning Blood of Christ mountains, we thought were well named, for their snowy tops were stained blood-red by the setting sun.

It is 30.8 miles from the interstate to the hamlet known locally as Picket-wire, a corruption of the name of the Purgatoire River. The sparkling

The Stonewall

Marion Russell's headstone is second from left; that of her husband's is third from left.

Purgatoire will be followed all the way. The cemetery where Richard and Marion Russell lie is past the little general store on the left in Picketwire. Drive ahead .5 mile and turn right onto a dirt road. Cross a ditch and check a steel gate—it usually is unlocked. Open it, drive through, stop, and close it immediately. Right now good people may drive in without permission. This is likely to change if gate etiquette is not observed and the rancher loses some livestock.

Proceed ahead for .3 mile into a pine forest, where the road curves to the left. One-half mile from the highway is a gate into a small cemetery. Pass through, and turn half-left. The Russell graves are enclosed in an iron picket fence.

Marion and Richard had the misfortune to settle on the great Beaubein-Miranda grant, long after ownership was lost by Lucien Maxwell. They were squatters, no doubt about it. And the owners wanted all squatters removed. Richard Russell tried to act as a mediator but was shot down by the goon squad.

This is a solemn, sad place, but as Marc Simmons writes, it is also inspiring. After he had finished the afterword for the new edition of her *Land of Enchantment,* which had been long out of print, he is said to have come here alone. When he was certain nobody was near, he shouted, "Marion—you're back!"

Return to Route 12 and turn right. Proceed .8 mile to the great Stonewall described by Marion Russell so long ago.

Kit Carson statue in Kit Carson Park, Trinidad

The Hough-Baca House

Return to Trinidad. Drive beneath I-25 and continue until reaching a four-way stop near the Colorado Welcome Center. This is now Animas Street. Follow Animas south to Main Street. Turn left on Main and proceed .1 mile to Commercial. Turn left there and drive .5 mile ahead to the traffic signal at Colorado, passing beneath I-25 again along the way. Cross that street. Commercial then becomes Arizona. Continue one more block ahead and turn right on Kansas Avenue. Drive one block, turn left, and park. On the right, in the center of Kit Carson Park, is the magnificent equestrian bronze of the kid from Old Franklin. Tell him I sentcha.

Return to downtown Trinidad via Commercial Street south to Main. Turn left on Main and drive east to the 300 block. Behind a retaining wall on the south side of the street are two magnificent examples of early Colorado architecture, now preserved and interpreted by the Colorado Historical Society.

The Baca House, on the near corner, was built by trail merchant John S. Hough in 1870 and purchased by Maria Dolores Baca in 1873. It is a two-story territorial-style adobe, historically furnished as the home of a prosperous Spanish-American family of this area.

The towering Second Empire mansion to the east was built by Frank G. Bloom in 1882. He was a Trinidad banker and rancher. Between them is the one story adobe building which is now the Pioneer Museum. At one time it housed the families of the Baca farmhands and sheepherders;

now it is a museum with exhibits interpreting the history of Trinidad and southern Colorado.

The Baca-Bloom houses are open from Memorial Day weekend through Labor Day weekend, 10 A.M. to 5 P.M. Monday through Saturday, and 1 to 5 on Sunday. There is a small admission charge. The noted Santa Fe Trail authority, Mark Gardner, is the administrator.

Continue east on Main, which is also U.S. Highway 160. Drive 6.7 miles, where Highway 160 turns to the right.

At this point a decision must be made. The directions which follow lead to the ruts of the Military Road, which proceeded south from the Union Pacific railhead near old Granada, Colorado, to Fort Union. This road carried an enormous amount of freight, and many trading caravans, too, during the last decade of the life of the Santa Fe Trail.

After visiting those ruts, the explorer could return to continue pursuit of the Mountain Branch, or continue south to follow the Military Road through Emery Gap and Tollgate Canyon. Again, one could return from that point.

Or, to complete a long loop drive, it is interesting to drive to Folsom, and then to Capulin Mountain National Monument, to hike down into the crater of a volcano. And then over to Raton and back to this point. The loop, including the Capulin visit, takes about four hours.

To visit the Military road, stay on 160. Exactly two miles to the east a gravel road comes in from the left. If the explorer intends to return to the Santa Fe Trail from any point on the Military Road, it is here that a turn should be made, to get to the town of Hoehne. But to continue the Military Road exploration, proceed east for 29.4 miles to Colorado Highway 389. Continue on 160 for another 1.1 miles and look to the right. There, in a gap in the mesa, is the cone of Sierra Grande, the same mountain which was so dominant along the Cimarron Cutoff.

Drive 2.7 more miles ahead and turn right onto the road marked 147.0. A sign identifying the Sharp Ranch is on the left, and a direction sign for the Louden Cattle Co. is on the right. Proceed south for four miles and turn left onto a two-track along the fence line. This is private land—get permission first. Drive east, twisting and turning, for 1.7 miles and stop. The ruts of the Military Road are all around here, heading due southwest. They are continuous for about four miles northeast and intermittent for nine miles to the southwest.

Return to the gravel road and continue south. The Military Road crosses 2.2 miles ahead. The ruts themselves are not easily seen from the road, but there is a strip of grass slightly more green winding toward Emery Gap, due southwest of there. That is the route of the Military Road. Continue 3.6 miles farther south and turn to the right. Drive 4.5 miles west to the town of Branson and turn left onto Colorado Highway

389.

Ahead is Emery Gap, named for Madison Emery, a pioneer rancher in this area. Richard Louden, whose grandmother recorded the recollections of the Emery family, said that the Tollgate route was pioneered by Madison Emery in the late 1860s.

> The road was refined by Basil (Missouri Bill) Metcalf and opened as a toll road in 1872, or possibly 1873. It does appear, on the basis of recollections of the Emery family, that the original military road went up the Gleason Canyon, a tributary of the Cimarron, about a mile east of Tollgate Canyon.

Pass through Emery Gap and into New Mexico just 1.7 miles to the south. At that point the highway number changes to 551. Drive ahead for 4.7 miles. On the right is a turnout for Tollgate Canyon, and a New Mexico historical sign:

> Between 1871 and 1873, Bazil Metcalf constructed a toll road from the Dry Cimarron through Tollgate Gap, providing one of the few reliable wagon roads between Colorado and northeast New Mexico. This road remained an important commercial route until the Colorado and Southern Railway came through this area in the late 1880's.

A few yards south is the ruin of the tollgate house. It is on private property.

Continue ahead for 1.6 miles to a stop sign and turn right onto New Mexico Highway 456. Proceed eight more miles to Folsom. This is perhaps the most important archaeological site in the United States, for it was near here about 1908 that a black cowboy, George McJunkin, found New Mexico's Folsom site. A strange assortment of amateurs—not one of them with a college degree of any kind—gradually worked in the site to find projectile points in matrices with bison bones, proving that man occupied this continent about 10,000 years ago. They held out against a disbelieving professional archaeological establishment until the pros, who clung to their position that man was here no longer than 3,000 years, eventually discredited themselves. A nice little museum is to the left at the intersection of New Mexico Highway 325. A donation is requested.

A nice side trip from here, which has absolutely nothing to do with the Santa Fe Trail, is to Capulin Mountain National Monument. Turn right in Folsom onto New Mexico Highway 325. Drive six miles southwest to the monument entrance.

Capulin Mountain is one of the few places in the world where a visitor may walk into the crater of a volcano. A fine blacktop road twists up to a parking area near the top of the volcano. One foot trail leads from there around the rim of the crater, a little more than a mile. Another is from the parking area only .2 mile to the bottom of the crater to the capped vent, an easy hike. Down. Not so easy back up, however.

Return to the fine National Park Service Visitor Center. (On the way down, it is a good idea to put all transmissions—automatic or manual—in low gear, to save wear on the brakes.)

Proceed south another 2.7 miles from the monument entrance to the town of Capulin, and there turn right onto U.S. Highways 64-87. Drive west for 26.6 miles to join I-25 south of Raton. Proceed up over the pass to Trinidad, and take Highways 160-350 north. Close the loop at U.S. 160, 6.7 miles north of town.

Only this time, instead of turning right onto 160 from 350, continue on 350 for 2.5 miles and turn half-left onto a gravel road marked 85.0. Cross the Purgatoire about a mile to the north, then proceed a half-mile farther to a T in the road. Turn left there, onto County Road 75.1, and proceed to Road 40.3 in Hoehne. Turn right and drive straight ahead to cross the Santa Fe tracks to the east side of town. Arrive at another T in the road the turn right onto the gravel Road 83.3.

About .7 mile ahead there is a Y in the road—bear right onto a road marked 42.0. This road slants to the right—the Santa Fe Trail and this road probably are one and the same.

A DAR marker is on the left side of this road. Proceed a half-mile from the last corner—the road turns left there. Continue north another half-mile, and the road turns right. Follow it east just .2 mile, to where it turns left. Then drive .4 mile north. Take an odometer reading here and proceed about .3 mile ahead, doing some some gradual twisting along the way. Just .3 mile ahead look to the left.

There is one of the most striking, non-eroded swales of the great Santa Fe Trail, probably thirty feet wide from shoulder to shoulder and a good five feet deep at the center. And filled with trash. Old washing machines, tires, refrigerators. The nation's most honored pioneer highway has been turned into a dumping ground for the detritus of civilization.

That swale continues for more than seven miles, virtually unbroken, but from here on access is very difficult. It is at this point that the Mountain Branch leaves the valley of the Purgatoire.

Backtrack to Highway 350 south of Hoehne and turn hard left. Drive 3.8 miles and cross the Purgatoire River for the last time. The town of Model is eight miles ahead—the visible ruts which came into view north of Hoehne stop two miles west of Model, but they are very hard to reach.

This is the area of the Hole-In-The-Prairie—nothing more than a pond in trail days. The actual stage station site evidently has been drifted in with dust, and the evidence—building stone and broken blue glass— probably is far beneath the surface. The area was located in the sum-

This magnificent swale of the Santa Fe Trail north of Hoehne, Colorado, is filled with trash.

mer of 1989 by Marc Simmons, Mark Gardner, Paul Bentrup, Jessie Scott, and the Louden brothers, Willard and Richard. It is on private land and can be reached only after a torturous 4x4 drive over the desert.

Proceed six miles to the northeast. There the trail is just to the left of the railroad tracks, but there are no visible ruts.

Proceed 7.4 miles northeast to the non-town of Thatcher, turn left off the highway onto a gravel road, cross the tracks, and the road curves to the left. Continue past a large, abandoned schoolhouse and drive toward a farmyard. Before reaching it look to the right. There is the ruin of a stone barn, once believed to have been part of the Hole-in-the-Rock stage station. Conversations with local ranchers by Paul Bentrup reveal that it actually was built for the Circle Diamond Ranch, a post-trail operation.

Continue ahead on the gravel road and turn to the right past the farm buildings. Proceed to a point twenty yards before reaching a small bridge over Timpas Creek. That is just .6 mile from the highway.

Take a bearing of 340 degrees, or a little west of northwest. About a quarter-mile along that line is the site of the Hole-in-the-Rock.

Timpas Creek, whose watershed sheltered the Santa Fe Trail where the Purgatoire left off, was an unreliable water source. But even when the creek was dry, there was water in a hole in the rock floor of this canyon.

Susan Magoffin stopped here:

Timpas Creek Canyon

"Hole in the Rock" Rather a place of some celebrity our camp is
in tonight.

I have not yet visited the "great well" . . . but from what others
say it is a large "hole in a rock" filled with clear, cold water, and
to which a bottom has never as yet been found. . . . [later I] found
[it] pretty much the same as described: the scenery around it is quite
romantic—high rocks covered with cedar trees; shelving and craggy
precipices; pearly brooks, and green groves, through which are seen
bounding the stately antelope and timid hare; while the ear is greeted
by the soft warble of feathered songsters.

Others who visited found the water stagnant. The water in pools of
Timpas Creek, however, was always bad.

What happened to Hole-in-the-Rock? The Santa Fe Railroad needed
water for their steam engines so they built a dam 193 feet wide across
the narrowest part of the canyon, less than a half-mile to the northeast.
Spillways are on either side of the dam. The canyon silted in over the
years. The floor is now level with the top of the spillway, some six feet
below the top of the dam; Hole-in-the-Rock is buried forever.

Drive over the bridge and note the power poles alongside the road.
Stop between the first and second poles and look north to several corrals.
About seventy-five yards beyond those corrals is the site of the Hole-in-
the-Rock Stage Station. The foundation ruins are behind the corrals and
virtually impossible to see from the road. Mark Gardner and the land-

Colorado Historical Society

The ruins of the stage station at Hole-in-the-Rock are shown, at top, in a photograph from 1915, and at bottom, as they appear today.

Colorado Historical Society—Mark L. Gardner

Members of the National Park Service survey group examine the site of the Iron Springs Stage Station. From left: Bonita Oliva, Betty Burnett, John Paige, Dr. Jere Krakow, Paul Bentrup, and Dr. Leo E. Oliva.

owner, Butch Hall, walked over there to see portions of the foundations. Much of the rock has been bulldozed away to form a diversionary dam, to keep rainwater from flooding the corrals.

Return to Highway 350 and continue to the northwest for exactly sixteen miles. Turn right there on a gravel road—it is hard to see and it comes up fast, but there is a mailbox perched atop an old oil drum next to the road. Proceed between .3 and .4 from the road, and a person with a good eye can detect a faint trace of the Mountain Branch crossing the road. Continue a total of 1.1 mile south of the highway, cross over a small bridge, and stop. This is private land, but it is a public road. Nevertheless, it would be a good idea to continue ahead and ask permission to visit the site from the nearest ranch house.

On the left are two round stock tanks. Several yards to the right of them is a large cube of concrete. Beneath that cube flows the Iron Spring.

Water from the spring is piped underground to the stock tanks. Nearby are the foundations and scattered rocks from the buildings of the Iron Spring Stage Station. It was built in 1861 and attacked by the Cheyenne three years later. It is hard to burn out adobe and rock buildings, so the station was back in business shortly thereafter. There are good ruts up on the ridge to the west of the road and a little south of the spring.

They are headed due west. This is a trail which detoured from the Mountain Branch to take advantage of the Iron Spring.

Return to the highway and along the way take a last look at the Spanish Peaks, far to the southwest. (They are usually lost in the haze during midsummer, but in spring and fall their shadowy forms can be seen.) Take an odometer reading and turn to the right. Four miles ahead three knobs will come into view on the right. The stage road went between the first and second of those knobs. They are about four miles to the northeast. Just 7.8 miles northeast of the Iron Spring road the Mountain Branch crossed, to be on the east side of the highway. Another 1.5 miles and it veers back to the northwest side of the road, but then the trail split—part of it will be on the right and part on the left side of the highway. Proceed ahead to La Junta—the intersection of U.S. Highway 50 and Business Route 50 is twenty-seven miles northeast of the Iron Spring road.

Proceed east 1.1 miles and turn right on Colorado Highways 109 and 194. Drive north for two blocks and turn left for one block. Then turn left again and cross the Arkansas River in the northeastern part of this beautiful little city. The Mountain Branch crossing of the river is only about 700 feet east of there.

Matt Field crossed the Arkansas in 1839:

> We had crossed the Arkansas at Bent's Fort, and the labor of the animals having been most severe, dragging the huge vehicles through the soft bed of the river, (eighteen mules were required to one wagon) we camped for rest upon the opposite side at a little after noon.

Susan Magoffin was in a reflective mood on August 8, 1846, when she wrote these lines in her diary:

> Left the Fort last evening at 6 o'clock, came six miles up the River to where we leave it finally. I am now entirely out of "The States," into a new country. The crossing of the Arkansas was an event in my life, I have never met with before; the separating me from my own dear native land. That which I love and honour as truly as any whole-souled son or daughter of the fair and happy America . . . ever did. Perhaps I have left it for not only the first, but the last time. Maybe I am never to behold its bright and sunny landscape, its happy people, my countrymen, again.

Just .6 mile farther the highways separate—turn right to follow 194 to the east for 6.3 miles and turn right into the parking area for Bent's Old Fort.

The decade of the 1830s saw the fur trade rapidly diminishing. The robe trade was flourishing, however. The powerful American Fur Com-

Colorado Historical Society

One of the most admired men of the Santa Fe Trail—William Bent

pany had aced out all competitors up on the North Platte, and its influence extended more to the west than to the south.

The Bent brothers—Charles and William—joined with fellow St. Louisan Ceran St. Vrain to work on the Indian trade far to the south. The white men felt they could do well on Timpas Creek, but the Cheyenne, their biggest customers, wanted an emplacement in the Big Timbers area, miles down the Arkansas from here. This site was a compromise—an art the company had honed to such sharpness that it prospered long after competitors had failed.

So it was here that they decided to build this adobe castle on the Arkansas River plain.

The company had its bets well hedged. They had carefully built up the Taos trade, reaching that ancient city over Sangre de Cristo Pass, a much easier traverse of that formidable barrier than Raton Pass. So when the Santa Fe market was glutted by a plethora of Missouri merchandise, Bent, St. Vrain and Company worked the Taos trade with virtually no competition.

The robe trade was prospering in this area—more revenue for the three partners. Traffic over the Mountain Branch was by no means insignificant, although in the 1830s more of that business rolled down the Cimmaron Cutoff than over the Raton. The beaver were pretty well wiped out in the Platte watershed, but there was still a good population in the Sangre de Cristo. The market had gone to pot when European dandies switched to felt, but there were some bucks to be gained there.

While the big fur companies were eating each other up out of Fort Laramie, and while the Missourians and Mexicans were saturating the

Santa Fe-Chihuahua markets, Bent, St. Vrain and Company were happily cleaning up with virtually no competition on the central plains. Their trade empire was vast. It extended into the panhandles of present-day Texas and Oklahoma, northern New Mexico, and virtually all of present-day Colorado.

Since William Bent was in charge of construction, the structure was known locally as Fort William. The building date is still a matter of conjecture, but Don Hill, superintendent of Bent's Old Fort National Historic Site, and his chief ranger, Bill Gwaltney, are comfortable with the year 1833. The principal structure measured 142 feet by 122 feet, with twenty-six interior apartments surrounding a *placita*. Corrals, wagon sheds, and other minor structures were outside the fort. Round bastions at the northeast and southwest corners commanded the walls and a watchtower surmounted the main gate.

About 1836 William Bent married Owl Woman, daughter of a Cheyenne chief. This was no marriage of convenience; unlike some mountain men he did not have an Anglo wife at home. His marriage involved much more than two people—it solidified the good relations between the tribe and the other people at Bent's Fort, and whites in general.

Susan Magoffin's description was long and colorful, and served as a guide for the restorers in the 1970s and for the interpreters of today. But the most poignant passage was written on August 6, 1846, one week after her nineteenth birthday:

> The mysteries of a new world have been shown to me since last Thursday! In a few short months I should have been a happy mother and made the heart of a father glad, but the ruling hand of a mighty Providence has interposed and by an abortion deprived us of the hope, the fond hope of mortals! But with the affliction he does not leave us comfortless!

There has been much speculation that the upset at Ash Creek had caused Susan's miscarriage. Had the pregnancy ended a day or two after the accident, that would have made more sense. Any number of medical circumstances could have transpired to cause the loss of the child. It is a good bet that the spill at Ash Creek had nothing to do with it.

In 1849, with the beaver trade long dead and Indian hostilities increasing, William Bent (by this time the sole owner) tried to sell the fort to the government. That attempt failed. Cholera shot west from St. Louis and swept the plains.

On August 21, 1849, William Bent took part in one of the most bizarre events in the history of the West. He ordered his employees to pack everything of value in twenty covered wagons, each pulled by a twelve-ox hitch. The perplexed drivers followed Bent five miles east and camped.

He rode back to the fort alone, and placed powder kegs all along the east wall. Then he torched the ceilings of other rooms. When he was some distance from the fort the powder ignited and Bent's Fort was no more.

Today the National Park Service has done an incredible job of reconstruction of the fort as it appeared in 1845-46, when the firm was at the zenith of its power. The best time to see the fort is perhaps an hour before dawn. Pull off the highway and park at the main gate, preferably in pitch darkness. Watch as the blackness of the Arkansas marsh eases, as the clouds turn from indigo to purple to red to white. The tungsten rays make the mud walls even more red than they really are. Crepuscular birds by the thousands swoop after mosquitoes and gnats by the millions, breaking the quiet of the dawn with a chattering cacophony.

Soon a lone park ranger will appear on the watchtower and the Stars and Stripes will be silently unfurled. There are days when the plains wind will stand it away from the staff like a board, but usually, in the hotness of the summer, it will drape motionless along the pole.

In summertime the great gates will swing open at 8 and the tours will begin. There is nothing quite like that experience on the face of the earth.

Continue east thirteen miles to Las Animas. Join U.S. Highway 50 there but follow the "50 West" signs instead of proceeding on east away from Las Animas. That highway turns south at the junction to cross the Arkansas. Continue south for 1.3 miles. At that point Highway 50 will turn back to the west. Follow it for a block, then turn left and drive south on Colorado Highway 101, or Carson Avenue. Cross the railroad tracks on the west side of the depot. Turn left and drive a block east to the Kit Carson Museum, another of the fine local museums which are along the trail in Colorado. Return to Carson Avenue and turn left. A Y is in the road about one mile to the south where the highway will curve to the left, but continue straight ahead on a blacktop road. Just .4 mile ahead turn left into the Las Animas cemetery. Guide to the right, proceeding east on the southernmost street, which is South Avenue. Continue east to 6th Avenue. To the left is the grave of William Bent. He was moved here some years after his death at his ranch on the Purgatoire in 1869. The ranch was about a mile northeast of here.

Drive north to the next street, Central Drive. The large monument on the corner marks the plot of the family of John Wesley Prowers. Prowers was a Santa Fe Trail trader and merchant who later became a pioneer settler of this area. Like his associate, William Bent, he married an Indian, Amache, who remarried a man named Kazee after Prowers's death. Her stone is behind the monument and to the right, with only the initials A.P.K. identifying her grave.

Dawn at Bent's Old Fort is a haunting experience.

Traders entering the fort would have gained this view of the placita.

The Thomas Boggs House, Boggsville, is being restored by the Pioneer Historical Society of Bent County.

Return to the Y in the road and turn hard right on the highway. Drive just .6 mile ahead to a monument on the right, which commemorates the site of Boggsville. Proceed another .1 mile and turn left onto a gravel road which leads to the only two houses left in Boggsville.

The first building, a U-shaped adobe, was the home of Thomas O. Boggs, who came to the area in the 1860s. The house was built in 1866. Like Prowers, Boggs was an associate of William Bent. The home to the rear was built by Prowers in 1867.

Kit Carson moved here in November 1867, after resigning his commission in the U.S. Army. His wife, Josefa, died here, and Carson also died while living in Boggsville. They were buried in their garden, but the bodies were moved the following year to a cemetery near their old home in Taos.

The twenty-acre site of Boggsville was acquired by the Pioneer Historical Society of Bent County in 1986. The organization, working with largely volunteer labor, has managed to do some stabilization of the buildings. Much archaeological work has taken place in Boggsville under the direction of the noted archaeologist Dr. William G. Buckles of the University of Southern Colorado, Pueblo. The location of Carson's house is one of the goals of the diggers. The long-term goal of the society is to restore the structures, furnish them authentically, and open them to the public. They need monetary help, and lots of it.

Return to Highway 50 and drive north out of Las Animas. Slow down when crossing the Arkansas River, and notice the character of the stream, and the abundance of wildlife on and above its banks. Better still, park on the approach and walk out on the span to study the ecosystem closely.

Drive 4.5 miles east from the bridge and turn right on Colorado Highway 183. Proceed one-half mile south; there is a DAR marker on

The Arkansas River, as seen from the Highway 50 bridge in Las Animas

the right. Continue ahead another .4 mile and turn half-left on Route HH to proceed to the main entrance of the Veterans Administration Medical Center, the site of New Fort Lyon.

Continue ahead on Gate Drive to C Avenue and turn left. At the far end of C Avenue, behind the large administration building, is a structure identified as Kit Carson Chapel. In the 1860s this was the quarters of the post surgeon. Upon his retirement Carson had been appointed superintendent of Indian affairs for Colorado, and early in 1868 he accompanied a delegation of Utes to Washington for treaty talks.

He returned to Boggsville by train and stage, deeply distressed by chest pains, terrible coughing spells, and a rapidly weakening condition. He moved to Fort Lyon, possibly in a room in this very building, and while in the office of surgeon H. R. Tilton on May 23, 1868, he made one last bloody cough and gave up the ghost.

His demise was caused by a ruptured aneurysm of the aorta.

In 1957, long before preservationists had much voice, the building's roof was replaced with this steeply-pitched roof and the decrepit old relic was converted into a chapel.

Return to Gate Drive and turn left. Follow it around behind the brick buildings to the south end of the fort. There are two old stone structures there which date back to trail days. Both were erected in 1867. The first is the commissary; the second is the quartermaster building. The

The Kit Carson Chapel today

Kit Carson died in the surgeon's quarters at New Fort Lyon. This photograph was made prior to 1910.

Red Shin's Standing Ground

stone which was in the gable to identify the first building is gone, but
that of the second structure is still in place.

Return to Highway 50 and turn right. Proceed ten miles northeast
to the center of the town of Hasty and turn right on a blacktop road,
following the signs to the John Martin Reservoir, administered by the
U.S. Army Corps of Engineers. Proceed south for 1.8 miles, where there
is a Y in the road. Veer left on the blacktop to avoid driving over the
dam and continue on the main road. Follow the main road for 1.3 miles
to a gravel turnout on the left, which goes up the near side of a startling
rock formation—a pedestal atop a high rock hill. This, according to
legend, is Red Shin's Standing Ground.

The legend is backed up in no fewer than six independent accounts,
all dug up by Paul Bentrup, so evidently it really happened. This account
appeared in the Kansas State Historical Society quarterly:

> In 1833 a camp of Cheyennes was wintering here, and Red Shin
> and another man in this camp had a quarrel over a woman, and
> Red Shin had rather the better of it until the other man called on
> his brothers for aid and they all ran for their arms. Red Shin then
> went to his lodge and got two flint-lock muskets, one bow, one quiver
> of arrows, two butcher knives, one tomahawk. Carrying this small
> arsenal he ran to a stone knob about twenty-five feet high standing
> out in the open valley, and from the top of this knob he called out
> in a loud voice and challenged his enemies to come and fight. These
> men quickly made their appearance and advanced to the attack.
> Bull-Cannot-Rise was one of them. He told George Bent years ago
> that when he and his companions started toward the stone knob
> Red Shin began shooting arrows at them. One arrow went right

Barracks at old Fort Wise, 1886

through Bull-Cannot-Rise's hair, and the other attackers also had very narrow escapes. The affair did not last long, for the attackers soon sought cover, and before the fight could be resumed friends of both sides interfered and persuaded the belligerents to arbitrate.

Many visitors park here and climb to the top of the formation. While up there, look to the east and note the occasional groves of trees along the river. This is the western edge of an area known as Big Timbers—a band of cottonwoods and willows which extended nearly twenty-five miles east, about to the mouth of Big Sandy Creek.

Return to Hasty and turn right on Highway 50. Proceed east for 9.5 miles and turn right on a gravel road. Drive south for one mile to a T in the road. From here on it is private land, so get permission before continuing.

Drive straight across the T and enter the field by means of a wire gate. The road is now a two-track. It splits into several branches just .1 mile ahead—take the one to the left. Proceed to the fencing by the ditch. Park and start walking east, along the south side of the ditch. About 200 yards ahead are many low mounds of dirt, linear in shape—the remains of old Fort Lyon. Fine ruts of the trail are about sixty paces to the north, on the other side of the irrigation ditch.

The army built this post here in the fall of 1860, shortly after the present Fort Larned was established. It included four rock stable buildings, five

Big Timbers, as depicted in John C. Fremont's Memoirs of My Life

sets of quarters, a guardhouse, hospital, and a stone corral. Usually when military posts were abandoned, as this one was after the floods in the spring of 1866, the building materials were up for grabs. Presumably nearby ranchers salvaged the stones to build structures of their own.

Return to the gravel road, turn right, and drive 1.2 miles on Road JJ to Road 35.25. (The half-mile road leads to the iron bridge across the Arkansas River.) Turn right onto Road 35.25. Drive exactly one-half mile to the south and stop. A wire gate should be on the right, leading up a substantial rise. On top of that hill is a utility pole, bearing 260 degrees from the gate. That pole is standing in one of the bastions of Bent's New Fort.

If permission to go to the fort has been gained, climb the hill and stare at the outlines of the fort, crisply defined by rows of rocks. A ditch-like moat still girdles the foundations on three sides. It was dug hastily in 1864, in anticipation of an Indian attack. The main gate faces north, but there obviously was a smaller east gate also.

William Bent began his new fort here in Big Timbers in the winter of 1852-53. Far smaller than the old fort, this one had but twelve rooms surrounding the placita.

It would serve as a pleasant stopover for traders and other travelers using the Mountain Branch. Bent had hoped, too, to regain the Indian trade he had lost, but things were not the same. The war against white incursions intensified. Wars between the tribes became fratricidal. The

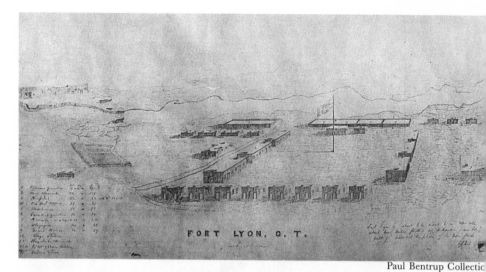

Old Fort Lyon

National Park Service survey team examines plat of Old Fort Lyon, on the site of the parade ground. From left: Dr. Jere Krakow, Paul Bentruip, Dr. Leo E. Oliva, John Paige, Don Hill, and Tom Betz.

trade with Bent never rematerialized. He rented the fort to the army and was paid for two years. He couldn't collect for the next five, because the army said it wasn't his to rent—those were Indian lands, they said, so he was, in fact, a trespasser. He moved to his stockaded ranch at the mouth of the Purgatoire and by 1867 was done with the fort business forever.

In May 1869 Bent attempted one more caravan east from New Mexico. The ugly weather took its toll and Bent contracted pneumonia. Feverish and delirious, Bent reached his ranch on the Purgatoire and his daughter sent for a doctor. It was too late. On May 19, 1869, at the age of 60, the great pioneer of the West passed away.

Return to JJ, turn left, and drive west only a quarter-mile. Turn right onto Road 35 and drive north one mile to Highway 50. Turn right and proceed 7.6 miles east to Lamar. Where the divided highway starts to curve to the south to go into the city, turn left onto Highway 196 and continue east for a block. Turn right and stop. This is Big Timbers Museum, a wonderful place to spend an hour or two. While there, pick up a copy of Ava Betz's thorough study, *A Prowers County History*. It contains much material on the Santa Fe Trail in this area.

Continue south on U.S. 50 through Lamar to the intersection of Main and Olive. Turn left and follow Olive east. Proceed seventeen miles east to the town of Granada and check the odometer. Proceed 3.1 miles farther east to the bridge high over the railroad. Continue only .4 mile. There a gravel road comes in from the south. Look, but don't leave the highway. Just .2 mile south of there is the site of old Granada, terminus of the new Goodnight Trail for cattle, which operated from 1873 to 1875.

Continue 2.5 miles ahead to the town of Amity. At that site an immense volume of military freight left the Santa Fe Railroad and was placed on covered wagons for the long haul over the Military Road to Fort Union.

Continue east along the north side of the river for three more miles to Holly. According to Ava Betz, Holly was the site of the Santa Fe Trail stop known variously as "Pretty Camp," "Pleasant Camp," and "Pretty Encampment." Lewis Garrard stopped here on his way home, in 1847:

> "Pretty Encampment," the loveliest on the river, with its glossy-leaved cottonwoods, was that evening early our home. Half a mile above was the Cheyenne village. Many of the savages who thronged the camp uttered the well-known *Hook-ah-hay, Numwhit*, as they took my hand. A party coming in from a buffalo hunt—the veritable John Smith at their head—stopped; we had a cordial embrace. His lodge, pitched with the rest, his squaw, son, and other "sign," proclaimed him an Indian—almost.

At the east edge of Holly turn left onto North First Avenue. Cross

Nothing but loose rock remains of Bent's New Fort today.

Tom and Ava Betz

This aerial view of Bent's New Fort shows the Amity Mutual Irrigation Canal headgates to the south. The army added the elaborate breastworks around the outside of the original fort.

a canal .3 mile ahead and immediately turn right onto a winding blacktop road which leads to a cemetery .8 mile away. Park, climb through the fence, and hike east of the east line of the cemetery. There are some good ruts there, spotted by Paul Bentrup.

Return to Highway 50, turn left, and drive twenty miles east to Syracuse. Take an odometer reading at the point where Kansas Highway 27 leaves U.S. 50 to head south, in the heart of town. Continue east on Highway 50 for exactly five miles. On the left side of the highway there is a steel bridge flanked with wood posts. Turn right at that point, onto an obscure gravel road. Cross the Santa Fe tracks immediately and proceed south for .2 mile, where the road curves to head straight west. Proceed west for one mile and then turn left again. Pull into a farmstead on the right. A DAR marker stands in front of an old farmhouse. This is private land; get permission before going farther.

Walk past the house and turn left behind the barn. This is the site of Fort Aubrey, built in September 1865 and in use only about a year. (The army misspelled the name of the fort.) Follow the left bank of the creek for about 200 yards and look around along the way. Several depressed areas in the form of irregular rectangles will be passed. These evidently are the remains of dugouts which housed the 220-man garrison stationed here.

There are some very good ruts on the north end of the Aubry Cutoff, which was established by Francis X. Aubry, certainly one of the most innovative of the Santa Fe traders.

Aubry, who set the Santa Fe-to-Independence speed record of five days twenty-two hours, was convinced that there must be a better route between the Arkansas and the Cimarron than the traditional Jornada crossings. After several false starts, he found a road which was clearly superior to any of the others, leading from the Arkansas to intercept the Cimarron Cutoff in the Oklahoma Panhandle, thus avoiding the Jornada and all its dangers entirely.

Until 1988 most Santa Fe Trail scholars believed that the Aubry Cutoff left the Arkansas from Fort Aubrey. (In other words, they felt Fort Aubrey was founded at the north end of the Aubry Cutoff.) However, this was doubted by Leo and Bonita Oliva. Their analysis of the terrain led them to believe the freighters would not have tried to plow through the rough sandhills south of Fort Aubrey—if any trail left from there they felt it could have been no more than a mule track.

Rancher David Brownlee, who lives one-half mile east of the site of Fort Aubrey, found some fine, sharp ruts leading along the north side of the sand hills, for several miles south of the river.

To see the ruts will require about twenty-two miles of driving on incredibly dusty gravel roads. Those who would rather not do this could backtrack from Fort Aubrey to Highway 50, turn right, and drive east for 6.8 miles—a point a half-mile north of the big grain elevators at Kendall. Turn right there and proceed to a gravel road which runs along the north side of the railroad, and turn left. That is the point where the alternate trip, about to be described, will end.

Those who would like to view the ruts of the Aubry Cutoff must return to Syracuse and turn left on Kansas Highway 27. Drive south and cross the Arkansas River. Just past the bridge, at a point 1.3 miles south of Highway 50, turn left on a gravel road. This road twists and turns for 6.6 miles, generally eastward, to arrive at a T. At that point turn right. Drive south for 2.8 miles. The single track of the Aubry Cutoff, which began two miles north-northeast, will cross the road. It may be followed either way, but permission to hike in the range must be obtained first.

A hiker may get in the ruts on the west side of the road, while a driver continues to the next corner, turns right, and stops .2 miles ahead, where the rut crosses the road again. It is a hike of about fifteen minutes.

Return to the T in the road (about four miles north) and continue straight ahead for another .1 mile. Turn right there and drive a mile to the east, passing through a farmyard along the way. The road then turns right—the Aubry Cutoff bisected that corner. Proceed south a half-mile—the ruts now are about .2 mile to the west. The road turns to the left there, to leave the area of the Aubry Cutoff.

Continue east for three miles, toward the grain elevators at Kendall. An intersection is there. Continue straight east for 1.5 more miles to a T in the road. Turn left, cross the Arkansas River and the Santa Fe tracks, then right again at the Kendall grain elevators.

Drive 6.3 miles ahead. On the left will be an abandoned farmstead. Get permission first, then drive in and park. Hike a half-mile due northwest and arrive at two or three sharp rut swales, some eroded, which may be followed for more than a mile to the northwest and west.

Return to the gravel road and continue east another 4.1 miles. A DAR marker will appear on the right. Keep moving to the east and scan the left side of the road. About a mile ahead a low hill will come into view—a hill with a marker on top. That, patient drivers, is the Indian Mound, which from the south appears to be only a fraction of its size when viewed from the north.

Continue east another .6 mile to be abreast of the landmark. Then on into Lakin, the end of the Mountain Branch, and the end of this twentieth century adventure—the revisitation of the Santa Fe Trail.

From here the northbound traders were on the main trail, and stayed on it all the way to Westport, Independence, or Old Franklin. This journey is over.

THE SPEED TRIP

It will take nearly four weeks to follow the directions in this book at a leisurely pace, seeing all the ruts and historic sites along the Santa Fe Trail. Some will have neither the time nor the resources to devote to the subject, so this Speed Trip has been devised to hit the highlights along the trail in about ten days.

In some cases, the directions given in the main text will be used. Refer to the index, using the italicized word, for the page numbers of those passages.

Leave Interstate 70 at the second Boonville (Missouri) exit, drive north over the Missouri River bridge via Highway 5, turn left at the first opportunity, which is Highway 87, and drive west one-half mile. This will be the heart of Old Franklin, the birthplace of the Santa Fe Trail. The trail continues to the west-northwest from there to cross the Missouri River at Arrow Rock.

Return to I-70. Drive west to Grain Valley and turn north there onto Highway BB. Drive to *Buckner* and follow the signs to Arrow Rock.

Return to Buckner and turn right on U.S. Highway 24. Continue west on 24 to the heart of Independence and turn right on North River Road to drive to *Independence Landing.*

Return to *Independence,* park, and walk around Courthouse Square. Drive a few blocks east to Noland Road, turn right, and proceed south for about three miles to I-70 and follow it west to 31st Street. Exit there and drive west for nearly four miles to Main Street and turn left. Drive south about nine blocks to Westport Road, turn right, and visit the *Harris House* and other sites in that old town.

Broadway is in the heart of Westport. Take it to the south. It will become J. C. Nichols Parkway. Turn right onto U.S. Highway 56, which becomes Ward Parkway, and follow it south to 83rd Street. Turn right there for about a block, then right again onto State Line Road, and visit the *Alex-*

ander Majors House at 8201 State Line Road.

Follow State Line Road south to 85th Street and turn left. Drive east about 1.5 miles to Holmes Road and turn right. Follow Holmes south for about 3.2 miles and turn left onto Red Bridge Road. Follow Red Bridge east for about a half-mile, past the *Minor Park* golf course, and turn into the park entrance on the right. Drive to the east edge of the parking area, park, and walk about 100 yards farther east to a wonderful swale of the Santa Fe Trail.

Return east on Red Bridge, turn left on Holmes, and drive south for about a mile to the 11900 block, which is Santa Fe Trail. Turn right and drive to *New Santa Fe,* on the Kansas state line.

Turn right on State Line and drive two miles north to I-435 and take it to the west. It will curve to the north gradually, and intersect I-70 about twenty miles from State Line. Continue ahead on 435 for another 2.5 miles to the Leavenworth Road and turn left. Drive about four miles west and turn right on Kansas Highway 7. Drive north about thirteen miles to *Fort Leavenworth.*

Drive south from Fort Leavenworth to the Kansas Turnpike and take it west to the Lawrence exit. Drive south there on U.S. Highway 59 for thirteen miles to U.S. Highway 56. Turn left and drive back to the east to Baldwin City. *Black Jack* Park is about three miles east of town. Turn right on the gravel road on the west edge of the park and drive south about 100 yards, and walk in the wonderful rut swales of the Santa Fe Trail.

Turn around and drive west on U.S. Highway 56. The *Simmons Point* Stage Station is about nine miles west of Highway 59, the road leading south from Lawrence. Continue west on 56, through *Burlingame.* Follow the directions to the *Havana Stage Station* and the grave of *Samuel Hunt.*

Continue on Highway 56 west to *Council Grove.* Plan to spend a couple of hours there. (The legend, "Birthplace of the Santa Fe Trail," which is on the signs leading to the city, will be removed the next time the signs are repainted. Old Franklin, of course, is the birthplace of the Santa Fe Trail.)

Follow 56 to the west, and as it turns south in Herington. The turnoff to the town of Lost Springs is about seven miles south of Herington. Turn right there, onto a paved road, and proceed west for three miles to the *Lost Spring.* Then follow the directions in the main text to the *Durham* ruts.

Return to 56 and continue south and then west through McPherson and Lyons. Four miles west of Chase turn right on the blacktop to *Ralph's Ruts.* Follow the directions in the text past *Gunsight Notch,* the *Plum Buttes,* and back to Highway 56. Turn right on 56 and follow the directions in the text to the *Fort Zarah* area.

Continue on 56 southwest through Great Bend and about thirteen miles farther to *Pawnee Rock*. Turn off the highway there and visit the landmark. Then continue southwest to Larned, and follow 156 from there. Proceed west for 2.6 miles to the *Santa Fe Trail Center* for a tour of that fine museum. Continue west on 156 for less than four miles to *Fort Larned National Historic Site*. Plan to spend from two to three hours there.

Follow the directions in the book from Fort Larned to the detached site, about five miles to the southwest. Continue south on the gravel to Garfield and turn right on 56. Proceed less than two miles to the southwest and observe the swales leading down to *Coon Creek*.

Continue along Highway 56 to *Dodge City*. There is a road on the east edge of town which cuts down to Highway 154. Take it to the south, then turn back east on 154 for about three more miles to *Fort Dodge*.

Follow the directions in the book from Fort Dodge to *Front Street*, then some ten miles west of Dodge City on U.S. 50 to the ruts owned by the Boot Hill Museum.

Proceed west on 50 to the city park in the town of *Cimarron*, near the principal crossing of the Arkansas River. Continue west from Cimarron to Pierceville and turn left, drive through town, cross the railroad tracks and turn right on Mansfield Road and drive west on the gravel to the site of *Pawnee Fort*.

Return to Highway 50 in Pierceville, drive through Garden City and Deerfield. About 2.5 miles west of that town stop at *Charlie's Ruts*.

Continue west to Lakin and turn south on Kansas Highway 25, and drive twenty-eight miles through the Jornada to Ulysses. Follow the directions in the book for eleven miles south of Ulysses to *Wagon Bed Spring*.

Return to Highway 25 and proceed on south to Hugoton and turn right on U.S. 56. Follow that highway southwest to Elkhart and turn right on Kansas Highway 27. Drive north eight miles, cross the Cimarron River, and proceed ahead to the overlook prepared by the U.S. Forest Service. Return from the overlook, following the directions in the main text, to *Middle Spring*, and then *Point of Rocks*.

Return to Elkhart and drive about thirty-eight miles into the Oklahoma Panhandle to Boise City. Turn north there on U.S. Highways 287-385 to *Wolf Mountain*. Return to Boise City, stop at the Chamber of Commerce office (in the red caboose) on the square, and check on visitation to *Autograph Rock* and *Cold Spring*.

Return to the Kenton Road and follow it west to *Mexhoma*, then another half-mile to view the ruts along the south side of the blacktop as it nears the New Mexico state line.

Jog to the left at the border for one-third mile, then turn east on New Mexico Highway 410. Follow it for two miles, then turn left on Highway 406. Follow the highway as it loops to the south, for about three miles to the entrance gate to *McNees Crossing*. Remember to close that gate! Return to Highway 406 and follow it south and west for about fifteen miles to U.S. 56, then turn right for about three more miles to Clayton.

Turn right in Clayton onto U.S. Highways 64-87. Drive northwest for twenty-seven miles to Grenville, then turn south onto New Mexico Highway 453 for 2.5 miles to *Round Mound*. Continue south and west for about eighteen more miles to U.S. 56 and turn right. Drive 29.4 miles farther west to a state roadside park, then follow the directions in the book to *Point of Rocks*. That is private property—get permission before visiting it.

Return to the highway. Drive west another 14.2 miles to an abandoned rock house on the left, sight over it to see the ruts leading to the *Rock Crossing of the Canadian*.

Continue another nine miles to Springer and turn onto Interstate Highway 25 southbound. Drive twenty-four miles south and exit at *Wagon Mound*. Proceed to the two cemeteries and get a close view of the rock mass.

Return to the highway and continue south to Las Vegas. Take the second exit, turn left, cross over the highway, and re-enter it northbound. Proceed ahead 1.3 miles, pull far over on the east shoulder, turn on the clickers, and stop. On the right is a deep swale of the Santa Fe Trail heading straight for the old plaza in Las Vegas.

Continue north to the next interchange, leave the highway, and remount it headed south. Take the center exit again, but this time drive to the right to the main street, Grand Avenue, and turn right for one block to National. Turn left on National and drive about a mile, crossing the Gallinas River, to the old Las Vegaz Plaza. It is one-way counter-clockwise. On the right are some single-story buildings numbered 210-218, believed to be the structures mounted by Gen. Stephen Watts Kearny when he declared to the townspeople that they were henceforth under the American flag.

Return to the highway and follow it south and west, around the "fishhook," for about twenty-four miles to the exit onto New Mexico Highway 3. Proceed south through the town of Ribera to *San Miguel*.

Return to I-25 and continue west to the Rowe exit about fifteen miles away. Take it to the north, following the signs past the *Forked Lightning Ranch* headquarters and on to *Pecos National Monument*.

From this point follow the main text to *Johnson's Ranch*. After viewing that site, get back on I-25 and drive on in to *Santa Fe*.

To follow the Mountain Branch, leave Santa Fe on I-25 eastbound, follow the "fishhook" route for about eighty-two miles, to Exit 366, Highway 161 to *Fort Union*. Plan to spend about two hours there.

Return to I-25 northbound and follow it for about forty-five miles to Springer, take the first exit, drive into town and turn left on New Mexico Highway 21. Follow that road twenty-three miles west to *Rayado,* and continue north to *Cimarron.*

Turn right at the stop sign in Cimarron onto U.S. Highway 64, and follow it north for about thirty-five miles, almost to I-25. Then follow the directions for finding the ruins of *Clifton House.*

Continue north to I-25 and drive through Raton and over *Raton Pass* into Colorado.

Follow I-25 into Trinidad and exit onto U.S. Highways 160-350, also Main Street. Continue northeast on Main to the 300 block, the *Baca-Bloom houses.* Continue northeast on Highway 350. Note the Spanish Peaks on the left. Drive eighty-one miles to *La Junta,* note the crossing of the Arkansas River, and proceed ahead to *Bent's Old Fort.* Allow at least three hours for this visit.

Continue east on Highway 194 to Las Animas, join U.S. Highway 50 westbound, and follow it through town to Colorado Highway 101. Drive south to the site of *Boggsville.*

Return to Highway 50 and take it eastbound for 4.5 miles, turn right on Colorado Highway 183 and proceed to *New Fort Lyon.* Return to 50 and continue east for another ten miles to Hasty, turn right on the blacktop in the center of town and drive about three miles south to the site of *Red Shin's Standing Ground.*

Return to Highway 50 and continue west for another 9.5 miles and turn south on a gravel road. Proceed to a T in that road and turn left on Road JJ. Follow it for 1.2 miles and turn right on Road 35.25. Drive one-half mile south, stop, and pay a visit to *Bent's New Fort.*

Return to Highway 50, turn right, and proceed into Kansas, to the Upper Cimarron Crossing west of Lakin, and the end of the Mountain Branch.

BIBLIOGRAPHY

Barry, Louise. *The Beginning of the West: Annals of the Kansas Gateway to the American West, 1540-1854.* Topeka, 1972.

Beachum, Larry M. *William Becknell, Father of the Santa Fe Trade.* El Paso, 1982.

_____. "To the Westward: William Becknell and the Beginning of the Santa Fe Trade." *Journal of the West* 28 (April 1989).

Betz, Ava. *A Prowers County History.* Lamar, Colo., 1986.

Boyd, Le Roy. *Fort Lyon, Colorado: One Hundred Years of Service.* Colorado Springs, 1967.

Brown, William E. *The Santa Fe Trail: National Park Service 1963 Historic Sites Survey.* St. Louis, 1988.

Buckles, William G. "The Santa Fe Trail System." *Journal of the West* 28 (April 1989).

Conard, Howard Louis. *Uncle Dick Wootton, The Pioneer Frontiersman of the Rocky Mountain Region.* Lincoln, 1980.

Connor, Seymour V., and Jimmy M. Skaggs. *Broadcloth and Britches: The Santa Fe Trade.* College Station, Texas, 1976.

Cordry, Mrs. T. A. *The Story of the Marking of the Santa Fe Trail.* Topeka, 1915.

Dary, David *True Tales of Old-Time Kansas.* Lawrence, 1979.

_____. *More True Tales of Old-Time Kansas.* Lawrence, 1987.

Drumm, Stella M., ed. *Down the Santa Fe Trail and into Mexico: The Diary of Susan Shelby Magoffin, 1846-1847.* Lincoln, 1982.

Duffus, R. L. *The Santa Fe Trail.* New York, 1934.

Fisher, Virginia Lee. *Arrow Rock Places: The Architecture and Environs of Arrow Rock, Missouri.* Arrow Rock, 1988.

Franzwa, Gregory M. *Images of the Santa Fe Trail.* St. Louis, 1988.

_____. *Impressions of the Santa Fe Trail.* St. Louis, 1988.

_____. *Maps of the Santa Fe Trail.* St. Louis, 1989.

Gardner, Kathryn Davis. "Conn and Hays: Council Grove's Trail Merchants." *Journal of the West* 28 (April 1989).

Gardner, Mark L. "The Glasgows: Missouri Merchants in the Mexican Trade." *Journal of the West* 28 (April 1989).

Garrard, Lewis H. *Wah-to-yah and the Taos Trail.* Norman, 1955.

Gregg, Josiah. *The Commerce of the Prairies.* Lincoln, 1967.

Gregg, Kate L., ed. *The Road to Santa Fe: The Journal and Diaries of George Champlin Sibley and Others Pertaining to the Surveying and Marking of a Road from the Missouri Frontier to the Settlements of New Mexico, 1825-1827.* Albuquerque, 1952.

Hall, Thomas B., M.D. *Medicine on the Santa Fe Trail.* Arrow Rock, 1987.

Hamilton, Jean Tyree. *Arrow Rock, Where Wheels Started West.* Marshall, Mo., 1972.

Hathaway, Ralph. *My One-Half Mile of Santa Fe Trail.* Ellsworth, Kans., 1984.

Hoig, Stan. *The Sand Creek Massacre.* Norman, 1961.

Horgan, Paul. *Lamy of Santa Fe, His Life and Times.* New York, 1975.

Kelley, Katharine B. *Along the Santa Fe Trail in Douglas County, Kansas.* Baldwin City, Kans., 1987.

Kimball, Stanley B. "Rediscovering the Fort Leavenworth Military Branch of the Santa Fe Trail." *Journal of the West* 28 (April 1989).

Krakow, Jere L. "Preservation Efforts on the Santa Fe Trail." *Journal of the West* 28 (April 1989).

Lane, Lydia Spencer. *I Married a Soldier.* Albuquerque, 1987.

Lavender, David. *Bent's Fort.* Lincoln, 1972.

Lecompte, Janet. "The Mountain Branch: Raton Pass and Sangre de Cristo Pass." *The Santa Fe Trail: New Perspectives.* Denver, 1987.

Martin, Gene and Mary. *Trail Dust: A Quick Picture History of the Santa Fe Trail.* Denver, 1972.

Mills, William. *The Arkansas: An American River.* Fayetteville, Ark., 1988.

Oliva, Leo E. *Fort Hays.* Topeka, 1980.

_____. *Fort Larned.* Topeka, 1982.

_____. *Soldiers on the Santa Fe Trail.* Norman, 1967.

_____. "The Santa Fe Trail in Wartime: Expansion and Preservation of the Union." *Journal of the West* 28 (April 1989).

Oliva, Leo E., and Bonita M. Oliva. *Santa Fe Trail Trivia.* Woodston, Kans., 1989.

Quaife, Milo Milton. *Kit Carson's Autobiography.* Lincoln, 1966.

Riddle, Kenyon. *Records and Maps of the Old Santa Fe Trail.* West Palm Beach, 1963.

Rittenhouse, Jack D. "The Literature of the Santa Fe Trail: An Introduction and Guide for the New Traveler." *The Santa Fe Trail: New Perspectives.* Denver, 1987.

_____. *The Santa Fe Trail: A Historical Bibliography.* Albuquerque, 1986.

Russell, Marion Sloan. *Land of Enchantment: Memoirs of Marian Russell Along the Santa Fe Trail: As Dictated to Mrs. Hal Russell.* Evanston, 1954.

Sandoval, David A. "Gnats, Goods, and Greasers: Mexican Merchants on the Santa Fe Trail." *Journal of the West* 28 (April 1989).

_____. "Who Is Riding the Burro Now? A Bibliographical Critique of Scholarship on the New Mexican Trader." *The Santa Fe Trail: New Perspectives.* Denver, 1987.

Schmidt, Shiela Sutton. *Pawnee Rock: A Brief History of the Rock.* Pawnee Rock, 1986.

Simmons, Marc. *Following the Santa Fe Trail: A Guide for Modern Travelers.* Santa Fe, 1986.

_____. ed. *On the Santa Fe Trail.* Lawrence, Kans., 1986.

_____. "The Wagon Mound Massacre." *Journal of the West* 28 (April 1989).

Soil Survey, Cimarron County, Oklahoma. Washington D.C., 1960.

Stocking, Hobart E. *The Road to Santa Fe.* New York, 1971

Strate, David K. *Sentinel to the Cimarron: The Frontier Experience of Fort Dodge, Kansas.* Dodge City, 1970.

_____. ed. *West by Southwest: Letters of Joseph Pratt Allyn, A Traveller Along the Santa Fe Trail, 1863.* Dodge City, 1984.

Sunder, John E. *Matt Field on the Santa Fe Trail.* Norman, 1960.

Tejada, David, F.S.C. *The San Miguel Chapel, Oldest Church in U.S.* Santa Fe, 1957.

Thompson, Enid. *Bent's Old Fort.* Denver, 1979.

Utley, Robert M. *Cavalier in Buckskin: George Armstrong Custer and the Western Military Frontier.* Norman, 1988.

_____. *Fort Union National Monument.* Washington, 1962.

INDEX

Other Western Books Published or Marketed by The Patrice Press

These books may be purchased by direct mail.
Order from:
The Patrice Press
1701 South Eighth St., St. Louis, MO 63104

WESTERN HISTORY

Exploring the American West: 1803-1879. William Goetzmann. 128 pages. Paper, $7.95.

Kansas in Maps. Robert W. Baughman. 104 pages. Cloth, $14.95.

The Beginning of the West. Louise Barry. 1296 pages. Cloth, $14.75.

The Latter-day Saints' Emigrants' Guide. Wm. Clayton; Stanley B. Kimball, Ph.D., ed. 107 pages. Paper, $9.95, ISBN: 0-935284-27-3.

The Overland Migrations. David Lavender. 111 pages. Paper, $7.95.

THE SANTA FE TRAIL

Following the Santa Fe Trail. Marc Simmons, Ph.D. 214 pages. Paper, $12.95.

Fort Union. Robert M. Utley. 72 pages. Paper, $2.95.

Images of the Santa Fe Trail. Gregory M. Franzwa. 114 photographs. Cloth, $29.95, ISBN: 0-935284-60-5. Paper, $19.95, ISBN: 0-935284-61-3.

Impressions of The Santa Fe Trail: A Contemporary Diary. Gregory M. Franzwa. 207 pages. Cloth, $14.95, ISBN: 0-935284-62-1.

Land of Enchantment: Memoirs of Marian Russell along the Santa Fe Trail. Garnet M. Brayer, ed. 163 pages. Paper, $12.95.

Maps of the Santa Fe Trail. Gregory M. Franzwa. Cloth, $24.95, ISBN: 0-935284-68-0. Looseleaf, $29.95, ISBN: 0-935284-69-9.

The Santa Fe Trail: The National Park Service 1963 Historic Sites Survey. William E. Brown. 221 pages. Cloth, $17.95, ISBN: 0-935284-64-8.

Santa Fe Trail Trivia. Leo E. and Bonita M. Olivia. 76 pages. Paper, $2.95.

There is a $2.95 shipping and handling charge for the first book and a 95-cent charge for each additional book. Missourians please add 6.1% sales tax. You may call toll-free to place your order:
1-800-367-9242

THE OREGON-CALIFORNIA TRAIL

Fort Laramie. David Lavender. 159 pages. Paper, $8.95.

Fort Vancouver. David Lavender. 143 pages. Paper, $8.95.

The Great Platte River Road. Merrill J. Mattes. 583 pages. Cloth, $36.95. Paper, $16.95.

Historic Sites Along the Oregon Trail. Aubrey L. Haines. 439 pages. Cloth, $24.95, ISBN: 0-935284-50-8. Paper, $12.95, ISBN: 0-935284-51-6.

Maps of the Oregon Trail. Gregory M. Franzwa. 292 pages. Cloth, $24.95, ISBN: 0-935284-30-3. Looseleaf, $27.95, ISBN: 0-935284-31-1.

Old Oregon Trail Map. 16" X 24". $2.95.

The Oregon Trail Revisited. Gregory M. Franzwa. 419 pages. Cloth, $14.95, ISBN: 0-935284-57-5. Paper, $12.95, ISBN: 0-935284-58-3.

The Plains Across. John D. Unruh, Jr. 364 pages. Paper, $12.95.

Platte River Road Narratives. Merrill J. Mattes. 672 pages, 8½" X 11". Cloth, $95.

The Pony Express. Merrill Mattes and Paul Henderson. 85 pages. Paper, $4.95, ISBN: 0-935284-66-4.

Pump on the Prairie. Musetta Gilman. 223 pages. Paper, $12.95.

Scotts Bluff. Merrill J. Mattes. 64 pages. Paper, $2.45.

Trail of the First Wagons Over the Sierra Nevada. Charles K. Graydon. 81 pages. Paper, $12.95, ISBN: 0-935284-47-8.

To the Land of Gold and Wickedness: The 1848-59 Diary of Lorena Hays. Jeanne Hamilton Watson, ed. 496 pages. Cloth, $27.95, ISBN: 0-935284-53-2.

The Wake of the Prairie Schooner. Irene D. Paden. 514 pages. Cloth, $24.95, ISBN: 0-935284-40-0.

Two wonderful associations
to enhance enjoyment of the trails:

The Santa Fe Trail
ASSOCIATION

Your membership will:
- ☐ Help with efforts to preserve the remaining ruts of the Santa Fe Trail and associated historic sites
- ☐ Bring you four issues of *Wagon Tracks* each year, with news of the association and the trail
- ☐ Enable you to attend the conventions and conferences of the association, where you can:
  - ☐ enjoy the field trips out on the trail
  - ☐ hear thrilling papers about the trail, and
  - ☐ enjoy the camaradarie of fellow trail students and scholars

OREGON-CALIFORNIA TRAILS ASSOCIATION

Your membership will:
- ☐ Help save the remaining traces of the trails and related historic sites
- ☐ Bring you four issues of the *Overland Journal* and four issues of *News From the Plains* each year
- ☐ Enable you to attend OCTA conventions in historic trail cities each year, featuring:
  - ☐ field trips to important trails sites
  - ☐ wonderful slide shows and papers on the trail and its history, and
  - ☐ the companionship of new and interesting trail friends

**For a free membership application
to both trails associations,
call toll-free: 1-800-367-9242**